Archaeological Theory and Scientific Practice

Is archaeology an art or a science? This question has been hotly debated over the last few decades with the rise of archaeological science. At the same time, archaeologists have seen a change in the intellectual character of their discipline, as many writers have adopted approaches influenced by social theory. The discipline now encompasses both archaeological scientists and archaeological theorists, and discussion regarding the status of archaeology remains polarised. Andrew Jones argues that we need to analyse the practice of archaeology. Through an analysis of archaeological practice, influenced by recent developments in the field of science studies, and with the aid of extensive case studies, he develops a new framework, which allows the interpretative and methodological components of the discipline to work in tandem. His reassessment of the status and character of archaeology will be of interest to students, scholars and professionals.

ANDREW JONES is a Lecturer in the Department of Archaeology, Southampton University. He has worked extensively on British prehistory (especially the Neolithic and Bronze Age). Among his many research interests are the history of representation in archaeology, the role of art and memory in archaeological research, and the archaeology of animals and food. He has contributed to a number of journals and edited volumes. This is his first book.

Topics in Contemporary Archaeology

Series Editor
Richard Bradley, University of Reading

This series is addressed to students, professional archaeologists and academics in related disciplines in the social sciences. Concerned with questions of interpretation rather than the exhaustive documentation of archaeological data, the studies in the series take several different forms: a review of the literature in an important field, an outline of a new area of research or an extended case study. The series is not aligned with any particular school of archaeology. While there is no set format for the books, all books in the series are broadly based, well written and up to date.

Archaeological Theory and Scientific Practice

Andrew Jones

Department of Archaeology, Southampton University

CAMBRIDGE
UNIVERSITY PRESS

PUBLISHED BY THE PRESS SYNDICATE OF THE UNIVERSITY OF CAMBRIDGE
The Pitt Building, Trumpington Street, Cambridge, United Kingdom

CAMBRIDGE UNIVERSITY PRESS
The Edinburgh Building, Cambridge CB2 2RU, UK
40 West 20th Street, New York, NY 10011-4211, USA
477 Williamstown Road, Port Melbourne, VIC 3207, Australia
Ruiz de Alarcón 13, 28014 Madrid, Spain
Dock House, The Waterfront, Cape Town 8001, South Africa

http://www.cambridge.org

First published 2002

Printed in the United Kingdom at the University Press, Cambridge

Typeface Plantin 10/12 pt.   *System* LaTeX 2_ε [TB]

A catalogue record for this book is available from the British Library

Library of Congress Cataloguing in Publication Data
Archaeological theory and scientific practice / Andrew Jones
     p.   cm.
Includes bibliographical references (p.) and index.
ISBN 0 521 79060 3 (hardback) – ISBN 0 521 79393 9 (paperback)
1. Archaeology – Philosophy.   2. Archaeology – Methodology.
3. Archaeology – Field work.   I. Title
Jones, Andrew, 1967-
CC72.J66 2001 930.1'01 – dc21 2001035689

ISBN 0 521 79060 3 hardback
ISBN 0 521 79393 9 paperback

Contents

Illustrations

Tables

Preface

Since the contents of this book are concerned so much with issues of biography, it makes sense to begin by saying something about the biography of both text and author. The subject matter – the relationship between archaeological theory and archaeological science – arose from my doctoral research between 1993 and 1997 at Glasgow University, which was supervised by Colin Richards and Richard Jones. The examination of the pottery assemblage from the Late Neolithic settlement at Barnhouse, Orkney comprised the central focus of the original thesis (see Richards forthcoming, and chapters 6 and 7 this volume). However I felt that wider and more fundamental questions lay behind my use of the techniques of materials science within a framework informed by interpretative archaeology and anthropology. It was for this reason that I began to write the first two chapters of the book in Glasgow, after the completion of the thesis. At this time the subject matter was written from a personal perspective derived from attempts to balance an interest in archaeological theory with the practical application of scientific techniques. This perspective altered when I took up a teaching appointment at University College Dublin, where amongst other things I was able to observe the pragmatic application of scientific analysis alongside archaeological theory under the aegis of the Irish Stone Axe Project, directed by Gabriel Cooney and Stephen Mandal. I began to see that the issues examined in the volume were more fundamental to archaeological practice, and in Dublin I completed the third chapter.

I was persuaded more firmly of the subject matter of the book when I took up a post-doctoral position at the McDonald Institute for Archaeological Research, Cambridge. In Cambridge I came into contact with a growing number of people who were attempting to utilise both archaeological theory and archaeological science. My perspective on the topic had shifted over the course of the book's inception in Glasgow to its completion in Cambridge some two years later. No longer did it appear to derive solely from personal experience; instead, it had become a topic that was of wider concern to a growing number of archaeological scientists and archaeological theorists. This was encouraging although, of course, this state of affairs had prevailed throughout, since in reality we are never writing in isolation, but are always situated in a wider discourse.

My immersion in this discourse is not solely confined to my engagement with issues of science and society, and science and the arts in the academic world; these issues have an increasing impact upon the world which we all inhabit. I write at a time in which faith in science as a force of emancipation has diminished and public confidence in the sciences has waned. Genetically Modified Organisms, the Human Genome project and the issues surrounding the cloning of human tissue from stem cells are at present regular topics of discussion in the media. The terms in which these critical issues are discussed remain polarised in the framework that I describe in chapter 1, with scientists in the media occupying a position of certainty and knowledge sealed off from the wider concerns of the public. Meanwhile, while concern grows for the ethical issues associated with the newfound capabilities of the biological sciences, there is a lingering assumption of the inexorable and progressive nature of science. The discussion of these issues is then caught in a problematic trap: while it is realised that at the ethical level society ought to have an impact upon science, there remains the feeling that science proceeds outside the influence of the social. On a lighter note, the significance of the relationship between science and society, and in particular science and the arts, is also being increasingly stressed in the form of a number of major visual arts exhibitions at venues ranging from the Hayward Gallery and the Natural History Museum, London to the Victoria and Albert Museum.

While the wider issues concerning the sciences in relation to society and the arts have affected me both negatively and positively, on an academic and personal level my perspective on the philosophical implications of these issues has fundamentally altered during the course of writing this book. I have become convinced of the necessity of taking account not only of the philosophical implications of our practices, an area traditionally studied by philosophers of science (Embree 1992; Kelly and Hannen 1988; Wylie 1992), but also to understand the historical precedents and trajectories of these philosophical distinctions. In this respect I have been especially influenced by Barkan and Bush (1995), Fabian (1983, 1991) and Stocking (1996), amongst others. Although the history of science is a relatively unexplored field in archaeology and remains fairly implicit in my text, I nevertheless feel it is critically important to be aware of the historical depth of the philosophical distinctions that we employ on a routine basis in our contemporary practices. Moreover I believe that it is important to reflect upon this awareness in the reformulation of our philosophical frameworks. That is really what this book is about, since the aim is to examine the philosophical distinctions that divide the arts and humanities from the natural sciences. In this regard it would have been relatively simple to write an account that 'took sides'. Radically different accounts could have been written had I taken up the view of the natural sciences in defining positivism or empiricism as definitional knowledge (for the most famous recent examples of this approach see Gross and Levitt 1994; Sokal and Bricmont 1998). Similarly, in taking up a perspective flavoured by post-modernism it would have been possible to write an account which considered knowledge to exist in solely representational form. Both of these approaches would have fallen foul of the epistemological traps that ensnare our discussion of topics such as rationalism and relativism, objectivity and subjectivity. With Fabian (1991, 193) I believe that 'it is a bad sort of critique that first needs to pledge allegiance to one or another school'; instead, I have attempted to develop a position that examines the nature of the connections between each order of knowledge, and my account is meant to alienate neither archaeological scientists nor archaeological theorists.

Due to the exigencies of space, this book focuses upon materials science. However I am aware that excellent work of a similar vein is also being undertaken in many other fields of archaeological science, such as environmental archaeology (Albarella forthcoming), soil micromorphology (Boivin 2000), stable isotope analysis (Richards and Hedges 1999) and Geographical Information Systems (Lock and Stancic 1995), to name but a few. Furthermore some of the themes addressed in this book are of wider concern to field archaeology, and these have been recently examined by Bender, Hamilton and Tilley (1997) and Hodder (1996, 1999). In terms of my theoretical emphasis, I have focused upon issues such as biography, consumption, technology and identity that are of pertinence to interpretative archaeologists and anthropologists alike. It goes without saying that the application of techniques derived from archaeological science to the examination of theoretical issues need not focus on these areas of interest alone. Rather it is the imaginative application of both existent and novel techniques to a plethora of theoretical issues that will promote the creation of fresh interpretative networks between researchers in different fields.

ANDREW JONES

Acknowledgements

Over the course of writing this book I have enjoyed chatting to numerous individuals about these topics. These people include Dean Arnold, John Barrett, Kishor Basa, Robin Boast, Dusan Boric, Richard Bradley, Emmet Byrne, Gabriel Cooney, Jo Sofaer-Derevenski, Chris Doherty, Bryan Hanks, Yannis Hamilakis, Andy Hoaen, Cornelius Holtorf, Andrew 'Bones' Jones, Stephanie Koerner, Mark Knight, Helen Loney, Kirsi Lorenz, Stephen Mandal, Lesley McFadyen, Stephanie Meece, Karen Milek, Preston Miracle, Lise Nordenborg-Myhre, Mike Parker-Pearson, Jenny Rose, Hannah Sackett, Katerina Skourtopolou and Mike Tite.

I must also thank the staff of the Glasgow University Archaeological Research Division (GUARD) for teaching me a number of valuable lessons regarding the nature of contract archaeology. My time in Dublin was made all the more pleasant by discussions with Gabriel Cooney, Seamas Caulfield and Muiris O'Sullivan, and the hospitality (intellectual and otherwise) of Margaret Coughlan and Tadhg O'Keeffe.

I am especially grateful to Dean Arnold, Jo Sofaer-Derevenski, Yannis Hamilakis and Mark Knight, all of whom commented upon parts of the text, and to David Williams for the loan of thin-sections. I am also grateful both to Chatto and Windus publishers and the executors of the estate of F. R. Leavis for their permission to quote from F. R. Leavis' *The two cultures? The significance of CP Snow*, and to Cambridge University Press and the executors of the estate of C. P. Snow for their permission to quote from *Two cultures*. Further thanks must go to Colin Renfrew for permission to use the illustration of the Quanterness Grooved ware assemblage.

Special thanks must go to two people: Richard Bradley, who has been a constant source of encouragement throughout the writing of the book and whose editorial comments have been both incisive and an inspiration to further work, and Hannah Sackett, who has kept me on the straight and narrow during the writing of this book.

Finally, the book is dedicated to two remarkable individuals. My father, Dr Edward Jones, a scientist with strong opinions on the certainty and reliability of scientific knowledge and a flair for art, and my mother, Felicity Jones, a historian with a sense of the value of history who also keeps an eye on the empirical matters of life.

1 The archaeology of 'two cultures'

I have had, of course, intimate friends among both scientists and writers. It was through living among these groups and much more, I think through moving regularly from one to the other and back again that I got occupied with the problem of what, long before I put it on paper, I christened to myself as the 'two cultures'. For constantly I felt I was moving among two groups – comparable in intelligence, identical in race, not grossly different in social origin, earning about the same incomes, who had almost ceased to communicate at all, who in intellectual, moral and psychological climate had so little in common.   (C. P. Snow 1959, 2)

The only presence science has is as a matter of external reference, entailed in a show of knowledgeableness. Of qualities that one might set to the credit of scientific training there are none. As far as the internal evidence goes, the lecture was conceived and written by someone who had not had the advantage of an intellectual discipline of any kind. I was on the point of illustrating this truth from Snow's way with the term 'culture' – a term so important for his purposes. By way of enforcing his testimony that the scientists 'have their own culture', he tells us: 'This culture contains a great deal of argument, usually much more rigorous, and almost always at a higher conceptual level, than literary persons' arguments'. But the argument of Snow's Rede Lecture is at an immensely lower conceptual level, and incomparably more loose and inconsequent than any I myself, a literary person, should permit in a group discussion I was conducting, let alone a pupil's essay.   (F. R. Leavis 1962, 14–15)

The extracts above are taken from two Cambridge lectures. The first, delivered by the late Sir Charles Snow, a scientist and author, sketches the problem which he considers to be inherent to twentieth-century academia, that of the 'two cultures', divided conceptually between those who study science, and those who study the arts. The outline of the lecture, as indicated from this extract, suggested that the two disciplines were simply not talking to each other. This extract illustrates quite clearly the point that I wish to make in this opening chapter with regard to contemporary archaeology; that is, that archaeological scientists and theoretical archaeologists are quite simply speaking in different languages and have

quite different visions of what the study of archaeology entails. This paradoxical disciplinary position has served to force both a vigorous critique
of positivism on the side of those practising interpretative or theoretical
approaches (see Thomas 1990) and a whole-hearted rejection of post-
structuralist theory on the part of those practising scientific archaeology.
Here the position can be summed up by Dunnell's assertion that 'the ef-
fort, rigour and cost of physical analyses are lost in a humanistic approach
where they serve only to aspire story telling' (1993, 164).

Of course, as Snow's extract indicates, the division of intellectual labour
between the arts and sciences remains a long-standing problem. However, very few disciplines attempt to bridge the intellectual gap between
these bodies of knowledge. The question I wish to ask in this first chapter
is do we bridge the gap or do we in fact practise two different kinds of
archaeology, each of which produces different orders of knowledge about
the past? The aim of this book will be an attempt to examine the problems
facing contemporary archaeology as a discipline that is essentially split
in its theoretical and methodological aims. The second question I wish
to consider is whether this split is theoretically and methodologically
surmountable, or whether the two orders of knowledge are ultimately
incommensurable?

The second quotation is from a lecture delivered some years later by
the late F. R. Leavis, a professor of English Literature and a prominent
literary critic. This second lecture inveighed against the coarse-grained
nature of Snow's argument, against Snow himself and, to some extent,
against science itself as the talisman with which to heal all ills. This extract illustrates the intensity that the debate between scientists and artists
often reaches. Such intensity of debate certainly has its parallels in the
archaeological literature since the 1960s.

While Snow was both writer and scientist, his sympathy lay with science. His interpretation of the problematic relationship between science
and the arts was simplistic; he saw science as the way forward, believing it to be more rigorous than the arts, and more capable of providing
both truth and answers for society's problems. Science would emerge as a
latter-day holy grail, enabling the gap between rich and poor to be finally
bridged. Leavis' main point concerned the quality and rigour of Snow's
argument, and he rightly noted that science by itself held little promise
if it was not linked to a clearer understanding of society. As we shall see,
the debates between the arts and the sciences over rigour, truth and the
application of science have considerable resonance with the problems we
need to face in examining the position of science and interpretation in
the wider archaeological programme.

The intellectual division outlined above is not peculiar to the subject of archaeology; rather, the epistemological division between arts and sciences is a major concern in the construction and understanding of all forms of knowledge. When discussing the different intellectual positions taken up in constructing different orders of knowledge, we find that there are a plethora of terms used to define these interpretative positions. The definition of terms is a traditional issue of contention for those criticising opposing knowledge claims (for example see Reyna 1995). Therefore, in the proceeding section I wish to clearly outline the major problems in our discussion of differing domains of knowledge, to define the terms in which they are discussed, and to examine the ways in which they relate to each other. This clarification exercise is necessary before we proceed on to consider how these varying theoretical positions have been discussed within archaeology. In the account below it will not be possible to define the precise details of each theoretical position; rather I intend to provide a broad overview of the epistemological problems which face both the natural and social sciences. Overall, I want to critically evaluate the practice of science and examine ways in which theoretical or interpretative archaeologists may engage with science. Meanwhile, I also wish to demonstrate the necessity of social theory within archaeology, and suggest ways in which scientific archaeologists may critically engage in social archaeology.

Objectivity and subjectivity

Conventionally, within Western philosophical traditions – at least since Descartes and the early work of Kant (see Toulmin 1990 for discussion of the historical origins of Cartesian dualisms) – the world has been perceived to be composed of two things with differing properties, generally described as objects and subjects. Nature – the world of objects – is seen as an inanimate and immutable essence that existed prior to its description by subjects. Subjects, on the other hand, are perceived as animate and are therefore invested with the ability to act and describe the inanimate world of objects. This section will consider the processes and methods by which scientists, philosophers and sociologists investigate this apparent division.

According to an objectivist position the world consists of objects which exist 'out there', beyond the internal world of human subjects. The relations pertaining between these objects can be adequately described, discussed and studied by perceiving them and then representing them through language. The relationship between our language terms and the existence of objects in the world is seen as unproblematic and one-to-one. The core concept on which much of the empirical position of objectivism rests is that of phenomenalism. According to this position, the world can only be perceived through its direct apprehension by the senses. Through the description of externally perceived objects, language allows a direct representation of what actually exists in the external world (see Rorty 1991, 1–20). The position of objectivism allows for the possibility of an outsider's view that is able to accurately describe the nature of the world (Putnam 1975). This view can be taken up simply because, as thinking and acting subjects, we have a privileged and external view of nature. When we view objects in this objective manner our sense data correspond exactly with what is found in nature, and the language we use to describe these sense data accurately depicts these data using words. The use of these words in language allows us then to define the boundaries around objects and establish the relations of sameness and difference between described objects. What is more, the relationships between objects perceived in this way are generally seen as causal; in other words, they can be described by simple cause and effect systems. This generalised position broadly encompasses a number of epistemological positions, and each is characterised by the a priori assumption that this general division of the world exists. For instance, logical positivism holds that through building observation-based theories about the world, and testing those theories against the observed world, we are able to adequately describe the true nature of the world (Hempel 1965).

These positions are viewed as essential theoretical tools for the natural sciences. The objective existence of a prior natural world is essential for carrying out science. This is because it is only by assuming the real existence of the natural world that scientists can feel secure that their knowledge provides a description of the world that is valid and consistent. Since the goal of science is the steady and cumulative accretion of knowledge, in order for science to be carried forward and reproduced it must accept the notion of nature as a constant. This constant, the natural world, can always be drawn on to back up arguments concerning the real nature of observations (Latour 1987, 94–100). There are two important points we must draw from this: first, in order to carry out science we must believe in the constancy of the natural world; and second, we must take up a detached position to accurately describe that world.

But there are problems with this view. What if we cannot extricate ourselves from the world in order to describe it? If we consider this possibility, we then have to consider that maybe our senses are conditioned by the position that we take up within the world. If this is allowed as a possibility, then it is also probable that we are not accurately describing our world, but categorising it in specific ways. If this is the case then our language cannot accurately represent the objects in the world. If we take all these possibilities into consideration, we can no longer consider the world as a constant. This is especially important if we wish to extend our analysis to animate subjects in order to examine their role in constructing society.

I will consider each of these points in order to explain the nature of subjectivism. At this point I wish to focus on the ways in which various processes of acculturation affect the way in which we describe and interpret the world. The main point here is that we can never step back from the world in order to describe and know it since the very apparatus we use to do so, our senses and our language, is determined by the cultural world in which we live.

I will commence my discussion with the problem of perception. Here the most important issue is the cognitive categorisation of our sense data and the subsequent categories we use to describe these data. Recent work by cognitive psychologists has questioned the notion that the categories we use to describe the world are essentialist in form. They concede that the mind has a particular and given structural organisation. However, the way in which this structure is ordered is dependent upon the cultural uses of devices such as metaphors in constructing relationships between perceived objects (Lakoff and Johnson 1980; Lakoff 1987).

If we consider the way in which we categorise the world to be determined not by a priori categories in the world, but by the metaphors we employ to describe those categories, then we reach a point at which the description of the world is contingent or emergent. Rather than viewing the world of objects and subjects as static, we have to see them as fluid and dependent for their apparently solid nature on our descriptions of them. Rather than accurately using sense data to describe objects, we are using culturally contingent values or metaphors. If we take this as a valid observation, then the language we use to describe those objects is also contingent. This point was made apparent through the early work of linguists such as Saussure (1916 [1966]) and philosophers such as Wittgenstein (1953). Importantly, Saussure noted that there was an arbitrary relationship between objects and the precise words used to describe them in language. There is nothing in the properties of objects that is reflected in the words used to refer to them in social language. For Saussure, language was an abstract code distinct from the world of objects.

This appraisal of language has given rise to two further important notions: most notably, structuralism (Lévi-Strauss 1966), the study of how such abstracts are ordered culturally, which is essentially a study of the codes employed in constructing culture; and semiotics, which has given rise to a deeper understanding of how symbols are used. Rather than considering symbols as entirely abstract, the focus is on how meaning is created through the codified use of such symbols (Eco 1979; Ricoeur 1976). This presents us with a double problematic: we are not only conditioned by the cultural world around us, and are therefore not perceiving the world directly, but we are also investigating the manipulation of objects as cultural symbols, as cultural meanings. Thus we arrive at a position where neither the senses used to report the natural world, nor the cultural devices used to describe it (language), relate to the objective world in a simple way. Rather they are determined by our cultural expectations. This leads us on to a further important point concerning our interpretation of the world.

I have outlined the problems surrounding our cultural understanding of the world of inanimate objects, and have observed that our subjective examination of objects is bound up with the manipulation of cultural meanings; however, further problems arise when we turn to consider the world of animate subjects. First, our positions as interpreters are not divorced from the subject that we are interpreting – human society – since the very apparatus we use to describe society are the cultural meanings from which society is composed. We are then in a situated relationship in relation to our subject of investigation, and we must be extremely careful about our interpretations with regard to this relationship. The study of this situated relationship and the nature of the interpretations we make while a part of this relationship are essential components of the process of hermeneutics (Ricoeur 1981). What is more, while I have observed that for natural scientists the world of objects is composed of static entities with fixed relations between them, for social scientists society can be considered to be composed of social relations; however, these social relations are never static or constant. We cannot objectify them; rather they are created through a continuous dynamic, described as social practice (Bourdieu 1977). If we are to study society, we cannot appeal to an objectified and constant nature. We are not considering something which has a priori existence; rather we are considering something which is continually being made and remade.

Rationality and relativism

To reiterate, then, we are confronted by a world-view that divides off objects from subjects. While the relationship between the two is seen as problematic, there are two broad methods for achieving knowledge of the world. The first, natural science, studies nature and uses its privileged position as an active subject in taking up a detached view of the external world. The second, social science, studies society and therefore cannot take up any such privileged position. Rather, it realises the conditional nature of the knowledge it produces while attempting to describe society. I now wish to explore in more detail two further theoretical positions taken up by natural science and social science, that is relativism and rationalism. Both of these positions focus on the nature of belief, certainty and the concept of truth. However, both positions rely on the assumption that the world is divided up into inanimate, essential nature and animate, contingent society, or objects and subjects.

Rationalism covers a wide series of debates (see Wilson 1971); however it is broadly concerned with the nature of belief, and how we arrive at that belief. Here rationalism overlaps considerably with the theoretical position of objectivism. According to a rationalist view, if we consider a priori that there is a nature that can be described, then the description of nature must follow a rational path. This in itself requires a specific form of reasoning that involves building up a series of law-like statements about the world. These statements follow an identical form in whatever context we care to consider them. For instance, if we believe p as a reason for believing q, then we will believe that p will equal q, wherever and whenever we observe either p or q. The connection between these two articles of belief is immutable and incontrovertible. A correlate of this is that if our knowledge is rationally constructed, then our beliefs can be considered as either true or false.

However, the relativist views things otherwise. Hollis and Lukes (1982, 5–10) define a series of relativist positions, including moral relativism, conceptual relativism, perceptual relativism, relativism of reason and relativism of truth. In the interests of space, the discussion here will focus on conceptual relativism, since this has most bearing on the issues discussed above. Put simply, relativist positions encompass the belief that 'people of different cultures live in different worlds' (Berger and Luckmann 1966; Sperber 1982). As Sperber (1982, 154) indicates, this does not mean that people literally live in parallel worlds, rather that they inhabit differing cognisable worlds. This basic position encompasses the idea that knowledge may be culturally constructed and that the very act of reasoning itself is culturally specific. Beliefs on a given topic can vary and the relations between knowledge are not, then, absolute. This position is particularly acute if we consider the way in which the world is categorised.

This view raises a series of problems. If the process by which beliefs are constructed cannot be viewed as following the same rational process in all parts of the world, how are we to assess competing knowledge claims? In other words, we can have no absolute rational knowledge and therefore no absolute incontrovertible truth. If we consider the possibility that belief is culturally contingent – a conceptual position – then this opens up the possibility that truth itself is contingent, a moral relativist position. It is due to the fact that conceptual relativism blurs with moral relativism in this way that the entire concept of relativism has received such bad press. If we throw out the possibility of an absolute transcendent system of knowledge, i.e. rationalism, then we also dispose of an absolute truth. Therefore, one of the major issues in the debate between relativism and rationalism centres on our ability to assess knowledge between systems.

Again we are faced with differences in the order and goals of differing forms of knowledge, characterised by the natural and social sciences. It is essential for science to retain the idea of nature being 'out there', prior to human experience, for if nature was constantly changing we would be unable to observe it accurately and objectively. However, it is also essential to retain the notion of a science that is ordered according to unassailable universal laws, since if we consider the possibility that these laws change according to cultural context, then we lose certainty in the application of these laws in the generation of further scientific theories. If scientists had to continually check and recheck the reliability and validity of these laws, science would be unable to get on with the task of scientific and technological advancement. The belief in the generation of valid laws characterises a rationalist or positivist science.

On the other hand, the concept of some form of relativism allows historians of science, and anthropologists and archaeologists studying other cultures to consider the possibility of other knowledge systems as discrete and coherent forms of knowledge, which each generate their own forms of logic. If the social sciences were to take up a rationalist position, it would be necessary to consider the beliefs of other periods of history, or other cultures, as irrational or misguided. This would amount to a form of rational imperialism which would debilitate the enterprise of understanding other cultures. Furthermore, due to the hermeneutic involved in the interpretation of cultural knowledge, the critical stance of anthropology is seen as an important viewpoint, since by studying other cultural systems we are able to critically reflect on our own. As Strathern (1995) has recently noted in relation to the issues of global and local culture, knowledge is generated through our ability to shift between different contexts. In this regard Tambiah (1990, 111) describes the interpretative position of anthropologists as a 'double subjectivity'. The anthropologist must subjectively enter the minds of the people they are studying in order to understand them according to their own categories, while simultaneously translating those categories as if distanced from them. The critical distance that an anthropological viewpoint provides enables us to contrast a variety of different orders of knowledge, but this position brings with it a whole series of problems. How are we to judge our knowledge systems against others? Can we utilise a single benchmark against which to judge other cultures? Is there any point at which knowledge may be considered as commensurable? Is there a core set of real or essential facts about the world from which the beliefs of other cultures are constructed?

The problem of how we go about judging knowledge claims has been tackled on a number of levels. I wish to examine this issue from a variety of angles by examining the problem of external perspective, as well as the difficulties surrounding the internal constructs used within rational statements. The major issue in the debate between rationalists and relativists concerns the nature of the paradigms, or the worlds, in which knowledge is constructed. Can we view these differing worlds as being composed of a core set of beliefs around which alternate paradigms are constructed, or do we simply classify alternate beliefs as equally true, equally false or equally true-or-false (Hacking 1982, 49). Each view leads us to an impasse.

First, we will consider the possibility that there is a core set of beliefs about the world that are incontrovertible. Such a view would propose that each alternate viewpoint was viewing the same set of data from differing perspectives, but that each of these perspectives could be bridged through an act of translation (Hollis 1982). For instance, both Kuhn (1970) and Feyerabend (1975) claim that differing paradigms can be observed within the history of science, and that such paradigms are incommensurable. In other words, the science practised by one set of practitioners, at a given period in time, could not be comprehended by another set of practitioners at another time. Each set of practitioners occupied differing worlds and the knowledge generated in each world was relative to that world. Here Kuhn (1970) indicated that each group was practising their own rational methods, but from our viewpoint the knowledge of each group stands in a relative relationship to the other.

For the rationalist, the view that these paradigmatic understandings can be translated and understood by us supposes that the two systems cannot be incommensurable. If we can translate between these two domains of knowledge, there must be some common ground by which the two belief systems can be compared. The assumption is that there is an external viewpoint from which we can measure the validity of either belief. But how do we externally measure the validity of either system? As Rorty (1991a, 49–50) indicates, there can be no position by which we can judge alternate paradigmatic positions, since such a position would involve taking up what he calls an 'ethnocentric' viewpoint in assuming that what we described as true or rational was actually true. On the other hand, if we take the relativist view that each paradigm or world has equally valid belief systems, we still run into a problem if we also believe that in each world we are viewing the same external reality. This is partly because such a view presupposes that cultural beliefs are simply an adjunct to external reality (see Berger and Luckmann 1966; Ingold 1990; Richards 1990). A number of writers have observed that there is a tendency amongst both relativists and rationalists to employ both forms of belief system simultaneously (see Elkana 1981, 3). Elkana (1981, 3–4) describes this intellectual position as 'two-tier thinking', and I will consider this in more detail below.

At this stage I simply wish to note that both the rationalist and relativist viewpoints leave us with a series of problems. The position of rationalism ultimately relies on the notion that there is a set of rational core beliefs which must relate to external reality in a precise and determined way. Belief systems that do not accept the existence of these rational core beliefs are either classified as irrational or are considered to be translatable to an immutable system of understanding. Meanwhile, the relativist belief leaves us with the possibility that each paradigm or world is incommensurable, and therefore each system of beliefs has its own coherence and rationale. Each discrete belief system is seen to relate to and to construct external reality in its own manner. The former position is most applicable to the study of the natural world, since it relies on the concept of a constant and immutable nature. The latter position is most applicable to the study of a constantly changing set of social relations, since it relies on the notion of cultural or social difference. The relationship between the two points is problematic since, any attempt to find a 'bridgehead' (Hollis 1982) must rely on the notion of an overall external and neutral viewpoint by which to judge them.

Piecing together the past

The previous section outlined the problems involved in the broad approaches of both the natural and social sciences. In this section I want to examine the way in which the issues of objectivity, subjectivity, rationalism and relativism have been considered within archaeology as a means of understanding the underlying roots of the divided state of scientific and theoretical approaches to the past. I wish to consider the ways in which archaeologists relate to, and interpret, the material residues of the past: the archaeological record. Linda Patrik (1985) has undertaken the most detailed account of the contrasting approaches to the archaeological record. Here I will draw out some of Patrik's observations regarding the differing approaches to the archaeological record and set them against some of the generalised observations I have already made regarding the natural and social sciences.

The notion of an archaeological record is used as a heuristic device by archaeologists, as a means of conceptualising the way in which they perceive past human action to operate in relation to the remains of the past. However, as Patrik observes, archaeologists have no unified notion of what they understand the archaeological record to be (1985, 29–31). She defines two contrasting conceptions of the archaeological record: the physical model and the textual model. The physical model is characterised as considering the archaeological record to be composed of physical objects and features that are static effects of past causes; the record is perceived as a direct record of physical objects and processes. Given this, both the features and spatial order of the record are seen to be due to physical and behavioural processes that exhibit causal regularities – in other words, they can be seen to operate according to universal or probabilistic laws. By way of contrast, the textual model views the record to be composed of physical objects and features that are material signs or symbols of past concepts. The record is seen to record human actions, ideas and events of human importance. Following on from this, the structure of the record is viewed as being composed of rule-guided behaviour which is expressed in culturally specific ways; or in other words, the record is viewed as contextually specific (for a summation of these views see Patrik 1985, 36). Both viewpoints have their roots in the contrasting epistemological and methodological positions outlined above.

The physical model of the archaeological record

Those archaeologists taking up the physical model treat the archaeological record as the natural substrate on which the objective knowledge of the world is founded. The physical remains of the past are objects that have been separated from us by the passing of time. This approach to the archaeological record is typified by two main schools of thought: culture-historical archaeology and new or processual archaeology.

The first school of thought is exemplified by the work of Vere Gordon Childe. Childe was expressly concerned with distinguishing objective reality from subjective experience. He was specifically interested in distinguishing between the nature of knowledge itself and the observation of 'reality' within the archaeological record. Childe was aware of the situated position of the archaeological observer, since he noted that while archaeologists are concerned with observing cultures, their principle instrument of observation is itself culture (1949, 5). He realised that the categories we employ to understand other cultures are necessarily derived from our own. McNairn (1980, 135) has observed that this intellectual realisation was critical to Childe's approach to archaeology. Since, due to the relative nature of the conceptual frameworks of culture, Childe was uninterested in reconstructing past cultures using our own conceptual frameworks; rather he was concerned with examining what he described as 'true knowledge'. This consisted primarily of practical or technical behaviour, since he proposed, quite reasonably, that technical behaviour was a distillation of cultural knowledge (see chapter 5 for a fuller discussion of this notion). Despite this theoretical position, Childe's writings embody some of the most imaginative reconstructions of the past ever to have been written. However apart from his use of Marxist approaches, Childe's theoretical approach to the study of past societies remains relatively implicit.

Much of Childe's writing on the nature of knowledge took special care to distinguish different orders of knowledge, specifically the magical and the scientific (Childe 1956). He was careful to distinguish the uniformitarian principles, which are observable in the present, from the cultural principles of action that he supposed to be both lost and moreover inconsequential to our understanding of past action. A similar position concerning the definition and verification of orders of archaeological knowledge was proposed by Hawkes (1954). Hawkes suggested that the degree of certainty or verifiability concerning statements about the past depended on the degree to which those statements were grounded in archaeological evidence. As statements moved further from empirical statements about archaeological remains, the inferences drawn from them could be made with less and less certainty. Interpretation progressed from the bottom up by a process of inductive reasoning based on the self-evidential nature of the evidence. It is notable in this regard that those domains of the archaeological record which remain closer to material 'reality' are most amenable to archaeological scientists. Since technological data are thought to be grounded in the material aspects of the record, the technological dimensions of archaeological materials provide the subject matter of much archaeological science.

A similar theoretical position persisted amongst new or processual archaeologists. This school of thought is exemplified by the work of Lewis Binford. Although, for processualists, knowledge about the past was also based on the foundations of the archaeological record, the possibility of reconstructing past social systems from this record was viewed with less pessimism. For instance, Binford noted that due to the static nature of the material remains of the past, the remains could not be treated as if they spoke for themselves. He correctly noted that the mere observation of remains was inadequate as a means of understanding the past (Binford 1983a and b). Rather, as with the subjectivist viewpoint outlined above, he suggested that the observations by which the remains of the past are apprehended are necessarily theory laden. Like Childe before him, Binford's main concern was with distinguishing between objective reality and subjective experience. However, unlike Childe, he sought to work from the objective reality to describe the subjective experience of past cultures (Binford 1962; Binford and Binford 1968). Rather than abandoning the interpretation of past cultures, Binford instead sought to make theory an explicit component of the process of interpretation.

In order to provide a firmer basis on which to discuss past social systems, much new archaeology was concerned with producing an objective account of material evidence prior to its involvement in interpretation. Given a view of the archaeological record as the static remains of past physical processes, the obvious step to take in the attempt to move from the physical remains of the archaeological record towards more generalised statements about past activity involved the creation of universalising laws. While new archaeologists realised their situated position with regard to the material remains of the past, it should be noted that all attempts to formulate universalising laws concerning the nature of the archaeological record were distinguished by a single objective. That objective was the attempt to be divested of this situated relationship with the aim of providing a more empirical account of the evidence.

The mode by which such laws were generated took a number of divergent courses. The first involved ethnoarchaeology, the observation of living populations creating material remains in the present. Here the supposition was that by observing the actions of various traditional populations in the 'ethnographic present', the archaeologist could provide an objective model of the kind of probable formation processes which make up the archaeological record (see Binford 1978; Gould 1980). I wish to say little about this field of archaeological enquiry here; however, I will note that such an activity, while providing increased knowledge concerning site formation, says little about the social structure which brought the site into being, to say nothing of the responsibilities and moralities involved in the exercise (Gosden 1999, 58–61).

Given the problems of ethnoarchaeology, a further field of enquiry emerged, involving the generation of laws that would more closely inform the archaeologist about site formation processes. This second avenue of study included two main strands of enquiry; the first of these, proposed by Binford (1983), became known as Middle Range theory. By employing the principle of the uniformitarian behaviour of certain mechanical and physical laws in the past and present, Binford sought to generate a set of laws relating to the behaviour of objects which could be observed in the present and related to the past. The central requirement of Middle

Range research involved archaeologists effectively stepping out of the pre-suppositions that bound them to the interpretation of the archaeological record. In other words, it supposed a position of absolute objectivity. As Barrett (1990, 33–4) notes, Middle Range research also relies on the objective observation of these laws in the present, a position of extreme empiricism.

A further attempt to formulate laws concerning site formation was made under the aegis of behavioural archaeology (Schiffer 1976). Here it was conceded that the record need not be a direct reflection of what happened in the past, and may be subject to numerous distortions, both natural and anthropogenic. Therefore, one of the primary and essential tasks for archaeological enquiry was the formulation of laws that would distinguish between the 'real' remains of the past and those that are the result of disturbance. The generation of laws of this nature is especially important with regard to attempts to understand the natural formation processes by which the archaeological record is itself created.

We can observe from this that those archaeologists who view the record as the trace of physical processes place a significant emphasis on distinguishing between the 'real' as opposed to the distorted archaeological record. As I have observed earlier, there are difficulties with this approach. However, we can observe its legacy in the work of many archaeological scientists, most of whom take post-depositional changes, or taphonomy, into account in presenting their data. Indeed, taphonomic problems are used as one of the major means of refutation when criticising the validity of a body of scientific data. Furthermore, taphonomy is often used as an explanatory device in interpreting the structure of certain aspects of the archaeological record (e.g. Todd and Rapson 1988). The absolute necessity of making an adequate assessment of taphonomic factors concerns much of the practice of faunal and botanical analysis (for example see Chaplin 1971; Dimbleby 1985; Evans and O'Conner 1999, 78–92). In these accounts the physical appearance of the archaeological record has very little to do with anthropogenic or cultural processes, and greater weight is placed on its formation by physical processes.

While much emphasis was placed on investigating the material nature of the archaeological record, in the attempt to move beyond the physical nature of the archaeological record much new or processual archaeology was also concerned with the interpretation of past social systems. A number of approaches were utilised in order to understand the nature of past social systems, but systems theory, ecological theory and cultural evolution were the most often employed. Systems theory was derived from biology, economics and computing (Watson *et al.* 1971). It conceived of any operating system, whether biological or man-made, as being divided into inter-related parts, or subsystems, which each acted to create a holistic working system. When utilised in archaeology, isolated elements of the system could be studied as interacting processes. This enabled archaeologists to consider the relationship between differing elements of the archaeological record. These elements were not conceived as possessing simple one-to-one causative properties; rather, systems were perceived as operating through a series of interacting elements. The analysis of such complex systems required the mathematical or statistical treatment of data in order to make them amenable to study. The interactions between elements in complex systems were often viewed according to a model based on feedback mechanisms, a notion derived from cybernetics (Watson *et al.* 1971; Renfrew 1984). By modelling these feedback mechanisms, it was possible to explain or predict change in the system. Since the effect of variables could be modelled in this way, the state of systems could be described graphically.

Cultural evolution and ecological theory were both linked to a broad systems theory approach. A cultural evolutionary approach was traditionally used as a means of classifying social systems as they move through time, into bands, tribes, chiefdoms and states (Sahlins and Service 1960). This approach allowed given states within the system to be characterised and was a powerful tool in explaining how specific social formations came into being (Renfrew 1973, 1979). While systems theory explained the way in which various elements of the system interacted, cultural evolution was a means of ordering the changes within a system and provided a useful conceptual anchor around which to arrange past social formations. Ecological theory was more closely applicable to the explanation of stasis and change. If the relationship between social systems and the environment was conceived as open, then the environment could be viewed as having a feedback effect on the system. Such a view was founded on the notion of culture as an 'extrasomatic', or extra-bodily, adaptive mechanism for coping with the environment (Binford 1965, 205). According to ecological theory societies were bounded systems and, like the more general aspects of systems theory, ecological approaches enabled the relationships between variable components of a system to be modelled (see Evans and O'Conner 1999, 17–60). As such, ecological theory was particularly useful as a means of examining the relations between components of settlement systems, between members of a trade or exchange system, or more generally between social groups and the environment (see Watson *et al.* 1971, 91–107).

Each of the general theories that are applied to either culture or society by new or processual archaeologists relies on a number of core assumptions. The problem with the physical model of the archaeological record is that, when we move away from statements concerning the regularities observed between static material remains and natural processes to consider the relationship between material remains and human action, it becomes necessary to also consider social relations as static. If we consider the archaeological record to be composed of static objects, and the relations between these objects as best studied through a theoretical framework which relies on the use of universal or probabilistic laws, then we run into a number of problems when we attempt to study society.

As noted above, an objective or rationalist viewpoint relies on the notion of nature as static and constant, yet society is neither static nor constant. However, the application of systems theory and its cognate theories, cultural evolution and ecological theory, all depend upon the notion of stasis. While systems theory attempts to describe the dynamics of systems, relationships between elements of the system are examined as if they were in distinct stable states. One of the core concepts of such a theory is the notion of homeostasis, the process of remaining stable. Ecological theory similarly relies on systematising and creating mathematical models as a means of understanding settlement patterns or trade systems. Finally, cultural evolution itself relies on the notion of stable bounded social formations such as tribes and chiefdoms.

Each of these theories carries with it a rationalist notion of being able to accurately map and model the world in a systematic way. In each case human societies are ordered according to a series of given absolutes, such as water, food source, etc. We can see then that those archaeologists who consider the archaeological record to be composed of relations between static objects must adopt two strategies for understanding the past. First, they systematise the physical objects from which the record is composed, by creating general laws applicable to the formation of the record. Second, because of adopting this viewpoint, they then find it essential to build on this approach by systematising social systems and creating laws that model the patterning of human behaviour in the past (see Toulmin 1990 for a discussion of the history of these ideas of society).

It is important that we should note the legacy of systems theory, and especially ecological theory, on the practice of archaeological science. An understanding of taphonomic factors provides a methodological backdrop for much archaeological science, especially faunal and botanical analysis. Ecological theory (Jones 1992) coupled to classical economics provides the theoretical framework within which the relations between humans and the environment are then studied (for example see Higgs 1975; Jarman, Bailey and Jarman 1982). Meanwhile, the systematic and law-like nature of systems theory and ecological theory provides much of the impetus for the study of exchange systems. Archaeological science operates within a framework which allows the possibility of systematically classifying the composition of the material nature of artefacts, and due to this there is a concurrent emphasis on a theoretical framework within which exchange can be systematically modelled. Thus archaeological science provides a number of physical and chemical characterisation techniques, such as petrology (Middleton and Freestone 1991), Neutron Activation Analysis (Hughes *et al.* 1991; Neff 1992) and isotopic analysis (Gale and Stos-Gale 1992), which allow a more or less accurate means of distinguishing materials of different types. These methodologies are also considered as a further means of classifying material. When these techniques are employed to make more interpretative statements concerning the past, such statements are often made within a theoretical framework which also allows for a systematic description of the past (for examples see Renfrew, Dixon and Cann 1966).

   The point here is not necessarily that all archaeological scientists are theoretically reliant on systems theory and ecological theory, but rather that the legacy of the concerns which were bound up with these theoretical frameworks have had an important bearing on the areas of study which archaeological scientists find of interest at present. Thus, much archaeological science is dedicated to the investigation of exchange networks or the interpretation of the relations pertaining between humans and the environment. While much archaeological science is eminently suitable for these tasks, one of the important questions I wish to consider in this volume is this: can archaeological science be employed to consider theoretical questions framed under a different philosophical background? In order to consider this possibility, I will turn to consider the textual model of the archaeological record.

The textual model of the archaeological record

As noted above, those archaeologists taking up a textual view of the past believe that the archaeological record is composed of the material remains of signs or symbols. The symbols are elements of a codified symbolic structure, and such signs or symbols are viewed as having operated in past communication systems. Therefore, the existence of material remains notifies us of events of significance. Given this, the record is viewed as structured, since each sign or symbol is seen to be a single element in a wider structure. The task of archaeologists with this viewpoint is to translate and read the past (Hodder 1986; Tilley 1991).

   An important point to note here is that, following on from the approach of structural linguistics, the relationship between the material world and the world of signs or symbols is not conceived of as one-to-one. Rather, the archaeological record is viewed as a representation. Like the earlier approach of Schiffer (1976), reading the archaeological record depends on translation (Patrik 1985, 50). However, unlike Schiffer, this translation does not involve distinguishing between the 'real' and the extraneous; instead this act of translation embraces the problems of discourse (see Ricoeur 1981).

Barthes (1977) notes the problem, common to the study and interpretation of cultural signs, that there is an interpretative distance between author and reader. Due to this interpretative distance, the validity of an interpretation is bound up as much with the expectations of the reader as with what the author wished to express (Ricoeur 1981, 131–45). Therefore, rather than searching for the underlying 'real' archaeological record, those archaeologists adopting a textual view of archaeology are interpreting the record at a distance; the interpretation of the archaeologist in the present is as valid as the meaning attached to the object in the past. The reading of the archaeological record therefore cannot be objective; at no point can the archaeologist step out of his or her interpretative relationship with the archaeological record in order to create a series of generalising laws. Rather, the process of reading the material remains of the past is conditional: it is conditioned by the prejudices, presuppositions and cultural values of the interpreter in the present (Shanks and Tilley 1987, 105–6). The interpretation of the past is then a political exercise (Shanks and Tilley 1990; Tilley 1989a). Archaeologists are bound up in an interpretative relationship, or hermeneutic, with the object of their study. Objects themselves are only given meaningful status through interpretation.

There are a number of important correlates of this view. First, the meanings attached to objects are not fixed. Instead, the assignment of meaning to objects involves a process of dialectics, a movement between the presuppositions of the interpreter and the material constraints of the object (Shanks and Tilley 1987, 110–12). Second, if we consider the view that meaning may be considered to change according to context (Hodder 1986; Barrett 1987a) then, rather than considering the assignation of meaning to an object as an entirely open and relativist exercise, meaning will be tied down and fixed by context. The process of interpreting the archaeological record is not a process of assigning fixed meanings to objects but rather of reading the patterns of structured differences between objects. If we consider the archaeological record as a text, then we can also consider this text to have a grammatical structure. Rather than considering the archaeological record to be composed of static objects with a fixed relationship to each other, the record is viewed as composed of objects whose relationships are constantly changing according to their contextual relationships.

Interestingly this emphasis on the archaeological record as a text privileges the symbolic nature of the record over the physical nature of the record. The textual approach allows sophisticated examinations of the symbolic nature of objects; however, since the relationship between the object and its cultural use as a symbol is considered to be arbitrary, the physical nature of the object has little effect on the way in which it is employed symbolically. This problem has been addressed in recent years (see especially Gosden 1994; Tilley 1996) and will be developed further in chapters 4 and 8. Nevertheless, it is easy to see why this view of the representational nature of the archaeological record has had little effect on archaeological scientists. This is because the contingent nature of meaning makes objective assertions concerning the physical nature of material remains difficult to verify (see O'Conner 1991 and Rowley-Conwy 2000 for clear delineation of these views). An initial proposal that archaeological assemblages be treated as culturally structured (Moore 1982; Richards and Thomas 1984) has had a relatively low impact on the analysis of archaeological materials. I feel that (*contra* Rowley-Conwy 2000) the notable exception to this is the analysis of certain kinds of deposit in animal and human osteological studies (Hesse 1995; Marciniak 1999). Here the concept of structured deposition is viewed as having important implications for our understanding of the significance of differing modes of deposition (see papers in Anderson and Boyle 1996; Hill 1995; Kovacik 2000; Renouf 2000; Serjeantson 2000). In contrast, there has been little discussion of the problems and possibilities of structured deposits in relation to the study of plant remains or palynology (with the notable exception of Butler 1995; Hastorf 1991).

This view of the changing nature of the meaning attached to objects engenders a quite different approach to the interpretation of society. If we view the relationships between objects to be in a constant state of flux, this then allows us to see how the meanings attached to objects may change over time. By conceptualising the meanings of and relationships between objects as constantly open to change and re-contextualisation, it is possible to see how this view allowed contextual archaeologists to reconsider the relationship between material culture and society. Rather than studying societies as bounded and static social systems, archaeologists adopting a textual metaphor viewed societies as constantly changing. Here the dominant views of society were derived from either Giddens (1984) or Bourdieu (1977, 1990).

Both authors broadly view societies to be composed of a set of social structures that are informed by a set of structuring principles. These

structuring principles are not unlike the set of codified rules of structuralist thinking. However, structures are not fixed, as in structuralism,
but are constantly being reproduced as individuals draw on them and re-
work them. This process is described by Giddens (1984) as *structuration*.
Therefore, the reproduction of society is not due to an innate tendency
towards homeostasis, as with earlier approaches, rather society is perceived to be in a constant state of flux. The constant process of making
and remaking the social structures of societies is what carries forward
social change. However, it is also this process which allows societies to
remain stable. According to this view of society, the structures upon which
individuals immersed within society draw, in order to act within the social
world, tend towards dispositions of stability, and it is this process which
is characterised by Bourdieu as *habitus*. However, while the process of
drawing on these structuring principles may provide stability, this process
may also provide the instrument of social change. Here the most important concept embodied in such a notion of society is that of agency; that
is, that societies are created and recreated through the active involvement
of knowledgeable and active human subjects (see Johnson 1989; Barrett
1994; Dobres and Robb 2000). In conclusion, then, society is not considered as static; it is considered to be in a constant process of flux. Both
the theoretical positions of Bourdieu and Giddens provide interpretative
archaeologists with a more refined view of both social stability and social change. Finally, rather than utilising external factors to explain either
social change or stability, the notion of agency allows us to understand
more clearly how societies are shaped internally.

Conclusion

At this point I want to step back from the details of these issues and provide an overview of some of the problems concerned with the attempt to
harmonise each view of the archaeological record. As we have observed,
each model of the archaeological record involves taking up an epistemological position which resonates strongly with the wider issues that were
considered at the beginning of this chapter. Thus those archaeologists
taking up a position which views the record as physical can be broadly
characterised as objectivist, empiricist and rationalist, while those archaeologists who consider the archaeological record as textual can be broadly
characterised as subjectivist and relativist. The labels are fairly broad,
but at this point they serve as a means of characterisation. Many of the
difficulties of integrating scientific archaeology with an interpretative archaeology based on a number of post-structuralist positions arise from
the conflicting nature of these positions.

I do not wish to say too much here about how this integration of knowledge may be achieved; rather I will focus on the problems and benefits of both archaeological science and interpretative approaches to the study of past societies. A number of authors have noted that while many archaeologists have abandoned the central tenets of objectivism and rationalism as valid means of judging the past, archaeological science has retained these theoretical standpoints (Thomas 1990; Edmonds 1990). Moreover, it has also been suggested that archaeological science is reliant on methodological critique as a substitute for interpretation (Thomas 1990). While this may be so, neither of these points should be entirely unexpected since, as I have already indicated, the natural sciences are epistemologically bound to an objective and rational theoretical position. Methodology, on the other hand, is simply a procedure for distinguishing and defining the objective nature of the data. The precise definition of methodology within the literature of archaeological science has its place within the theoretical framework of objectivism and empiricism. While I am not proposing a return to empiricism or positivism, I feel that it is the rigorous application of precisely defined methodologies that lends scientific discourse its strength. It is this aspect of science in archaeology that is essential to retain.

I am not interested in considering methodology as a validatory mechanism; rather it is a device, which allows certain aspects of the archaeological evidence to be reproduced with reasonable accuracy. Science operates most comfortably within the wider field of archaeology when we are able to employ well-defined and rigorous scientific techniques to the archaeological record. I am thinking here of some of the techniques routinely used in archaeology which have been imported from the physical sciences (Tite 1972), or from chemistry (Pollard and Heron 1996). In other words, these are instrumental scientific techniques that can be usefully employed in order to provide a more detailed characterisation of the archaeological object. The problems arise when we utilise a broader empiricist philosophy as a means of understanding society. As noted earlier, as soon as we begin to frame society as a possible object of scientific study we must begin to place artificial constraints on our understanding. We reify it, or make it into a static object. It is this method of studying society that Bourdieu describes as social physics (1990, 26–7, 135). The process of objectifying society and the concurrent methodologies and interpretations derived from this process are a reasonable description of what may be considered as scientism (Edmonds 1990; Barrett 1990).

It was precisely because of the problems inherent in viewing societies as static objects that there was such a major shift in the interpretative framework employed in archaeology (see Hodder 1982a). Rather than attempting to systematise society by viewing it through the lens of the natural sciences, archaeology moved to the interpretative position which had prevailed for a considerable period within a number of the social sciences (see Leach 1973; Gellner 1982; Miller 1982). One of the major strengths of an interpretative archaeology that embraces a variety of post-structuralist approaches is the rigorous nature of its theoretical frame-work. We are now able to begin to reconsider the complexities involved both in understanding how societies operate and in understanding the way in which the social operates to structure the archaeological record. What is more, interpretative approaches also allow a more critical under-standing of our social position as interpreters.

In conclusion, I would like to propose that in order to begin to consider the possibilities of relating scientific archaeology with interpretative archaeology we must retain an aspect of each. The strengths of scientific approaches are reflected in their methodological rigour and reproducibility, while the strengths of interpretative approaches are reflected in their theoretical rigour and their ability to provide a coherent and satisfying account of society. The problems of embracing these two aspects of contemporary archaeology are manifold, and we must move through a difficult epistemological minefield in order to provide a more satisfying account of the past which encompasses both approaches. That will be the subject of the next chapter.

2 Science as culture: creating interpretative networks

Reviewing the record

The previous chapter broadly reviewed both the physical and the textual approaches to the archaeological record, and was intended as an assessment of many of the debates prevalent in the archaeological literature. This re-examination had an important aim: by broadly characterising the two main approaches to the archaeological record and providing a brief account of the problems with each position, I drew out the differences between the two approaches. These distinctions are crucial since I feel that the source of the rift between archaeological scientists and theoretical archaeologists lies, at a fundamental level, with the starkly different philosophical approaches each group employs as a means of understanding the past. On one side, we have a viewpoint which regards the archaeological record as the product of physical processes which can be examined empirically and objectively using the sense data derived from the description of objects. These descriptions and measurements can then be built up into generalising laws that can be applied in all archaeological contexts. On the other side, we have a viewpoint which considers the archaeological record to be the product of meaningful social action. As such it can be considered to be composed of a structured set of differences, like a text. In this case, each sentence of the text, or part of the archaeological record, is contextually distinct.

There are two important points here. First, if we focus our intellectual efforts not just on the objective description of objects, but on the interpretation of past societies through the medium of objects, then we are placing ourselves in a situated, hermeneutic position in relation to these past societies. Second, if we regard societies as something more than static objects which can be classified into cultural evolutionary stages, and we dispose of the view of society as something we can describe mathematically, then we must begin to consider each society as culturally different and historically contextual. We cannot then apply a self-evident rationalist procedure to describe these societies, since this would be denying each society its cultural specificity.

If, on the other hand, we consider the material remains of the archaeological record to be the result of meaningful actions, then we must also consider the cultural logic which brought these material remains into being. In order to do this we must consider the possibility that our interpretations reflect the cultural specificity of the remains. By interpreting the remains in so many differing ways, we abandon the idea of a universal and rational mode of cultural understanding. This then opens up the problem of cultural relativism (Kohl 1993), which is especially problematic in an archaeological context. If we consider the possibility that differing orders of knowledge may be responsible for the patterns of material we observe in the archaeological record, how do we validate our interpretations of this material evidence, and which paradigm provides the best interpretation of the evidence? If we abandon the notion of a rationalist yardstick for interpretation, does this mean that all interpretations are equally valid?

Here it is essential to return to the issue of paradigms and the commensuration of knowledge. If we consider Kuhn's view of paradigms, then each body of knowledge generated within a paradigm is structured by the concerns of that paradigm and is therefore distinct. This approach serves to perpetuate the dichotomy that is evident between the two models of the archaeological record, since according to Kuhn neither domain of knowledge is commensurable with the other. Interestingly, Patrik (1985, 546) considers the possibility of utilising both models of the archaeological record simultaneously. The physical model would provide information regarding the physical behaviour of artefacts, taphonomy and site formation, while the textual model would be used as a means of understanding the structured nature of the archaeological record, which would thereby allow a clearer interpretation of the social action represented by the record. Although this seems a profitable way forward, there are problems with employing both models of the archaeological record in this way. This is because, according to such a view, we would retain the notion of a core set of beliefs regarding the 'reality' of the archaeological record and onto these our textual or interpretative approach would construct its culturally specific worlds of meaning.

As an alternative I wish to reconsider Tambiah's notion of a 'double subjectivity' (1990, 1–11). This concept allows us to consider interpretation as an act that results from the process of translation. Such a translation occurs, for example, when anthropologists place understandings generated by culturally specific categories within a framework generated under the preconceptions of Western thought processes. What might this activity look like in the context of archaeology? One possibility may be to adopt the interpretative methods considered by Barrett (1990). Barrett's ideas regarding the interpretative process arise out of a critique of the empiricism inherent in Binford's project of Middle Range research. Rather than simply applying empirical observations to data, as Binford's conception of Middle Range research requires, Barrett suggests a movement back and forth between the theoretically informed notions of how society is reproduced (notions which embrace an understanding of how human action relates to material conditions) and the material evidence. The dialectic involved in this process allows for the possibility of making more theoretically informed statements concerning the nature of past social action.

A similar approach is suggested by Wylie (1993), who pays close attention to the way in which interpretative statements about the past are validated through the use of data. Wylie suggests that, rather than making statements about the past through a series of inferential steps (a process she describes as chaining), we make statements by a process of tacking back and forth between theory and evidence. This allows us to follow a series of strands of evidence to create something like a web of meaning. This process involves drawing on interpretations made at a general level, and following through the effect these interpretations have on the conceptualisations of the evidence at a more particular level. The advantage with this interpretative process is that while chains of inference may be easily broken down by the removal of a single link in the chain, the process of tacking back and forth between theory and data involves developing many more or less concrete links between theory and data. The validity of these multiple links depends more on the number of their associations than on their testability. In effect, we create networks in which our theories and data are inextricably linked within a web of significance. Tilley (1993, 18) has likewise proposed a process of interpretation which stresses the importance of the values of connection, heterogeneity and multiplicity as aspects of an interpretative process which creates networks of significance between concepts. This process of interpretation has overall similarities with the interpretative activity described by anthropologists as 'thick description' (see Geertz 1973).

Wylie's approach to interpretation has been criticised for its noncommittal to one epistemological position or another, in which aspects of both positivism and relativism are retained (Fotiadis 1994; Little 1994). However, if we enter into this argument there is a danger of an infinite regress into the epistemological definition of precisely where the core of rationalism might stop and relativism might begin. These are considerable problems if we wish to remain within the domain of philosophy. Instead, I want to shift the argument slightly to what I hope is a more productive level by examining how it is that we create knowledge, through exploring the practices of scientific knowledge production.

To reiterate, we have seen that the interpretative positions of archae-ologists broadly rest on the premises which characterise the natural and social sciences; that is, that the world is divided into inanimate objects and animate subjects. Each is studied in different ways, using differing methodologies. But this interpretative fault-line is problematic, especially if we are attempting to write an interpretative archaeology which incor-porates knowledge produced using a scientific methodology. We have also seen that one way out of this impasse is to develop an interpreta-tive strategy that involves moving back and forth between theory and data, developing weaker and stronger connections between each strand of knowledge. In the next section I will develop this approach to inter-pretation by examining the way in which networks of interpretation may be understood within scientific practice.

Science and culture

In order to reconsider the position of science within the interpretative practices of the social sciences we need to interrogate the theoretical position of science in greater detail. The central problem with science is that its entire practice has traditionally been treated as if it were in a privileged position with regard to interpretation. While other forms of knowledge are treated as paradigmatic, scientific knowledge is treated as distinct, being beyond the problem of paradigms. In short, scientific knowledge is true knowledge with a privileged access to nature 'as it really is'. As a correlate of this, scientists themselves are considered to be neutral and unaffected by cultural presuppositions. Notably, Binford (1983, 45–57) developed exactly this kind of argument in relation to New Archaeology's position with regard to the interpretative position of Hodder and others. Similarly, although Kelley and Hanen (1988, 99–165) pay attention to the social context of archaeology, they are also interested in distinguishing between the 'logical' and 'non-logical' aspects of scientific endeavour, an endeavour aimed at retaining an objective core for the discipline.

As Rorty (1991, 46–7) notes, much of the discussion related to this problem has focused on the attempt to demarcate science as a partic-ular form of activity, defined by a special method or a special relation to reality. For instance, he notes that Hempel (1965) solves the prob-lem by constructing a logical method of confirmation without worrying whether this was scientific activity or not. Others, such as Quine (1966), conflated the whole of knowledge with science by supposing that the vocabulary of the natural sciences provided the true understanding of reality. It is precisely this position which brings with it a whole series of problems since, as science explodes outwards to include all human action and knowledge, much of that activity and knowledge must be described as irrational since it will not fit with the vocabulary of the natural sciences. Quine's proposition takes us no further since we are still unable, from this definition, to solve the problem of competing claims to other forms of knowledge. If all knowledge is rational, then how do we treat the knowledge claims that do not fit with this image of rationality, except by classifying other knowledge systems as pre-rational or misguided.

Objections to the attempts of science to define itself as special or definitionally rational have come from a number of quarters, including recent work in the anthropology of science. The aim of such studies has been to oppose the sort of definition proposed by Quine. Rather than viewing science as a special form of activity divided off from society, the emphasis has been on considering science as simply another form of activity which is conditioned by culture (Elkana 1981; Franklin 1995). For instance, Martin (1990) has demonstrated that the language used to describe the science of immunology is shot through with metaphorical statements of a gendered nature. Fahnestock (1999) develops this argument through an analysis of the tropes – or modes of description and rhetoric – used in the construction of scientific facts. In a similar vein Strathern (1992) has investigated the constitution of the notion of 'natural facts' concerning biological reproduction and shown them to be cultural products bound up with our culturally specific notions of kinship and genealogy. Furthermore, Haraway (1989) has suggested that science, rather than being a unified and rational procedure, contains concepts that are structured by gender biases which actively affect the construction of scientific facts. Each of these works indicates that the very construction of scientific concepts cannot be seen as value neutral and unaffected by culture (see Longino 1990). Thus, much of the critique of science has involved bringing science closer to culture, and bringing science and its practice into line with society as an object of study.

These studies are important, in that their central area of study is the way in which scientists represent knowledge (Bloor 1976). However, a problem still remains. The problem stems from the fact that such studies simply use society as a means of understanding science. What these studies are in effect saying is that although scientists think they are representing nature accurately they are in fact representing nature through the distorting lens of either culture or society (but see Haraway 1991,

1997; Strathern 1991). This still leaves us with the problem of nature. In each case nature is still perceived as having a prior existence. In one case scientists view themselves as having a privileged knowledge of nature; in the other case social scientists indicate that scientists' representations of nature are distorted. However, in this second case the notion of nature as an immutable entity is still retained (see Latour 1993, 91–9). In order to solve many of the problems of relativism and rationalism, and in order to enable science to be integrated within the interpretative positions of social theory, we need to dissolve the distinctions which are held to obtain between nature and society, and between objects and subjects.

Latour (1993, 91) has observed that it is precisely the demarcated nature of scientific knowledge and its privileged access to nature which causes so many of the problems surrounding notions of relativism and rationalism. This is due to the fact that if we consider science to have a privileged access to nature then the knowledge constructed through this privileged position also allows us to view culture as demarcated, since those who are able to 'see' nature in its true form are also culturally exemplary or special. As Latour notes, one of the major achievements of our rational and modern view of the world is our ability to demarcate ourselves off from other cultures. Thus we achieve the view that, while there are innumerable other cultures within the world, these cultures can all be set up in opposition to Western culture, since only the West has a knowledge system – science – which directly represents nature (1993, 100–4). It is this point which lies at the heart of rationalism.

If we wish to integrate interpretative and scientific methodologies, we need to re-conceptualise these relationships. What if there is not one single nature, but multiple natures each conceived differently by multiple cultures? We have already considered this possibility under the aegis of cultural relativism. But rather than retaining the rationalist concept of a priori nature – as a means of judging cultural constructions against – we must now entertain the possibility that nature is contingent rather than constant. Thus, nature as well as culture and society might be considered to be in a constant state of flux. Such a theoretical position allows for the possibility of studying both inanimate and animate objects and subjects, or as Latour puts it object-subjects or nature-cultures.

But this position brings its own difficulties. If we consider not one nature, but multiple natures, each placed in relation to multiple different cultures, how do we consider science to actually operate? If we no longer retain the notion of a single constant nature how do we explain science, and what is more, how do we explain the rationalist dictum that science works in multiple cultural contexts? In order to solve these problems we need to study in detail exactly how science does work. In other words, we need to perform a more detailed enquiry into the anthropology of science.

Science in action

By examining the approaches of the anthropology of science (Latour and Woolgar 1986), I want to draw out two things. First, I wish to attempt to elucidate some of the problems we may encounter if we consider both societies and natures to be contingent, and second, I wish to examine how we may use these theoretical viewpoints as a way of integrating scientific practice with the interpretative social sciences. I wish to consider here three main issues: the construction of facts, the issue of translation and the creation of networks.

We have already observed in the previous chapter that one of the most important theoretical standpoints available to the natural sciences is the notion that nature is constant. It is this standpoint that enables natural scientists to create 'facts' through the observation of nature and then utilise them in further study. Latour (1987, 1–17) describes this process as the creation of 'black boxes'. These 'black boxes' may be considered in precisely the same way that scientists traditionally conceive of them – they are concepts or devices whose workings are too complex to explain; all that is understood of them is the relationship between input and output. One of the defining features of the methodology of the natural sciences is that once facts are created they are very rarely re-examined – they are effectively 'black-boxed'. This is in contrast to the social sciences, where previous ideas are constantly being reviewed and argued over. While scientific facts are seen to be the product of the direct observation of nature, Latour shows that this process of observation is far more complex. In opening up the 'black boxes' he reveals the symmetry between the involvement of animate subjects, in other words scientists, and inanimate objects, the instruments with which they view the world. Once facts are created the role of the former is underplayed and the role of the latter is promoted as supreme. In a similar vein, Callon, Law and Rip (1986) suggest that rather than considering facts as static pieces of information, they should be considered as active. In other words, facts gain their power in scientific practice through their social use by people (see also Haraway 1989, chapter 1).

In order to understand more fully the process that goes into the creation of facts, we must examine the issues of translation. Facts are typically presented in paper form, as published articles. Once they are created, they become incontrovertible. While the arguments contained within these texts are themselves open to textual analysis (see Latour 1987, 21–62), it is not possible to critique factual information itself – this must be treated as a given. In order to understand the production of factual information, we need to progress from the texts in which facts are presented to the laboratories in which these facts are created. Instead of facts being self-evident and directly observable, Latour (1987, 64–70) notes that facts are actually translated or transformed into factual information through the use of scientific instruments.

In order to clarify this point I will use an example from my own work using Gas Chromatography (for detailed methodology see Evershed *et al.* 1990; Jones 1997). If I wish to demonstrate the existence of cattle milk within a pottery vessel I am required to do a number of things. First, a section of the vessel is drilled and an amount of pottery fabric is retained. This is then refluxed in organic solvent for six hours and the resulting mixture is then reduced. The mixture is then reduced over nitrogen and dissolved in ethanol. It is then reduced to dryness and derivatised. The derivatised sample is then reduced to dryness, redissolved in ethyl acetate and then injected into a High Temperature Gas Chromatography unit, which is linked to an integrator. After an hour eluting through the column, the derivatised fatty acids present in the mixture will be indicated as peaks of varying height and width which are printed out on paper by the integrator (see Fig. 2.1).

For more detailed confirmation I may decide to inject a different sample of the same mixture into a Gas Chromatography unit linked to a Mass Spectrometer. In this case I will be presented with peaks which represent the fragmentation pattern of the fatty acids on a computer screen. Finally, if I wish to be certain about the existence of cattle milk, I will compare my results against those of a sample of cattle milk that has undergone the same procedure. At no point am I directly observing fatty acids. Rather, the presence of fatty acids has been indicated to me by a process of transformation afforded by a set of instruments both chemical and electronic. These results will be presented in a quite different format, as a series of histograms (see Fig. 2.2). The 'raw data' will have been 'interpreted' – transformed and cleaned up for publication. This is a critical element in the rhetorical methods we employ to persuade our peers of the validity both of our methodologies and of our resultant conclusions. It is part of what Lenoir (1998, 4) describes as the 'materiality of communication' – what and how the material means of communication represent when we communicate with others.

At no point am I observing nature directly during this process. More importantly, this process cannot be easily criticised by an outsider, especially one who is unaware of the procedures of transformation and translation. Latour (1987, 21–62) makes the important point that in

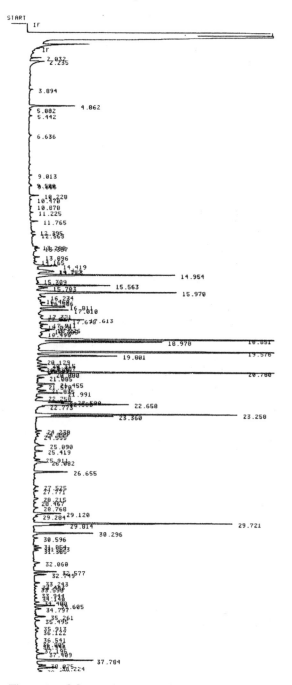

Figure 2.1 GC retention graph of sample SF 2,000 from a GC integrator

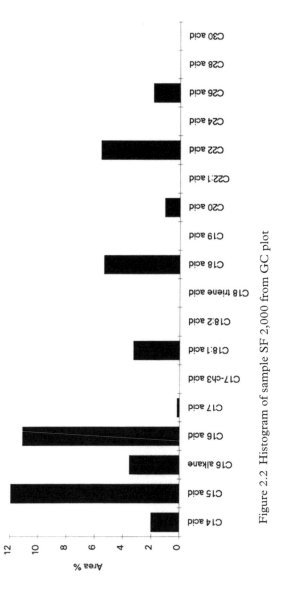

Figure 2.2 Histogram of sample SF 2,000 from GC plot

order to criticise scientific facts it is necessary to carry out the same procedures yourself. For most people this would be a costly and impractical
business, so facts are taken on trust and become unchallengeable. This
brings me to a further point, regarding the creation of facts and concerning the earlier discussion of facts as 'black boxes'. The production
of my facts concerning the presence of fatty acids which indicate cattle milk within the pottery vessels I was studying involves the drawing
together and articulation of a whole series of other facts. These facts
are effectively 'black boxes' that have been previously generated and on
which I rely in order to generate further meaningful factual information.
If I were to re-examine these 'black boxes' from the point of view of fatty
acids, I would be forced to re-examine the chemistry of fatty acids, which
would ultimately lead me into a review of the chemistry of carbon, hydro-
gen and oxygen and ultimately to sub-atomic physics. If I want to enquire
about the validity of the Gas Chromatography unit or the integrator, this
would lead me into the elution characteristics of various gas phase particles on capillary columns, or for the integrator into the characteristics
of microchip technology. However, my interests are in the generation of
information concerning food use in a particular period of human history. Like most scientists concerned with the generation of more factual
information I have neither the time nor inclination to investigate these
other avenues of information. Instead, I take them as read; I 'black-box'
them. We can observe from this example that prior factual information
is tied together to make a seamless whole. It is this process of tying information together which allows scientists to proceed with the creation
of more facts. It is this process of tying information together which we
may describe as a network, and it is to the working of such networks that
I will turn next.

   It is important to realise that networks are not just made up of facts and
instruments that articulate together in order to create a seamless working whole. Networks are also composed of people (Hughes 1983). This
point is crucial, since by looking at the role of people in the creation of
facts and the ways these facts are further used in the creation of more
facts, the analysis is biased towards neither objects nor subjects. Instead,
the analysis shifts between objects and subjects and looks at the way
in which they operate together. Science and the technologies produced
by science are not then simply the result of inanimate objects articulating together; rather, they are a product of the forces of both animate
subjects (people) and inanimate objects (instruments). It is the articulation of these processes together which creates a network, and networks
are composed of weaker and stronger associations between people and
things.

However, due to the fact that science and technology are 'black-boxed', the human factor in the process of technological production is removed from the equation. Technology is then perceived to have a life of its own; it has become an animate object (Latour 1987, 1993; Pfaffenberger 1992). Both the production and use of science and technology involve the articulation of a whole series of factors, some of which may be physical processes, others political, others economic. Yet all of these are brought together as part of a network in order to create a fact or to make things work. The key is to understand how the associations between these disparate social and physical factors create facts and technologies. Most important, due to the social nature of science and technology, and the accretion of facts as 'black boxes', we can begin to think of the process of technological advancement as something like the process described in the previous chapter as structuration (see Pfaffenberger 1992; Giddens 1984). Thus new technologies are structured by, and built up from, the available factual and material resources that surround them, rather than always being conceived in a scientific and technological vacuum.

In order to clarify the set of assertions made above we need to turn to an example. Using the example of Diesel, the inventor of the diesel engine, Latour (1987, 105–6) notes that the products of scientific technologies do not simply emerge fully formed. While Diesel had the initial idea of creating an engine that ran according to Carnot's theory of thermodynamics, this was not the end of the process of creation but the beginning. His first ally was Lord Kelvin, a reviewer of his ideas who placed his considerable scientific weight behind the notion. However, in order to build the engine he had to enlist the services of MAN, a German machines firm. They were involved because of their own wish to develop a more efficient steam engine. During the testing of the engine there were considerable problems with fuel combustion that required building an elaborate system of pumps and cylinders, making the engine less efficient and more bulky. Therefore, Diesel's task was to tie together Carnot's thermodynamics, Lord Kelvin, the German machine firm and the fuel combustion problems. Only by doing this could he create a 'black box' – a working object. As Latour illustrates, the finished machine had severe problems and its use as a taken-for-granted, a fact or 'black box' did not take place until some years later, years in which Diesel had a nervous breakdown and was close to suicide. The object was only 'black-boxed' some years later, and by this time it was so transformed that its relation to Diesel was scant; it had become transformed through the operation of many other objects and subjects.

This example demonstrates that networks are not simply the result of the operations of machines or inanimate objects; they are also made to operate through the ideas, politics and economics of people. What is more, networks are composed of stronger and weaker associations. For instance, the association between the fuel combustion and the German machines firm was weak, while the association between Diesel and Carnot's thermodynamics was strong. In order for something to be made to work these associations must articulate together, and as Latour notes, the network is only as strong as its weakest association (1987, 121–2). Finally, we can observe that science and technology are drawn on in human life as a series of animate objects, whose practicality, usefulness and utility are already predetermined through the earlier role of human beings in their creation.

Theoretical implications of an anthropology of science

What does all this mean in relation to the problems we have been discussing for the past two chapters? Well, the most important point to arise from this elucidation of science is the notion of *associations*. Rather than considering objects and subjects as distinct and immutable entities, in order to understand how science works we need to examine the associations between them. By examining the set of associations set up between animate subjects and inanimate objects and interpreting them through the same analytical procedures, we are able to begin to understand how science and technology work. The important point here is that we treat objects as social in the same way we treat people as social. Objects are always bound up in the social projects of people, and it is this that makes them animate. This theoretical and methodological treatment also allows us to solve a number of the problems that have been a motif of the previous chapter, namely the distinction between objects and subjects, rationality and relativism.

We can now observe that the distinction between objects and subjects has become less rigid, and we are therefore in a better position to assess the way in which scientific practices interlock with the interpretative practices of social science. We can side-step the problem of retaining a rationalist core of knowledge onto which cultural specific understandings are constructed. By doing this we are able to re-evaluate the positions of rationalism and relativism. Rationalism can be seen to be a product of the series of associations that go to make up scientific practice, especially the process of transformation and the setting up of associations into networks. Science works because our networks of scientific practice are extensive; these networks can be seen to extend at different scales. The political and economic networks of capitalism extend further and with stronger associative links between them than the networks of associations which characterise traditional and small-scale societies (see Latour 1993, 107–11).

In order to clarify this point we need another example, again drawn from Latour's work. If we consider, for example, the highly specific categorisation systems which anthropologists have described as ethnobotany or ethnozoology, and then we compare these with the categorisation systems we use within Western botany or zoology, we have a contradictory set of categories. However, if we consider the scale of these categorisation systems then the problem becomes clearer. It is not that the native system is wrong and that ours is right, rather that these two systems are working at two different scales. The native system is using and comparing a restricted set of plants and animals as a means of categorising the world. In contrast, our categorisation systems compare plants and animals from around the world, since Western botanists and zoologists regularly meet to compare, discuss and standardise their collections. Our categories are then operating at a quite different scale, and because of this our network of associations is more extensive. It is no surprise, then, that our categorisation systems work throughout the world, for they are drawn up using comparanda from varied environments across the whole world. Furthermore, as Strathern (1992, 17) observes, 'A world made to Euro-American specifications will already be connected up in determined ways.' This is the illusion of rationalism – everything in the world works in the same way because everything in the world has been made to work in the same way.

Our task in comparing these networks of associations as anthropologists or archaeologists studying other cultures is in comparing the relationships between associations, and in comparing the scale and strength of these associations. Latour describes this as relationism. By considering both cultures and natures symmetrically and by examining the creation of networks of associations between the two, we will no longer be studying either one side of the equation or the other. Instead we will examine the nature of the connection between the two, and the mode by which this connection is articulated in practice. The stability of the terms nature and culture begins to erode, and we begin to understand science as a set of practices which create associations between things and people.

For example, Franklin (1997, 212–13) makes the point that Darwinian notions of genealogy and kinship have now been rendered artefactual within the biological sciences since the advent of IVF (in vitro fertilisation). This technique enables conception outside the human body and thereby detaches gestation and genealogy from the reference point of the female body. The practices of contemporary biological science have altered not only our understanding of cultural practices such as kinship, but also such natural processes as fertilisation.

Implications for scientific and interpretative archaeology: putting science into practice

So far the anthropology of science has provided insights into some of the practices of science. We now need to move back from the theoretical problems discussed in previous sections and consider how to operationalise these ideas. I wish, therefore, to return to some of the problems presented in the first section of this chapter and consider how we may reconcile both sides of the theoretical divide. I noted that one way of reconciling the divide between the physical and textual models of the archaeological record might be to retain the physical model as a method of approaching the mechanics of the archaeological record, while simultaneously using the textual approach as a means of understanding the social practices that are represented by the record. As indicated earlier, this approach was seen to be problematic since it consisted essentially of constructing a cultural shell around a realist core. Rather it was proposed we should consider an approach that sees interpretation as a process of creative tension in which interpretations arise from the movement back and forth between theory and data.

One of the simplest theoretical positions available to interpretative archaeologists involves the rejection of positivist science as an explanatory framework for human action in the past. Traditionally, the rejection of positivism involves adopting a theoretical position that leans heavily on some form of theory which views human action as culturally specific. However, there is a problem with doing this in archaeology since, as we observed above, positivist or empiricist ideas form the primary framework of much archaeological science. In order to carry out practical or field-based archaeology, scientific procedures will be utilised. These procedures will be formulated using something like a positivist or empiricist approach. The interpretations made under the suppositions of scientific archaeology will be effectively 'black-boxed'. This 'black-boxing' has an interesting effect, since it allows these parcels of positivist knowledge to be safely digested by interpretative archaeology. As Wylie (1992) notes, both new archaeologists and interpretative archaeologists subscribe to the existence of a core of objective or rationalist beliefs.

On the other side of the theoretical divide, we observe the familiar problem of scientific archaeologists producing knowledge up to a certain level and then simply hitting an interpretative brick wall. It is at this point that the evidence will be 'black-boxed'. Once the evidence cannot be described with certainty, or is not amenable to generalising laws, then interpretation ceases and the evidence is handed over to the theoretical archaeologist, who then constructs a series of interpretations derived from a quite different theoretical framework. The utilisation of archaeological science in these ways is jarring, since the conditions under which each form of knowledge is constructed are positively antagonistic. As an alternative we need to employ a strategy which uses archaeological science in quite a different way.

The critique of science explored above was crucial, since it highlighted a number of important points concerning scientific practice. Under the aegis of the anthropology of science we can see that the interpretation of scientific data can be considered to operate in a manner akin to hermeneutics. The most important points to emerge from this discussion are that the creation of factual information and the creation of novel technologies are not simply the result of the measurement of a prior and immutable nature. In order to understand how facts or technologies are created it is essential to understand the social conditions of production. The process of understanding the links between the social and the material is symmetrical: that is, the same analysis was conducted on both sides of the object–subject equation. What is more, as we move away from a concern with an explicitly epistemological position to one concerned with the process of interpretation, we need to worry far less about the problems of validating our paradigmatic positions through data manipulation. Instead, we become more explicit about the links between our theoretical suppositions and that data (Rorty 1980, 315–56). In the next chapter I will examine some of the problems inherent to an objectivist approach to archaeological practice and explore ways in which we may move towards an approach that embraces an interpretative framework. In doing this I want to examine the institutional position of archaeological science within the wider field of archaeological practice.

3   Archaeology observed

In this chapter I will take a broad view of some of the problems associated with archaeological interpretation by examining the relationship between archaeological science, the archaeological specialist and the practice of archaeology as a whole. My account will provide a *situated* perspective of archaeological practice (see Harding 1991 and Haraway 1997 for a discussion of situated knowledge). My situated knowledge is derived from the experience of working within the field of post-excavation analysis in Britian as both a materials specialist and an archaeological scientist. While this knowledge is specific to this context, more general points may be extrapolated from my account which can inform our understanding of wider archaeological practice.

Throughout, I want to examine the process by which we come to make archaeological interpretations. In doing so I will consider a wide range of questions: How are archaeological reports constructed? Who provides the information that makes up the archaeological report? What are the conditions under which this knowledge is constructed? Is there an interpretative distance between those who have a primary engagement with the site, and those who report that encounter? How is this knowledge deployed in the construction of subsequent archaeological knowledge? Simply put, I will consider how it is that we create accounts of past societies using the medium of material culture.

For the purpose of discussion, archaeological practice can be divided into three broad enterprises: excavation, post-excavation and publication. These are crude divisions, but they will suffice for the present. Two of these enterprises, excavation and publication, have come under considerable critical scrutiny over recent years, while the other has remained strangely absent from critique. During the course of this chapter I want to arrive at an understanding of why this might be the case, while outlining some of the problems associated with the normative perceptions of each of these enterprises. Traditionally, excavation has been perceived as an activity that simply involves a process of objectively recording the nature and extent of archaeological layers and deposits and the position and status of the material objects found within them. In the same way, post-excavation is considered as a series of objective analytical procedures, which allow us through observation and description to more-or-less accurately assess both the site and its material culture. Similarly, publication has been traditionally treated as a process that involves a presentation of the detailed objective descriptions of the results of excavation and post-excavation analysis. If a problem with publication was perceived, it was simply related to where the results of excavation should be presented (report or archive), the infrequency with which sites proceeded to publication, and the medium in which sites were published (e.g. Lavell 1981). In this chapter I want to consider some of the consequences of this objective view of archaeological practice.

Exploding excavations

Adams and Brooke (1995) have recently noted that archaeological practice is an essentially linear process that moves in an orderly series of stages from excavation to post-excavation to publication. Given this observation, we should consider the practices involved in post-excavation to be central to the construction of archaeological knowledge as a whole. If we wish to investigate the disciplinary position of post-excavation we need to examine the effects of the linear nature of archaeological research as a whole. While the linearity of archaeological practice is the paramount structuring principle affecting the production of archaeological knowledge, the linear structure of archaeological practice also produces two further structuring principles, which have an important effect on the way in which archaeology is practiced and the way in which that practice affects our interpretations as archaeologists. These structuring principles include *fragmentation*, which manifests itself in the manner in which archaeological information is both created and presented, and *hierarchy*, which manifests itself in the organisation, management and dissemination of archaeological information. The hierarchical and fragmented nature of archaeological practice operates in tandem, one serving to reinforce the other.

Prior to excavation the archaeological site is a holistic entity. Layer covers layer, deposit is stratified against deposit. Material culture, animal bones, seeds and pollen lie within these layers and deposits. The layers and deposits are contextually related to each other, as well as to the material that lies within them. However, excavation is a destructive and non-reproducible process. As it is generally practiced, excavation involves the careful removal of layer after layer of both anthropogenic and non-anthropogenic deposits (Drewett 1999, 107–18). The extent of each deposit is recorded spatially through the use of site grids and temporally through the use of surveying equipment such as theodolites or levels or of standardised excavation units such as spits. The relationship of each layer or deposit to each other is established by sections cut through each layer or deposit in order to establish a two-dimensional picture of temporal sequence (Drewett 1999, 115). During the excavation process these layers and deposits undergo a transformation; they shift from being represented physically to being represented in the abstract (Harris, Brown and Brown 1993). Through the process of excavation, the layers and deposits are physically disassociated. They now only have meaning because of their representation in plans, sections or as a set of figures and measurements on paper (see Drewett 1999, 143–4). They have no material existence beyond this. The material within these deposits or layers, whether manufactured by past human activity or biologically or physically produced, is again recorded spatially and temporally. Unlike the layers and deposits, the archaeologically significant material obtained from these features still retains some semblance of physicality after the excavation process; however, the material is disassociated from the features and contexts in which it once lay. It only retains any relationship to these layers and deposits through its depiction on maps, plans and sections and through a set of three-dimensional coordinates. Occasionally an area will be sampled for subsequent detailed examination by sieving either on-site or within the confines of the laboratory. Alternatively, sections of the site will be sampled for subsequent laboratory analysis procedures such as soil micromorphology or heavy residue analysis. Again the location of the sieved or sampled zone will be recorded spatially and temporally. In this instance, elements of the original deposit may be retained for inspection. In the case of laboratory samples, once again this is an abstracted quantity of material that has no real physical relationship with the layers or deposits from which it was derived, and any anthropogenic or non-anthropogenic material obtained from such a sample will be decontextualised.

Through the process of excavation the site has become fragmented. Physically, the site now only exists in the form of the individually bagged and labelled material remains removed from the site. The recorded material created by the archaeologists who excavated the site provides information on where the material remains came from and on the spatial and temporal layout of the excavated features. However these features, and the relationship that once pertained between them, no longer exist. What happens to this fragmented information once it has been obtained? In order to understand this, we need to turn to examine the nature of the post-excavation process.

Post-excavation is characterised by a further act of decontextualisation. The site has been utterly fragmented; it no longer has spatial or temporal integrity. The post-excavation interpretation of the site occurs at a remove from the site itself. Due to this, the information derived from excavation is now spread out and further fragmented as it is handed over to archaeological specialists. The plant macrofossil remains are handed to the palaeobotanist, the pollen samples to the palynologist, the animal bones to the archaeozoologist, the snail shells to the mollusca specialist, the human bones to the human anatomist. Material culture is also divided amongst specialists. The flint, chert or obsidian will be handed over to the chipped stone tool specialist, the ground stone tools will be handed to the ground stone tool specialist, metalwork will be given to the metalwork specialist, while the ceramics will be handed to the ceramics specialist. Often the material may be further dispersed by period, with particular specialists with defined period specialisms working on particular classes of object. Thus in Britain and Ireland ceramics may be divided between a prehistoric and Medieval specialist, depending on the expected classification of the material from the site.

What happens next? We find yet more processes of fragmentation at work when individual elements of the material residue of the site are given to the archaeological scientist for analysis. Stone tools or ceramics will be thin-sectioned and examined by a petrologist, ceramics may be examined using Gas Chromatography in order to determine function, and this may be undertaken by a biochemist or organic chemist. Metalwork may be examined using a variety of techniques such as mass spectrometry, inductively coupled plasma emission spectrometry, x-ray fluorescence or neutron activation analysis; this will often be undertaken by another archaeological scientist with a background in physics or inorganic chemistry. The interpretation of the results is again distanciated from both the object of analysis and the site it was derived from.

So there are a number of levels of fragmentation involved as we move from excavation to post-excavation, with each layer of analysis involving a further process of abstraction in which the site, the objects from the site, and the scientific analysis of those objects are gradually pulled further apart. As this process continues, the connections between them become more abstract and less well defined. In effect the site has *exploded* – the constituent elements of the site and its artefacts have become disengaged (see Fig. 3.1). This process of 'explosion' has serious implications when the time comes to publish the site. As noted above, archaeological excavation is often presented as an objective technical exercise. We simply observe what we excavate and then present the results of those observations in our detailed publications – the site is simply recreated on paper. But let

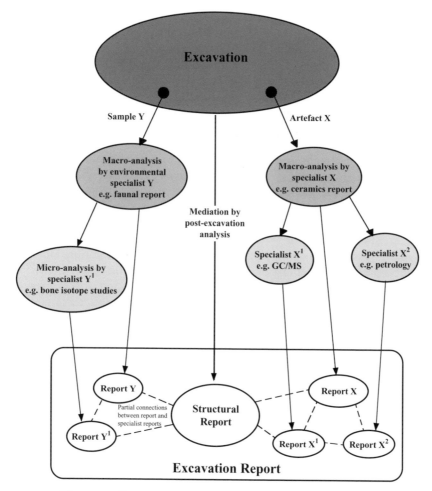

Figure 3.1 Exploding excavations

us examine this claim in more detail. I have presented a familiar view of the excavation and post-excavation process above. In each case features, objects and their contexts are gradually prised apart in order to better understand them. However in doing this we effect a process in which our interpretations of the site become ever less grounded on the primary observation of the site itself. Rather than presenting the holistic site that we began with, excavation reports present something quite different. The formula for publication generally involves publishing the site and its features along with a detailed finds catalogue. Finds are published according to category: we have ceramic reports, chipped stone reports, ground stone reports, metalwork reports, plant macrofossil reports, pollen reports, animal bone reports, human bone reports, etc. Onto each of these will be tacked, as something of an afterthought, the scientific analysis pertaining to each material. Somewhere near the end of the report we generally find a short synthesis placing the site into its regional or archaeological context. The publication of various elements of the site, such as particular classes of finds in microfiche or fascicule form, is a more extreme manifestation of this process of compartmentalisation in which elements of the site are physically discrete from the site even when in published form.

This form of publication is a *representation* of the site that was excavated. However, this is *not* the site which was originally excavated; it is a site which has been frozen on paper in a very specific form. What is represented is a frozen moment in the process of 'explosion'. The archaeological features, along with the material and biological remains which go to make up the site, are presented in decontextualised isolation. The publication of site reports in this way embodies a mode of representation viewed through the lens of objectivist or rationalist science. It is a representation of the past lives of people through a body of material culture that, I argue, would be unrecognisable to those that had inhabited the site.

Fragmentation and hierarchy in archaeological practice

Nevertheless the conceptual fragmentation of objects and the analysis of those objects at a distance from their contextual relationship with specific on-site features is part of the practice of contemporary archaeology. What causes this process of fragmentation? How has this fragmented knowledge been produced? In order to answer these questions, we need to examine the organisation of the excavation itself. What we find is that knowledge is generated in a hierarchical framework. Individual areas of the site are excavated by groups of individual excavators, and these may then be supervised by an area supervisor or site supervisor. This person is in turn overseen by a site-director. Interestingly, we find that the primary interpretative engagement with the site is the domain of the individual excavator (Chadwick 1998; Challands *et al.* 1998). These people may also undertake the recording of the features they have personally excavated; nevertheless the process of recording is often undertaken by the person who is on the next rung of the ladder of hierarchy – the area supervisor. Despite the fact that this division of labour exists on all archaeological excavations, it is traditionally the site-director, the person most distanced from the primary engagement with the site itself, who collates the interpreted information from the site for publication.

The hierarchical process of excavation consolidates the process of fragmentation. Excavation involves a process of double fragmentation: first the site is disassembled through the process of excavation and then the process of recording that process of fragmentation is divisive (Chadwick 1998). The most important point to note, however, is not only that this process of fragmentation occurs, but rather that this process is crystallised within publication. This is due to the fact that both the primary excavation of the site by individual excavators, and the interpretation of the materials excavated from the site by post-excavation specialists and archaeological scientists, are divorced from the final process of interpretation involved in publication.

The methodology I have characterised represents empirical and objective archaeological practice. Obviously not all archaeologists work in this way and this approach to archaeological practice has been criticised (Hodder 1989, 1999). Nevertheless, this is the procedural prototype from which much archaeological practice is judged; canonically it is the 'correct' way to do things. Yet, as I have shown, there are obvious problems with this methodology. Not only is this approach to the interpretation of material culture and archaeological sites a barrier to the holistic and integrative interpretation of the site itself, but also this form of interpretation is a conceptual barrier to the interpretations of sites, forms of activity and types of material within their wider archaeological context. These points will be discussed later in this chapter. Here I simply wish to ask the question, why is archaeological practice ordered like this?

To answer this question, we need to examine a number of problems encompassing the disciplinary organisation of archaeology and the philosophical underpinnings of that organisation. To begin with, excavation has been traditionally treated as the prototypical, or defining practice of the discipline of archaeology (Tilley 1989b). The results of this highly visible activity are traditionally disseminated to a wider archaeological public through the medium of publication. Therefore the twin practices of excavation and publication are closely bound up with the measurement of academic prestige. Archaeologists have traditionally forged their careers through the excavation of prestigious sites and through the publication of those excavations. No such disciplinary honour is associated with post-excavation, and it is for this reason that post-excavation has remained a peripheral activity. It never has been perceived to be central to the construction of archaeological knowledge; indeed, during the emergence of archaeological science as a routine part of post-excavation analysis, the task of analysis traditionally fell to those outside the boundaries of the discipline – zoologists, anatomists, botanist and chemists. Bluntly put, it is due to the peripheral nature of scientific specialists, as well as other materials specialists, that scientific analysis and specialist reports are often marginalised in contemporary forms of archaeological reportage.

What is post-excavation analysis?

At a disciplinary level we see a distinction between those who excavate and publish sites and those who analyse the material recovered from those sites. When post-excavation analysis is undertaken by archaeologists (ceramic, lithics and metalwork specialists for example) they are often individuals who have not been involved in the primary excavation of the site from which material was recovered. We have seen that if we take a strictly linear view of archaeological practice, the task of post-excavation analysis should be central. However, due to the fragmented nature of archaeological practice, post-excavation analysis is in fact at the periphery of the interpretative process.

Despite a critical awareness of the problems associated with excavation and publication, there has been little comparable criticism of the processes involved in post-excavation. Yet if we are to consider some of the problems associated with integrating archaeological science with an interpretative approach to the past, then post-excavation analysis requires careful consideration. It is during post-excavation that the detailed analysis of artefacts occurs, and it is as a result of this process that many interpretations become crystallised. As important as this process is, however, little disciplinary interest appears to exist in the processes by which the results of excavation move from site to publication. Indeed we might easily characterise post-excavation as a form of 'black box' (Latour 1987) in which the material results of excavation results are simply produced from excavated sites for post-excavation analysis at one end, while the results of this post-excavation analysis are reproduced in publications at the other (Adams and Brooke 1995). Post-excavation practices remain untheorised and incoherent; post-excavation is simply a stage between the tasks of excavation and publication.

Here I wish to consider a definition of post-excavation analysis that includes the analysis of archaeological materials, bones, seeds, pottery, stone tools, etc., as well as materials science, which includes a range of instrumental scientific techniques. I want to consider a number of problems concerning post-excavation analysis. First, what is post-excavation analysis and how does it operate? How does post-excavation analysis intercede in the interpretation of the site as a whole? We have seen that in general post-excavation analysis is distinct from the process of excavation. This image of post-excavation is enduring and characteristic of almost all forms of post-excavation analysis. The process of post-excavation is itself surrounded by an aura of objectivity, and herein lie many of its problems. The analysis of material excavated from an archaeological site is traditionally understood to be the domain of objective or empiricist scientific practice. Materials, whether biological or cultural, are handed over to individuals with a high level of expertise. These individuals are considered to be in possession of wide-ranging knowledge concerning their object of study. Most post-excavation analysis proceeds by a combination of observation and description. Through the process of empirical observation an accurate description of the material being studied is made, and these observations are then compared against other known objects within the class of materials being studied. It is against this background that a series of objective recording methodologies have been developed. Knowledge concerning different classes of archaeological object is published in journals or monographs, or detailed knowledge is simply stored within the memory of the individual post-excavation specialist. This model of post-excavation analysis works just as well for the analysis of archaeological materials both through macroscopic identification and through instrumental scientific analysis. Both of these aspects of archaeological science operate within a well-established, independent body of data concerning the phenomena that they are attempting to observe and measure. Faunal specialists and human anatomists employ collections of skeletons as comparative material, while they also utilise other forms of information including broad ecological and morphological data on animal species and more detailed osteological data such as that for tooth eruption and epiphysial fusing derived from zoological analysis (Rackham 1987, 51). Palynologists and plant macrofossil specialists utilise collections of known pollen or seed species. Materials scientists, on the other hand, draw on a more abstract body of data in order to assess their observations. Such data encompasses the known characteristics of sub-atomic particles, biochemical molecules, etc. (Pollard and Heron 1996).

Often the post-excavation specialist is in possession of little or no information concerning the context or nature of the feature from which the material they are analysing was obtained. Once an interpretation of the object is made, based on comparison with other phenomena, this information is then passed on to the site excavator who uses it to confirm or refute their initial observations. This image of post-excavation conforms very well with the inductive logic of objectivist science. Post-excavation is then treated as a form of independent process against which the material and the site itself are tested. It is according to this philosophical model that artefacts are simply used as a means of dating sites, in precisely the same way that the techniques of radiocarbon dating and dendrochronology are used as chronological indicators (Blinkhorn and Cumberpatch 1997).

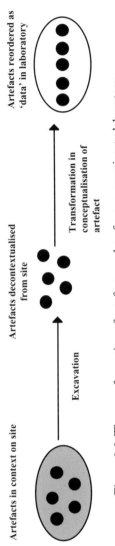

Artefacts in context on site

Artefacts decontextualised from site

Artefacts reordered as 'data' in laboratory

Excavation

Transformation in conceptualisation of artefact

Figure 3.2 The transformation of artefacts as data from excavation to laboratory

There are obvious problems with this approach to post-excavation. The most immediate of these is that this form of analysis presupposes a large body of site-independent information against which to compare the analysis of materials or phenomena. With this approach, we are unable to deal with materials or phenomena that have been barely studied or are entirely unique. Even if this information exists, this methodology leads to stultification in the nature and level of knowledge that we are able to develop concerning certain classes of material.

Transforming the laboratory

One of the critical points arising from the twin processes of fragmentation and hierarchy in archaeological practice is that the constituent elements of the site are prised apart through excavation in order to uncover and analyse them. Moreover, as I noted, a necessary part of the process of analysis involves the transformation of the physical components of the excavated site into representational data. Here I want to further consider the process of transformation that occurs during excavation and its problematic relationship to the notion of the archaeological laboratory.

The main point to note, when we wish to consider archaeological practice as a science, is that scientific veracity is traditionally dependent on the existence of a reproducible set of results from a given body of data. The ability to conduct experiments, and to witness and thereby judge the results of repeated experimentation, lies at the heart of science as a cultural endeavour. As a cultural practice science is characterised by the testability of its knowledge. However archaeology does not conform to this model of scientific practice. There is no such entity as a site-based archaeological experimental laboratory in which conditions can be controlled in order to reproduce testable knowledge. Where we do observe controlled experimentation, this occurs in the present and the results of experiments are related back to past processes through analogy.

Archaeological sites are individually distinct. After excavation the site no longer exists in physical form. The archaeological site does not then conform to the definition of a laboratory since through the practice of excavation the laboratory has been destroyed. Due to this the results of the experiment cannot be tested. But what does remain from the site? The site has become transformed and exists only as a series of representations as plans and section drawings. Despite this, some physical remains are preserved in the form of artefacts and environmental samples.

With the transformation of the site, the archaeological site-as-laboratory has effectively disappeared. However in order to retain an attachment to scientific objectivity a further interesting transformation takes place (see Fig. 3.2). Although the site-as-laboratory has disappeared through the practice of excavation, we witness the creation of a new kind of archaeological laboratory out of the transformed (decontextualised) physical remains derived from the now extinct site. These remains are taken into archaeological laboratories and they are subjected to analytical techniques that allow for reproducibility and testability. Although the site-based archaeological laboratory has disappeared, out of its physical remains (artefacts and environmental samples) the laboratory has been reconstituted.

But the problem still remains that the archaeological site is both unique and non-existent. Therefore we cannot consider it to be a component of objective discourse since it does not conform to the basic tenets of objectivity – it is non-testable and can no longer be empirically observed. The observations made on site have become transformed, and those artefacts and environmental samples that do remain have themselves undergone a transformation since they are only related to the site through the annotation of site plans and sections of three-dimensional coordinates. Furthermore these too are unique; they are recovered from specific locations around the site and are often derived from distinct contexts within the site. There is little room then for statistical comparison of comparable contexts; rather most sites are characterised by zones of contextual difference. It would appear that the practice of archaeological science is a transformative process in which artefacts and environmental samples are changed from decontextualised objects and samples into meaningful objects and samples by virtue of their status as objects of analysis in the laboratory. It is due to this process of transformation that we find artefacts, faunal remains and botanic samples discussed in terms of the induction-driven methodologies described earlier. It is precisely because artefacts and environmental samples are divested of their context that scientific analysis is required to situate them within a wider framework of objective knowledge. I will examine ways in which we might re-contextualise scientific knowledge in more detail below.

How do we define objective analysis in archaeology?

As archaeologists we state that we are producing an objective account of the past in our excavation reports. But how do we define objectivity, and whose definition of objectivity are we employing? One of the serious problems inherent in the concept of objective data-recording is that, once we believe that we have an adequate definition of objectivity, we do not feel the need to reflect on it; instead we crystallise it, or 'set it in stone'. For instance, while we have retained a notion of standardised or objective recording, many of the principles guiding what we deem worthy of record and publication have themselves been retained from an earlier vision of archaeological objectivity. One obvious example of this concerns the nature of reportage required in British and Irish excavation reports. In excavation reports in these countries it is *not* deemed to be a necessary component of an objective archaeological report to conduct a detailed spatial analysis of the site and its artefacts, while it *is* deemed to be a requirement of objective analysis to list parallels for site types and artefact types found on other, more distant, sites at great length and in some detail. In other words, despite the latent empiricism of much archaeological enquiry, it is not deemed to make good sense to compare and contrast empirical observations made between objects at a directly observable intra-site level, although it is deemed to make good empirical sense to compare and contrast both sites and objects at the inter-site level. This is in part due to our attempts to create an objective scientific discourse that is both generalising and testable as opposed to particularist and contextual. While this understanding of objectivity underpins much archaeological practice, we also observe that the notion of objectivity we retain in archaeological discourse is historically contingent. It is a notion of objectivity that has been retained from culture-history, in which it was a requirement, under the aegis of a normative vision of culture, that individuals should catalogue and list parallels for sites and objects as a means of defining and dating cultural units. Despite the widespread criticism of this view of culture both archaeologically and anthropologically, the requirements of culture-historical analysis are fossilised within the objective discourse of adequate site reporting. Here we observe an earlier set of disciplinary practices simply 'standing in' for objectivity. This is a form of statutory objectivity; it does not characterise objectivity in its strictest philosophical sense.

It is the issue of statutory objectivity that lies at the heart of our problematic use of the results both of specialist analysis and of scientific analysis within excavation reports. This is because the use of specialist reports and scientific reports often becomes disengaged from the interpretation of the site itself. Reports on archaeological materials and their scientific analysis are often undertaken as a 'matter of course', with little reflection on how this information will integrate with the broader interpretation of the site. An example of this non-reflective use of science may be drawn from some of the published excavation reports for the Orkney Neolithic. Many of the excavation reports from Orkney include a mandatory petrology report for stone tools and ceramics (Williams 1976, 1979, 1983). These reports are insightful in themselves, however the results of these reports, if integrated into the body of the excavation report, generally state that the pottery or stone tools are simply 'locally derived' (Ritchie 1983).

While this may be considered to be a legitimate result, when these results are integrated with a wider series of interpretative questions petrological analyses may be of considerable interpretative value themselves, as we shall see in chapters 6 and 7. In the instance of these reports it would appear that, for the archaeologist interpreting these results, petrology was treated as a simple technical procedure: a procedure which 'ought to be done', but whose value had been overlooked or simply forgotten at the wider interpretative level.

A similar example arises when we come to look at the nature of animal bone reports incorporated within many excavation reports. Faunal reports are an interesting form of reportage since they often appear to embody a series of requirements that have little relationship to archaeology in the strictest sense (Legge 1978); that is, if we define archaeology to be an investigation of human activity in the past through the medium of material culture. Many animal bone reports include minute comparative details describing the morphological differences between bone material using metrical analyses. These details are often used to provide information on the level of domestication, the habitat of animal species, etc. While these reports provide some information on archaeological details such as economy, they also appear to indicate a preoccupation with interests of a more broadly zoological nature (Legge 1978). All too often, few faunal reports do not pay sufficient attention either to the context from which material was derived or the intra-site spatial organisation of animal deposits (see Legge, Payne and Rowley-Conwy 1998 for a discussion of the necessity of intra-site contextual differences in the study of past diet). Here it is important to reiterate that we cannot simply read off economy from site assemblages, as if sites themselves had economies (Barrett 1989). Sites are not uniform entities, which means generalising statements that rely on conditions of uniformity are problematic in the reconstruction of economic regimes. Instead we need to embrace the heterogeneity of contexts in an attempt to understand both the differences and similarities between different sites in terms of consumption practices (see chapter 5 for further discussion; see Meadows 1997 for an example of this approach).

Each of the examples discussed above calls into question the nature of the definition of objectivity embodied in many specialist reports. My point here is that criticism does not solely rest with the specialist or archaeological scientist, it resides as much with the field archaeologist. We have to ask ourselves whom these reports are for, what questions they are required to answer, and how the results of such reports are deployed within the site report as a whole. We must remember that there is no such thing as an objective scientific report, rather many reports purporting to be objective are simply reproducing a previous set of disciplinary concerns. Due to the contingent nature of these definitions of objectivity there can be no 'correct' and objective manner in which to publish our interpretations (Barrett and Bradley 1991), except when publication becomes a prescriptive exercise enshrined in rigid policy (Adams and Brooke 1995).

Science in its broadest sense may be employed as a means of understanding a very broad series of questions. There is not a set of statutory questions that we should feel impelled to ask of archaeological science or the archaeological specialist; rather the questions that we ask of science constrain the nature of the answer that we receive (Bradley 1998). We need to think very critically, then, about a number of issues. What questions do we wish to ask of the archaeological scientist or archaeological specialist? Can the particular techniques used provide answers to these questions? In short, our expectations are intimately bound up with our observations. Moreover, these questions will alter depending on the historical period we are studying (see Bayley 1998). We need to be aware of this and consider what kinds of archaeological reports we actually want, rather than simply persisting with reports that reproduce an outmoded vision of archaeological objectivity.

The philosophical nature of archaeological practice

There are a series of problems, then, in the way in which archaeological knowledge is constructed. If we are to comprehend the construction of archaeological knowledge in more detail, we need to examine why it is that archaeological practice is conducted in this way. I will begin by looking at the distinction between excavation and post-excavation. While the peripheral nature of post-excavation in relation to excavation and publication may be explained by a recurrent distinction between field archaeologist and archaeological specialist, we need to examine the ideas that underpin and structure these distinctions. If we return to the arguments outlined in the opening chapters, we observe a practical application of the distinction between the social/human sciences and the natural sciences. At the most basic level this involves a disjunction between those who do field archaeology – the province of cultural analysis – and those associated with the natural sciences – the province of scientific analysis, effectively archaeological scientists.

While a fundamental distinction remains between those who practice archaeology in the field and those who practice archaeology within the laboratory, when we come to examine the division of labour within the 'archaeological laboratory' at the post-excavation level we see further fine-grained distinctions (Sofaer-Derevenski forthcoming) between those who examine the cultural aspects of archaeological data (pottery, lithics, met-alwork, glass, etc.) and those who study the biological aspects of archaeo-logical data (seeds, pollen, human and animal bones, etc.). Finally, we also see a division between those who study the cultural aspect of objects – finds specialists – and those who study the physical aspects of objects using procedures derived from materials science, engineering, chemistry and physics. Again we observe the fundamental distinction that pertains be-tween the two domains of knowledge – the social sciences and the natural sciences.

At another level we see yet further distinctions between the individuals who study different forms of archaeological material – finds specialists tend to be categorised by the material they study. What we are observ-ing here is a categorisation scheme that is based on the material nature of the object of study. This form of categorisation is itself based on an objective understanding of the world in which artefacts may be divided according to their essential natures. According to this view objects are classified in bounded sets according to the possession of a series of mate-rial attributes (Lakoff 1987). Each of these levels of differentiation goes some way towards understanding why we observe a fragmentation of the archaeological site through archaeological analysis.

We might consider the possibility that our fragmentary mode of analy-sis is due to our belief in a set of overarching disciplinary divisions. This is interesting, but we also need to consider the whole process of frag-mentation in and of itself. Fragmentation is a characteristic aspect of objective analysis in which one breaks down, or compartmentalises, the world in order to define it. Once this is done, as rationalists we build up generalising laws concerning the way in which each isolated unit ope-rates in relation to its neighbours. This kind of analysis comprises the central tenets of systems analysis. A characteristic of systems analysis is that each component of the system and each constituent element is treated as a discrete unit in order to aid comprehension. This then al-lows the analyst to understand the articulation of these elements together as part of a working model. Indeed the matrix analysis of Harris *et al.* (1993) may be considered to be the archetypal form of systems anal-ysis applied to archaeological stratigraphy, in which each stratigraphic unit is broken down and understood in relation to its nearest neighbours on the site. However, although the aim of the systems approach is to create a working model, in the realm of archaeological practice this fun-damentally objectivist procedure rarely leads to detailed model-building. Instead we might argue that many archaeologists proceed as if, after hav-ing laid the components of the site open to the empirical gaze, this was sufficient.

There are serious problems raised by our decontextualised mode of representation within excavation reports. The most pressing of these is that the objects and remains that we excavate are meaningful; they are contextually related to the features, layers or deposits in which they were originally found. More importantly, when these objects actively intervened in the lives of past peoples they were bound up in networks of meaningful connections. If we are to recover and interpret these aspects of the past, we must realise that we need to begin to create interpretative connections between different kinds of material, rather than simply studying material in isolation and then presenting these isolated studies in publications as objective reality.

Problems in the reproduction of objective knowledge

An objective approach to archaeological practice produces a report that fragments archaeological knowledge. However the problems that this fragmentation of knowledge brings with it does not stop with the excavation report. This form of knowledge production can be shown to be unproductive to the reworking of subsequent archaeological knowledge. At the level of primary interpretation, the disjunction of materials from their original context prevents their contextual re-association. It is often difficult to locate artefacts spatially and stratigraphically within excavation reports, which prevents the interpretation of the functional and social analysis of different areas of the site (Allison 1997). Hill (1995), for example, draws our attention to the difficulties involved in reintegrating finds from different contexts in his analysis of structured deposition in the British Iron Age. A greater concern is that the decontextualised nature of our reporting also structures the way in which we set about writing wider accounts of the past based on site report data. This form of reporting in fact creates a number of problems, since it forces us to retain a vision of artefacts and sites in the abstract. While it allows us to dislocate material from its context and compare that material across widespread geographical regions (a major component of culture-historical analysis), it simultaneously structures the nature of wider archaeological discourse. It is due to this fragmented view that we have societies and symposia devoted to distinct specialisms: metalwork analysis; ceramic analysis; lithic studies; environmental analysis; and the chemical analysis of archaeological materials. It is also the reason we find volumes devoted to prehistoric ceramics, medieval ceramics, prehistoric metalwork, stone axe studies, flint and chert analysis, etc. Clearly, the way in which the discipline is structured at the specialist level is divisive (Bradley 1987) and we see little cross-referencing between areas of specialisation.

The point here is that many of the problems we perceive as archaeologists are created by the manner in which we structure our discipline. What is more, this structure pervades the discipline at the most fundamental level (in the organisation of archaeological practice according to the triptych of excavation, post-excavation and publication) and at the specialist level (symposia, societies and publications devoted to particular kinds of archaeological data). As Evans (1998) notes, we practice archaeology in relation to other practitioners: 'There are not just lineages of discovery but matrices of interpretation' (*ibid.*, 198). The highly specific manner in which we structure archaeological discourse affects the way in which we write archaeology at the wider synthetic level; it allows some problems to be examined while systematically closing off other areas of research. Most syntheses tend to present the evidence from a series of different and discrete strands of material. Rarely do we see synthesis examining the systematic connections between different classes of material.

The creation of archaeological truth

The concept of 'objective' analysis throughout the various areas of archaeological practice has brought with it a series of problems. Rather than creating an objective standpoint by providing a unifying interpretative perspective, as initially proposed in Britain by Clarke (1973), it has enabled archaeological practice to fragment along a series of fracture lines which produce a dislocated vision of the past. There are further aspects of objective analysis that are worth considering here. As noted in chapter 1, objectivity presupposes the existence of the real material world beyond the gaze of the subjective observer. Objective analysis requires that there is a real world 'out there' to be examined. One of the peculiarities of objective analysis is that any contradictions in the analysis are considered the result of problematic relationships in the real world, not in the nature of the expectations and presuppositions of the observer. The presentation of the results of objective analysis does not tend to include the analysis of contradictions or problems; instead, peripheral contradictory conclusions are jettisoned, while a single unified conclusion or explanation is retained (Clifford 1994). Without this unified conclusion, any objective analysis could not truly be counted as objective, since objectivity presupposes the notion of certainty. Due to this notion, objective archaeological reports tend to present a single interpretation of the site. Due to the hierarchical production of archaeological knowledge this interpretation is usually that of the site-director/site-publisher. Since the aim is to create an objective record of the site, any contradictions inherent in the individual analysis of various specialists, archaeological scientists, etc., will be concealed or removed entirely from the text of the report (Hodder 1989). It is precisely because of this problem of ahistorical objectivity that Barrett (1987b) suggests that we need to carefully consider the suppositions and expectations of fieldworkers before re-analysing excavation reports. In precisely the same way, while Evans' analysis of Bersu's Manx excavation campaign offers an insight into the ethnological presuppositions behind his interpretative excavation strategy, it is unable to supply us with a list of the artefacts discarded by Bersu as worthless due to this interpretative strategy (Evans 1998, 193–8). We cannot simply consider site reports as statements of fact. It is the process of creating truth through publication that lies at the heart of the fragmentary and hierarchical procedures of archaeological practice. I will interrogate this view of archaeological practice by focusing on a series of issues discussed in chapter 2, including the creation of 'facts', the problem of translation and the creation of interpretative networks.

Facts are created when information derived from one particular form of analysis is 'black-boxed' and then utilised in further analysis. It is precisely this process that occurs throughout archaeological practice at a number of levels: at the level of the individual on-site excavator who digs the site, at the level of the site supervisor, at the level of the individual specialist, and at the level of the archaeological scientist performing an analysis on the archaeological object. Each of these individuals produces a series of discrete and objective bodies of information or 'facts' concerning the site and its artefacts. These 'black-boxed' facts are then employed by the site-director to create the site report. The site report itself then becomes a fact and is utilised in subsequent archaeological analyses and syntheses. It is this process of bringing together the individual 'black-boxed' facts that involves a form of transformation or translation of knowledge.

In chapter 2, I discussed the way in which, during scientific analysis, this translation process was undertaken by a series of analytical instruments. This also occurs in archaeological analysis in which archaeological scientists employ a variety of instrumental techniques as a means of analysing archaeological materials. It is not only scientific instruments that are involved in this process of translation. More subtle – or less obvious – processes of translation may occur using simple graphic media. Many graphic systems of representation are used in the presentation of archaeological facts: the site plan, section drawings, plans and elevations of buildings, drawings of artefacts, graphs, text, etc. These are devices that allow us, as archaeologists, to translate the physical world of the archaeological site into a graphical and textual form. Each 'black-boxed' or translated component of the site is drawn together in these representations as components of an objective record of the site and its artefacts.

This form of 'black-boxing' is a necessary requirement of the form of systemic approach that I suggest characterises the organisation of archaeological practice. Although the goal of systems analysis is to create a coherent model of the given field of study, the practice of 'black-boxing' each unit of analysis appears to have had the opposite effect. This is because the knowledge associated with each component of the archaeological site and its artefacts is produced in isolation and then 'black-boxed' and used elsewhere. It then becomes extremely difficult to present a coherent picture of the site as a whole – each piece of knowledge is produced under a different regime of expectations and judgements. Without critically examining these expectations it is very difficult to bring each fragment of knowledge together. While the fragmentary process is embedded in the structure of archaeological practice, it also becomes embedded in the presentation of the final publication.

Writing material culture: archaeological practice and subjectivity

It is obvious from the critique I have undertaken throughout this chapter that we need to think differently about our methods of archaeological practice. Rather than considering either excavation or publication as objective and technical exercises, a number of authors have suggested that instead we bring a whole series of disciplinary expectations and prejudices to the exercise of excavating a site (Tilley 1989b; Richards 1995; Hodder 1999). What is more, if we treat publication as the presentation of the results of excavation, then we need to be clear under what conditions these results are constructed. We cannot treat excavation reports as if they were neutral and ahistorical evaluations of 'what was found' on excavated sites. As we have seen, excavation reports, like other forms of archaeological endeavour, are historically contingent; they crystallise the expectations and concerns of the paradigm in which they are produced (Barrett 1987b). Within their pages excavation reports should embed some of the expectations and uncertainties involved in excavation. In short, they should involve an adequate presentation of, and reflection upon, the conditions upon which the knowledge contained within the report is based. Yet while much recent critique has focused on the twin practices of excavation and publication, we must also be signally aware of the interpretative nature of post-excavation practices, especially the relationship between science, excavation, post-excavation and the process of interpretation.

The issues outlined above concerning the nature of excavation and publication encompass a wider critique of the way in which we construct and represent knowledge about other cultures. Much of this has focused on the anthropological problems of providing an account of other cultures (Clifford 1986). This discussion has focused upon the position of the observer in relation to the observed, and the process by which field observations are transformed into ethnographies; a process which carries with it claims of objectivity and authority (Clifford 1994). The problems associated with reporting the results of excavation are, in many ways, parallel to this, but there are further problems in our engagement with past cultures. We are not simply interpreting one set of cultural idioms through encounter and observation and then translating these experiences through the medium of language and written text (Asad 1986). Rather we are interpreting the nature of past cultural activity, through an encounter with physical objects, and it is this understanding which is then translated into a textual form. We are then transforming the nature of our encounter with past cultures from a set of experiences which relies on the physical nature of the archaeological object, into a descriptive account of these experiences through the medium of texts and graphic representations. We cannot simply treat our encounter with past material cultures as a process of direct translation (Barrett 1994; Hodder 1986) because by necessity we bring our own prejudices and expectations to bear when interpreting material culture. It is due to the expectations bound up in our interpretations that we need to critically assess the nature of the interpretative accounts of our encounters with the residues of past cultures.

If we are to examine the way in which we create archaeological information, we need to consider in more depth what it is we are doing when we encounter the residues of past human activity. Why do we think we are competent to write about past material culture? In considering this question I want to develop the ideas of both Barrett (1995) and Richards (1995) with regard to the problem of interpreting excavation data. Both authors have considered the nature of the experience involved in excavation. Colin Richards has characterised it as an experience which embodies all the interest, excitement and intellectual challenges of an ethnographic encounter with another culture. John Barrett has discussed the fascination embodied in the process of discovery, a fascination heightened by a 'feeling of otherness or difference' (1995, 6). For both these authors excavation is felt to be primary to the process of interpretation, as it is during excavation that our first interpretations about the past are formulated. However, as Barrett notes (1995, 6), this initial engagement with the past, through archaeological excavation, begins to stale as the remains of the past are filtered through the processes of post-excavation and publication. The excitement and interest engendered in the primary task of excavation is rarely communicated in excavation reports. As we have seen this is due, in part, to the processes of fragmentation, hierarchisation and transformation. As the remains of the past are filtered through the various stages of archaeological investigation, they are gradually dislocated from the site itself and the knowledge concerning them is ordered according to a hierarchical interpretative convention. Interpretation at this stage is quite simply divested of its interest – the past has become entirely abstract and objectified. To paraphrase Barrett (1995, 6), it is only when material is placed in a frame of reference other than our own that it gains its historical significance. It is precisely this frame of reference that is lacking when we shear material from the site and subject it to a series of objective analyses.

I want to begin to reconsider these problems through recourse to an analysis of the parallel problems encountered by anthropologists. As I have noted, one of the principal problems which anthropology has confronted in the late twentieth century is precisely how, as observers of other cultures, we are able to provide accounts of our experiences and encounters with other cultures. That is, in essence, what we attempt to do as archaeologists. In the opening chapters of this book I noted that, following Tambiah (1990), one of the views available to anthropologists was to employ what he described as a 'double subjectivity'. This viewpoint involves attempting to understand the intentions of people inhabiting another cultural setting, while simultaneously taking up a neutral stance removed from this cultural setting. This ability to occupy a position both within and without a given culture enables the anthropologist to translate or write the experience of that culture within the terms of our own culture. As both Asad (1986) and Tambiah (1990) indicate, it is through this process of translation, through an attempt at understanding the idioms of another system of thought, that we come to understand ourselves. The interesting point about this form of enquiry, as it applies to anthropology, is that it presupposes that at each stage of interpretation, from the primary encounter to the publication of a monograph, the anthropologist moves back and forth between native cultural understandings and the understandings of the anthropologist's own conceptual system. It is this movement back and forth which is the essence of translation.

I noted above that one of the effects of fragmentation and hierarchisation through excavation was the shift in emphasis in the status of what we might describe as the 'archaeological laboratory'. The excavation site as the object of analysis disappears, and we are left with the tangible physical remains of the site in the form of artefacts and environmental samples. At this point the remains of excavation are transformed; as they enter the laboratory in which archaeological scientists work, they become the objects of scientific analysis. They are then resituated within the wider discourse of archaeological science, and their nature is determined through recourse to extensive bodies of independent scientific data. If we are to adopt the mode of enquiry suggested above, we need to be aware that artefacts and environmental samples are physically situated within the realm of objective scientific analysis, while conceptually they are simultaneously situated within the contextual parameters of the archaeological site. Moreover, the artefacts and environmental samples were once contextually situated in, and intervened in, the lives of people. Hodder correctly notes that both object and context are mutually constituting – the meaning of the context is provided by the objects found within that context and vice versa (1999, 84–6). It is critical, then, that the physicality of the object to be studied is taken into consideration as well as its physical, historical and cultural context.

How does this viewpoint affect the way in which we practice our analyses in the laboratory? While the transformation of artefacts and environmental samples occurs from the site to the laboratory, archaeological scientists need to consider re-contextualising artefacts and environmental samples both during and after analysis in the laboratory. Both the object of analysis and the interpreter (the archaeological scientist) need to be at once situated – like the anthropologist – within Western conceptual systems and non-Western conceptual systems. By doing this during the process of scientific analysis, material will be placed in a very different frame of reference, and will thereby regain its historical and cultural significance.

One way of accomplishing this change is to alter our view of archaeological practice. Rather than simply viewing excavation to be the site of primary interpretative encounters with the physical remains of past cultures and post-excavation analysis in the laboratory to be the domain of objective analysis, we need to cultivate each element of archaeological practice as part of a single interpretative process. At each stage of the interpretative process we need to consider how it is that we formulate interpretations as we move back and forth between our observations of material and our theoretical assumptions about that material (Barrett 1990; Wylie 1993).

However the crucial moment in the process of reworking our relationship with past material culture arrives with publication. We need to be especially aware of the kinds of narratives that we employ in writing about archaeology (Pluciennik 1999). I have argued that it is through excavation publications that we not only reproduce particular kinds of knowledge but also particular modes of archaeological discourse. The narrative forms that we deploy in excavation reports are therefore crucial. As Pluciennik notes (1999, 655), narratives are constituted of characters, events and plots. Importantly each element of a narrative is linked together by different levels of scale and context that ultimately lead to different kinds of explanation. I will take this point up in the next chapter; here it is sufficient to point out that in excavation reports we need to experiment with the inter-relationships between these elements of narrative. The process of excavation lends itself to a variety of plot devices. We need not simply write reports as the presentation of data recovered by a linear scientific methodology. There are other ways of telling that include the usage of narratives about the excavation process (Bender, Hamilton and Tilley 1997). Other modes of writing might employ artefacts and environmental samples as components of the story, used to describe significant kinds of on-site events, such as processes of building or rebuilding, or other fundamental alterations in the site. Alternatively artefacts, architecture and environmental evidence may be used to explore specific kinds of social practice, such as food production and consumption, the social construction of the body, hunting and agriculture, defence and warfare, etc.

Earlier in this chapter I employed the metaphor of 'explosion' to describe the effects and after-effects of archaeological excavation. Here I am advocating that writing excavation reports should involve the opposite of 'explosive' linear narratives; they should encompass a process of re-connection that involves the creation of interpretative networks. This process of reconnection should be twofold. First, it is essential that we recreate the connections which defined the relationships between site and artefact. By doing this we will go some way towards providing a clearer picture of the site that was excavated. Rather than presenting a picture of the site with its compartmentalised artefacts and scientific analyses, we need to create an image of the site with its components in context, either in the order and sequence in which they were excavated or according to an order and sequence that makes sense within the overall interpretative framework of the report. By doing this we will also be creating interpretative connections by bringing together the various analyses undertaken at both the excavation and post-excavation level in an inclusive form of interpretation. Rather than prioritising one element of the site, or one interpretation, over the other, we need to be aware of the dynamic that exists between them.

4   Materials science and material culture: practice, scale and narrative

In the account I have provided so far, science has been represented as a somewhat monolithic entity. However, if we consider scientific practice to have a critical effect on the kinds of knowledge generated, then it follows that different sciences engender quite distinct cultural practices and produce distinct forms of knowledge (Knorr-Certina 1999). This means that we cannot assume the existence of a unified laboratory-based practice known as 'archaeological science' that unites archaeobotanists, zooarchaeologists, soil micromorphologists, ceramic petrologists, etc. Within the next two chapters, I will set aside other areas of archaeological science in order to focus on the practice of materials science – the study of archaeological materials using techniques derived from engineering, chemistry and physics (Kingery 1996). In taking this step, I do not wish to present a further divisive view of archaeological practice; rather, I want to examine how we might re-orientate materials science analysis in terms of the wider goals of interpretative archaeology. In order to undertake this task I will focus on the *interface* between these branches of archaeology (see Renfrew 1982).

Hand in hand with the creation of the archaeological laboratory we observe the conceptual transformation of the physical traces of the site (both artefactual and environmental) as they become the focus of objective scientific analysis. In order to re-contextualise artefactual and environmental samples within a historically and culturally meaningful framework, I advocated a mode of enquiry that takes account of both context and content, both the physical dimensions of artefacts and environmental samples and their cultural and historical dimensions.

This methodology can be described in terms of a process of translation in which alliances are created between observations and interpretations on a step-by-step basis. In other words, an interpretative analytical process for archaeological science that requires simultaneous attention both to the rigour of scientific analysis and to the rigour of cultural and historical understanding. Such a framework of analysis attends to the traditional explanatory mode of analysis of science, in which the veracity of results are judged by empirical analysis and reproducibility, while at the same time attending to the interpretative mode of analysis promoted in the social and human sciences, in which analysis is judged according to the kind of framework of understanding in which it is situated and depends much on the clarity and persuasiveness of the discussion (Toulmin 1990).

If we are to examine this mode of enquiry, it is necessary first to concern ourselves with the practices of materials scientists. First, we need to focus on the nature of the problems that materials scientists study, and second on how they go about solving those problems at the practical level. In previous chapters I noted that epistemologically there were a number of alliances made between science and certain kinds of archaeological theory. For example palaeobotanists and zooarchaeologists often ally themselves with ecological or Darwinian approaches, and materials scientists often ally themselves with broad-based studies of exchange networks or studies of ancient technology. However I also noted that there appeared to be an interpretative 'brick wall' created between the kinds of analysis found in much recent interpretative archaeology and that traditionally allowed for in scientific analysis. Certain theoretical approaches appear to articulate better, or more solidly, with the results of certain kinds of scientific analysis than others. If the practices of materials scientists are to articulate differently, we need to understand how the connections are made in practice between different kinds of scientific and theoretical knowledge. We need to consider what it is that we might want to know at the theoretical level and examine how our practices as materials scientists might be modified in order to create clearer articulations between one body of knowledge and another.

In this chapter I want to develop this methodology by examining three main points which arise from this proposal. First, I want to examine the nature of the relationship between materials science and material culture as a means of highlighting some of the possibilities open to archaeological scientists in the integration of analytical approaches from both the human sciences and the natural sciences. Following on from this, I want to look at the important issues of scale and resolution. These issues are critical if we are to fully realise an alliance between material culture studies and materials science analyses. Finally, using a short case study, I will explore what such a scientific analytical process might look like.

What is material culture?

The field of material culture studies has grown considerably over the past twenty years or so. Due to this we tend to take the term 'material culture' for granted (Prown 1996), but I believe we need to scrutinise the term in more detail. An objective view of the world would see a logical distinction between inanimate objects, which are part of the *material* world, and animate subjects, that are part of the *cultural* world. The concept of 'material culture' fuses these distinct elements of the world together in a single term. From an objective viewpoint it appears logically inconsistent. If we are to employ the term, then we may be required to embrace an element of subjectivity if we are to proceed with our enquiries. We are required to take on board the view that the material world is apprehended through a series of cultural devices, including perception and language, and that the way in which we engage with this world is heavily laden with social and cultural significance. More maturely, from a perspective informed by an understanding of the philosophical tenets of phenomenology, we might view the material and cultural aspects of the world to be mutually constituted and mutually specifying. As Christina Toren (1999, 5) puts it: our ideas, the cultural aspects of life, are constituted in material relations with each other, and we communicate with each other in and through the materiality of the world. Or, to put it another way, people and things are mutually constructed; things are enmeshed within human affairs (Latour 1999, 174–215; Strathern 1998). In short, in order to propagate social relations between each other, people use things.

However, this proposition poses a considerable puzzle. In many ways we might think of socially constructed things as mediators of social relations. But if things are socially constructed and therefore composed of social relations, why do we need social relations (in the form of things) to mediate with another set of social relations? One way of reorienting this conundrum is to consider the possibility that we might view the construction of things as one technique by which humans make society more durable (Latour 1991); since things retain, in material form, the ideas and notions that make societies operable and reproducible. If we take this idea on board, we then need to consider *how* it is that things mediate *for* humans.

This exploration of both how and why alliances are constructed between people and things is what makes the field of material culture studies so dynamic. Importantly this theoretical perspective places archaeology at centre stage, since it is one of the few disciplines dedicated to exploring the relationship between people and things. Furthermore, the development of this outlook within archaeology has led to increased discussion at a theoretical level with those working in other disciplines, such as anthropology, history of science and technology, human geography, design studies, art history and museum studies (see Miller 1987; Gosden 1999, 152–79). Moreover, since the discipline of archaeology encompasses an interest in the social and physical dimensions of the material world, it is critical that we engage with these ideas not only at a theoretical level but also at a practical level. We are required to consider simultaneously how it is that artefacts are socially and culturally constructed, while also taking into account the physical and mechanical construction of artefacts. We do not need to study these two aspects of artefacts as separate and distinct entities. Materials science and material culture studies are therefore engaged in the same project of enquiry, as we will see in this chapter.

Sampling, scale and abstraction

How are we to relate these points to the concerns and expertise of the materials scientist? First, materials science provides a series of techniques for characterising the physical and material basis of material culture; these range from image intensification techniques, such as low power light microscopy, to high intensification techniques, such as scanning electron microscopy (SEM). A series of techniques are also available to determine the material composition of artefacts (for overviews see Kingery 1996; Pollard and Heron 1996; Wachtman 1993), ranging from thin-section petrology to more complex analytical procedures such as neutron activation analysis (NAA), inductively coupled plasma spectroscopy (ICPS) or x-ray fluorescence spectroscopy (XRF). Each of these techniques is aimed at providing precise data on the major, minor and trace elements from which an object is constituted. Second, through techniques based on the principles of engineering, the physical properties of material culture may also be determined (Cotterell and Kamminga 1990). Fundamentally aspects of cultural choice determine both the material composition and the mechanical properties of material culture. If we are to understand these aspects of material culture, then materials science has a critical role to play (Kingery 1996, 176).

If we are to gain an understanding of the manner in which cultural choices have been made in relation to the material construction of artefacts, we must be especially aware of the scale of analysis at which we operate. In general we can distinguish between techniques designed to examine the elemental basis of artefacts, the microstructure of artefacts, and those used to determine the macrostructure. Different scales of analysis require different instrumental techniques in order to describe the details of artefact composition (see Kingery 1996; Killick 1996). Our task remains to move between our interpretation of objects as determined by material science techniques and what these interpretations might tell us

Scale   Analysis of artefact

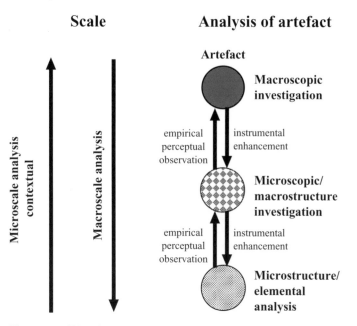

Figure 4.1 The changes of perception allied to changes in analytical scale

in terms of the intentional and meaningful aspects of material culture. Herein lies a problem.

As a broad rule of thumb, we appear to observe an interesting relationship between scales of analysis and scales of resolution (see Fig. 4.1). As we deal with the elemental and microstructural properties of artefacts, the finer-grained and more abstract the scale of resolution (e.g. trace element analysis, stable isotope analysis or scanning electron microscopy) the less inclined we feel to interpret our results in terms of past social practices. What is more, the more abstract the results, the greater the scale of the interpretative framework we feel we need to operate at in order to make sense of the results. Conversely, as we turn to deal with the macrostructural properties of artefacts, the less abstract our object of analysis (e.g. microwear analysis on stone tools) and more coarse-grained our resolution, the more we feel inclined to interpret our results in terms of past social practices.

For example, when we employ elemental analyses of pottery we tend to situate our results in very broad schemes of interaction and exchange (Tite 1996). We tend to say less about individual acts of pottery production; rather, we feel more secure discussing production in terms of very broad frameworks. On the other hand, when we employ much more coarse-grained techniques such as petrology we feel more confident in assessing strategies of pottery production in a localised framework.

This problem is demonstrated by the recent work of Arnold *et al.* (1999, 2000). Their work involves the use of instrumental neutron activation analysis (INAA) as a means of determining discrete compositional groups of pottery collected during ethnoarchaeological fieldwork from Guatemala and Yucatan. Their work was aimed at testing the ability of INAA as a means of resolving groups of pottery at a number of levels of interaction. The results of this analysis indicated a high degree of resolution in distinguishing between communities of potters working in different regional centres of production. The results were also able to distinguish *between* communities that used at least one resource in common. However, the analysis was unable to distinguish between different production households *within* a single production community. This example indicates that while studies that utilise elemental analysis are extremely useful in resolving differences between the characteristics of materials at the macroscale level over a large geographical scale, the same technique is unable to resolve differences in the composition of objects at the microscale or local level. I use this example not to indicate that either the technique or its application should be viewed as problematic, but rather to illustrate how closely we need to be aware of how our techniques relate to our scales of analysis.

There is a further rule that applies to the issue of abstraction. Often there is a tendency to feel that the more complicated our techniques, the better our science. Simple techniques are associated with crude levels of analysis; complex techniques are associated with sophisticated analysis. This is obviously a generalisation, but we need to critically examine our tendency to relate complexity with sophistication, since on critical examination there is no obvious correlation between complex analytical practice and sophisticated analytical interpretation. If we are to give this point serious consideration, we need to be aware that there are two crucial issues we must tackle. First, we need to consider what it is that we want to say with materials science in terms of past social practices. Second, we need to be aware that, as indicated in the previous chapter, materials science techniques are situated within the broader process of interpretation. If we take this on board, we might judge the sophistication of our analytical techniques not just by the complexity of our results but by the sophistication of the resultant interpretation. In other words, we need to consider not just the technique, but how we interpret the results of that technique. This symmetrical mode of analysis therefore pays attention to the mode by which we tie the analytical results together with our interpretative frameworks.

Narratives: scientific facts and interpretative fictions

The historian of science Donna Haraway (1989) points out that in the modern West we have tended to rigidly divide fact from fiction. She argues that, in order to maintain a belief in the veracity of science, we have created a distinction between the results of scientific practice and the results of imagination created by novelists. We have maintained a rigid divisive line between the non-constructed and the constructed. Facts are hard-edged, real and non-constructed, while fiction is soft, related to fantasy and entirely constructed. Throughout this book I have suggested that scientific facts are in some ways socially constructed. The intention here is not to pour scorn on the truth or falsity of scientific knowledge, but to draw attention to the way in which we practice the creation of scientific facts. One of the most important aspects of this argument is that once we realise that we are constructing or creating facts we become aware that we may, within reason, construct them in multiple ways. In other words, we need to consider what it is we want to know before we begin the practices of fact construction. If we take this argument on board, we need to realise that just as fictions are created within certain narrative frameworks, so facts are situated in certain narrative frameworks. As Knorr-Certina (1981, 88–91) has it, all scientific facts are situated within wider frameworks associated with broad-based research goals and problems that transcend the individual laboratory or fieldworker.

The proposition that we might treat facts as constructed should not be perceived as a degradation of the veracity of facts; rather it provokes an awareness of the relationship between our analyses and wider scientific questions. Equally we may note, with Ingold (1993), that fiction need not be perceived as entire fabrication, a process of covering up or concealing the raw facts. Rather fiction may be considered as a device for opening up or providing an entry into an argument. We need to embrace the realisation that both fact and fiction are equally constructed, although they are constructed in different ways and for different audiences (Knorr-Certina 1981, 94–133). Our task then is to critically reconsider the relationship between different types of construction and the kinds of statements we might make using knowledge of different qualities.

A consideration of narrative leads us to think about some of the issues related to the nature of abstraction, and the narrative and analytical scales at which we operate. The issue of narrative forces us to realise that we need to be mindful of what it is that we are trying to say about the past;

we have to concern ourselves with the kind of *narrative scales* at which we work. Pluciennik (1999) notes that different types of narrative relate to different scales of analysis. We might usefully distinguish between two broad narrative scales, the macroscale and microscale. Macroscalar narratives include those in which events are abstracted and linked to common processes. We can recognise this form of narrative in the generalising approach of rationalism in which human activity may be linked together by a series of cause-effect laws. This is the narrative scale at which much culture-history operates; cultures are used to stand in for characters on the world stage. Similarly this narrative scale is often deployed in processual archaeology, since the aim is to work towards building a series of generalisable laws of human behaviour. Such laws of behaviour are often set within broader narrative schemes, such as those of social evolution (Pluciennik 1999, 662).

On the other hand, microscalar narratives emphasise the individual or historically specific, events are linked by very specific reason-action explanations and there is little claim to extrapolate to wider causal explanations. Microscale narratives are context dependent, and we can see an obvious alliance between this scale of analysis and relativism. Such approaches have been employed most readily in post-processual and interpretative accounts of the past in which human action is viewed as situated in, and structured by, local cultural and historical contexts.

But are we required to operate with just two polarised scales of analysis, or are the different narrative scales interlocking? These questions have had a considerable currency within both history (Braudel 1980; Ginzburg 1982) and archaeology (see Bintliff 1995; Knapp 1992 for archaeological overviews). But they have recently been re-appraised by a number of authors (Dobres and Hoffman 1994; Gosden 1994; Hodder 1999). Hodder (1999, 130–1) suggests that the two narrative scales are incommensurable since localised events are underdetermined by large-scale structures – we can never determine all the factors that lead to events, and they cannot be explained by large-scale structures alone. Despite this pessimism Hodder goes on to describe, using the example of Otzi the ice-man, how individual actions are related through practice to long-term structures. Dobres and Hoffman (1994, 213), discussing the scales of analysis required in technological studies, suggest that while microscale and macroscale analyses are different, it is possible to work from the local, microscale towards the macroscale. They suggest that 'dynamic social processes operating at the microscale may have impacted upon or substantially contributed to more macroscalar processes' (*ibid.* 213). Similarly Gosden (1994, 15–17) notes that each action is linked in space and time to other future or past actions. These actions form chains which together form networks, and these networks form what Gosden describes as 'frames of reference'. It is these frames of reference that together make up large-scale structures of action. Our conceptualisation of scales of analysis must therefore encompass the point that, both historically and geographically, the scales within which individuals act are constructed by societies, and these prescribed scales of action are both monitored and transformed by the individuals that act within them. The scales within which we act are multidimensional – for example, the same individual may operate simultaneously at the level of personal interaction, as a member of a localised social group, and as a member of a larger social group, such as a nation-state. At each point the ability to work within and transform these scales depends on the action taken with regard to these various scales of analysis.

We need to keep in mind the point made by Barrett (2000, 63) that 'it is possible to write narratives which mark the passing of time but without reference to agency. Such narratives work at a level of abstraction – economic processes operate without labour, ideologies arise without the struggle to maintain belief – and the reasons for choosing such abstractions must be explicitly understood.' Therefore we need to remind ourselves that, although macroscale processes may provide a basic level of explanation, our analytical framework should commence by bringing into focus the scale of human endeavour and interaction – at the microscale level – that provide the structural conditions that inform these wider processes.

How do these issues relate to the analyses performed by materials scientists and why are they important? I have already argued that the material world is not socially and culturally neutral: it is imbued with meaning. However the ways in which we can 'get at' some aspects of the meaningful nature of the material world using materials science techniques depend very much on the type of technique that we use and the analytical scale at which that technique operates. This problem is again illustrated by the work of Arnold *et al.* (1999). The samples collected for analysis were microscale in nature – they were derived from individual potters in each area – but the technique employed (INAA) to analyse the samples, although successful at distinguishing compositional difference at the macroscale level, was unable to distinguish between samples at the microscale level at which they were sampled. The technique therefore restricted subsequent analysis to the discussion of broad macroscale processes.

The main point I am making here is that if we undertake our analyses within a narrative framework that only attends to the macroscale, our interpretations will tend to be restricted to this scale of analysis. If our analyses attend to the microscale, then our analysis may also be able to inform us about processes that occur at greater scales. I would argue, then, that the microscale represents the most appropriate scale with which to initiate our analyses. This is because attention to fine-grained microscale analysis will not only allow us to consider fine-grained localised differences in material culture patterning, it will also enable us to 'scale up' our discussions to consider localised differences within a wider macroscale framework. This attention to scale has important implications with regard to our sampling procedures and the subsequent analysis of results.

Scale, structure and narrative

Curiously, we tend to see *macrostructural* analyses of artefacts associated with *microscale* narratives, and *elemental* or *microstructural* analysis of artefacts linked to *macroscale* narratives. Why is this? Because as we move away from the tangible (and observable) analysis of material culture towards more abstract modes of analysis, we begin to suffer a crisis of confidence. We begin to question our ability to assess the significance of our results within the framework of human observation. This is due to the fact that when we analyse the concrete macrostructure of materials such as potsherds or flint flakes our results are amenable to empirical observation. This observation may be with the naked eye, or it may be enhanced (or transformed) by optical instruments. Furthermore, the practice of analysis does not require the destruction of the artefact in order to produce results. Therefore our interpretation of these results can be reassessed at any time hence.

However, when we consider abstract elemental and microstructural analytical procedures, such as stable isotope analysis or trace element analysis or petrology, designed to examine the microstructure of materials, the destructive nature of our analytical techniques requires that we *sample*. Significantly, each distinct sample is derived from a different location and therefore no two samples are coterminous. Each sample is unique. This means that not only is each sample non-observable in the empirical sense, but also we cannot return to the same sample location on the artefact and reassess it at a later stage.

We employ a number of devices in order to circumvent this problem. When we present the results of our analyses, we filter them through a series of inscription procedures. The analysis of concrete observable artefacts, such as potsherds and flint flakes, is fairly straightforward. We simply observe, measure and sketch the artefacts. The relationship between our observations and our interpretations is viewed as reasonably unproblematic. We present a text-based interpretation of our analysis alongside a quantitative analysis, employing simple histograms related to minimum number of vessels, or numbers of different types of flint instrument. We also use a further mode of representation – artefact drawings – which are presented as accurate and conventionalised representations of artefacts 'as they really are'. These drawings provide an illusion of concrete familiarity. Because we are trained to recognise and interpret these drawings, we therefore 'see' these artefacts in their natural state much as if we were observing them in reality. For us they are real and empirically observable.

When we come to examine more abstract modes of destructive analysis, our observations are filtered through far more complex inscription devices. First, as noted in chapter 2, instrumental techniques such as XRF, ICPS, NAA and GC/MS encode information. They transform the raw material analysed into data. We observe further layers of encryption as data are transformed statistically. Finally these data are presented visually in the form of three-dimensional graphs or histograms. The material world has undergone a series of transformations as it changes from raw material to numerical data to graphic data. My point is that due to the abstract nature of this kind of information, and the destructive, non-repeatable nature of analytical practice, we employ a series of inscription devices, statistics and graphs, as a means of persuading ourselves of the veracity of our data. This is not to say that these results are not 'real', or do not adequately represent archaeological facts. Rather, I simply wish to point out that certain analytical procedures and the presentation of the results of these procedures are *constructed*. Not only this – they are also subject to multiple layers of construction.

To return to the first point made above, we have problems with employing abstract materials science analyses as a means of discussing past social practices. But this is precisely because of the nature of our analytical practices. We create a distance between past social practices precisely because we disassociate material from the artefact and subject it to a series of instrumental, mathematical and graphical transformations. A far greater number of stages of analysis and presentation (each associated with a fresh stage of transformation) lie between, say, NAA analysis of pottery and macroscopic analysis of pottery. Therefore we find it problematic to retrace our steps and relate our analysis to some form of past social practice. There are simply too many layers of transformation between specific social practices and the results of instrumental analysis.

We find it easier to start from a position in which we examine the microscale contextual differences between the observable macrostructural properties of artefacts. We then find it simpler to transform our understanding of this observable data to the next stage of interpretation, in which we try to say something meaningful about past social practices in relation to our empirical observations.

However if we start from an initial position in which we have already abstracted material from an artefact in order to examine the microstructural differences in artefact composition, we are then required to make a *far greater* series of inferential steps back towards the empirically observable artefact in order to say anything meaningful about past social practices in terms of our microstructural observations. Rather than torturously retracing our steps, we instead opt to fit our observations into wider generalised schemes of knowledge in order to make sense of them – we therefore rely on comprehending the results of our analysis in a macroscale narrative structure.

I argued above that attention to microscale contextual differences allows us to eventually fit our observations within wider macroscale narratives. While this is desirable, I have also outlined some of the problems we face when we attempt microstructural analyses of artefacts. We face problems because, due to our analytical practices, our results are abstracted from the artefact and we therefore find them difficult to interpret in terms of microscale contextual differences. The problems of transformation and subsequent interpretation arise in part because of the archaeological practice of shearing the object from its original archaeological context. As indicated in the previous chapter, not only is the material sheared from its context, but that context very rarely travels with the object through subsequent stages of analysis. This relates to my point that often materials scientists have little knowledge of the historical or cultural context of the material on which they base their analyses. The decontextualised object actively creates the 'brick wall' of interpretation that divides materials science from interpretative archaeologists. Again, our practices structure the mode by which we construct our knowledge.

If we are to get around this problem, and work towards knitting together tighter and more plausible alliances between materials science and interpretative archaeology, then we need to work back along the chain of transformations described above. At each stage the materials scientist must keep in mind two aspects of data:

1 While data are transformed through presentation, the artefact remains the same. The data are derived from an archaeological artefact of some form, and our interpretations must be plausible in terms of the material and physical nature of that artefact.
2 The artefact is grounded in a context. Just as the artefact remains the same, despite the subsequent alteration of the data derived from the artefact, so too the fixed nature of the context of the artefact must also be kept in consideration.

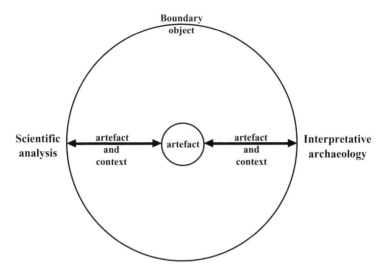

Figure 4.2 Artefacts and their contexts as boundary objects

Both of these features of analysis, the artefact and its context, provide what historians of science describe as 'boundary objects': an object that keeps its constancy, although the data and alliances surrounding that object change (Star and Griesemer 1989). Such boundary objects, in this case the artefact and its context, allow distinct groups of people, in our case materials scientists and interpretative archaeologists, to find some form of bridging device that provides some constancy of purpose and interpretation in what are otherwise distinct and contradictory projects (Fig. 4.2). In the case of archaeological analysis, the property that defines and maintains the constancy of the boundary object is the documentation that surrounds the artefact – it is this that gives it contextual definition. It is the methodological constancy – the retention of documents concerning context – at each stage of the analysis that allows us to begin to bridge the gap between the two approaches to the archaeological artefact. This constancy enables the results from the preliminary stages of laboratory analysis to have an effect on the subsequent stages of interpretative analysis, and vice versa.

There is, of course, a further important problem, and this concerns *resolution*. If the results of microstructural analyses are very coarse grained, then we feel little confidence in differentiating one set of results against another at the microscale contextual level (see Tite 1996, 241–2). This problem with resolution often affects the way in which we sample artefacts. As Tite (1999, 197) observes, the chemical analysis of artefacts using minor and trace element analysis may provide a compositional 'fin-gerprint' for characterising objects made of the same raw materials. How-ever in some cases, as with pottery and metals, we may have problems due to the variability in chemical composition of source materials. In an attempt to surmount this problem there is a tendency to sample large numbers of objects in order to place them in broad compositional groups. It is this practice of homogenising numerous samples that then prevents us from discussing differences between artefacts except in terms of wide macroscale geographical or chronological differences.

How are we to get round this problem? While problems of resolution are best solved by the application of alternate methodologies, we may also consider the possibility of multi-stage sampling procedures. These could commence with techniques designed to securely observe the differences between artefacts in terms of macroscale differences and then, armed with the results of this analysis, proceed to a stage in which more fine-grained microstructural techniques are applied. As Kingery (1996, 178) rightly notes, we need to be aware that no single technique is entirely secure in its ability to provide conclusive results. It is therefore beneficent to work with a number of complementary techniques.

A further problem also relates to the nature of the on-site sampling of artefact assemblages. Here I am not especially interested in the nature of sampling in terms of the recovery of a representative sample of the assem-blage population (Cherry 1978). Obviously these issues are critical to our understanding of any archaeological site; however, I am more interested in how we move from on-site sampling to the sampling required of ma-terials scientists in a laboratory setting. As the example above indicates, if we are to understand the microscale differences in artefact assemblages we need to consider sampling according to the contextual differences of the assemblage, rather than at random. It is only by adopting a contextual approach to sampling artefacts that we avoid the problems associated with homogenising artefacts in subsequent analysis. If we are to meaningfully categorise artefacts in terms of compositional groups and relate compo-sitional differences to decisions made in selecting materials for artefact manufacture, we must be careful in our use of this sampling procedure. As materials scientists, if our analytical results are to have any bearing on our understanding of issues of artefact categorisation and construction, we are required to tie the results of our analytical methods back to the specific raw materials that constitute the artefact.

We should conclude that these issues are critical to scientific analysis since the issue of narrative scale lies at the heart of what we sample, how we sample, and how we relate this analysis to a specific framework of un-derstanding. What I am suggesting here is that our attention to issues of scale as materials scientists needs to be manifold. We must relate our theoretical interests to a set of multi-layered practical considerations. First, we need to consider what kind of narrative scale we wish to operate with. Second, we need to decide what kind of techniques are most appropriate to answering the kinds of questions we are interested in, and how we may go about sampling a given artefact in order to produce the answers to these questions.

Linearity and reflexivity in practice

Having discussed some of the problems associated with the scales of scientific analysis in relation to material culture, I will now shift the discussion towards considering another scale of analysis – how this overall approach to archaeological science integrates with wider interpretative research questions. Traditionally scientific analysis has proceeded along a familiar path from hypothesis, to experiment, to the refutation or confirmation of the primary hypothesis. At this point the hypothesis is reformulated, abandoned or retained. This process of investigation is characterised by its linearity. Furthermore, as we saw in the previous chapter, a linear process of excavation, post-excavation and publication similarly defines archaeological practice. Here the analysis of objects and samples retrieved from the site is traditionally undertaken off-site and after the excavation process has ended. I have already argued that this rigidly linear structure promotes a series of problems in the subsequent interpretation and publication of archaeological data.

As an alternative, Hodder (1999, 80–104) has proposed what he describes as a reflexive methodology in which both description and interpretation are simultaneous. One aspect of such a methodology involves the classification and analysis of those objects and samples otherwise analysed under the aegis of post-excavation *at the stage of excavation* – in other words on-site – as objects and samples are retrieved from the ground. This process allows the interpretation of artefacts and environmental samples to actively reflect back on the methodology of excavation, allowing for an increased sensitivity to the exigencies of the site itself and thereby enabling a closer fit between the interpretation of site and artefact. This suggestion is commendable and certainly side-steps some of the problems associated with the process of 'explosion' outlined in the previous chapter. However we must be wary of two problems, the first philosophical, the second practical.

First, we must be careful when utilising the on-site expertise of archaeological scientists that science does not simply stand for objectivity and that the analyses of objects and samples do not remain as immutable statements of fact which are then deployed back on-site in a rigid and prescriptive manner. Rather we must be aware that, as suggested above, the formulation of scientific analyses must be structured as much by contextual considerations as by recourse to a set of objective scientific data. Second, the practical aspects of retaining on-site specialists depend very much on the contingencies of national laws concerning the exportation of scientific materials beyond national borders. More importantly, funding considerations may also hamper such an approach – since few funding bodies are prepared to part with post-excavation monies until the significance of the site has been established through excavation.

Nevertheless the broad notion of reflexivity may be harnessed in other ways. For example, it is common for many field projects to be conducted over a number of seasons, and it is entirely feasible that specialist scientific analysis may proceed off-site between excavation seasons. This process would potentially allow information from such an analysis to be fed back into the excavation process in subsequent seasons. Ultimately, while the place and position of the archaeological scientist or specialist is important, we also need to consider how interpretations are arrived at in practice and how these interpretations cohere with the results of others within the excavation report or within other mediums of reportage. The point here is that close contact between specialists and other practitioners is required at all stages of analysis in order to produce a coherent and satisfying account, an account in which knowledge is not presented as disparate and fragmented, but in which each area of knowledge mutually structures the other.

Case study: interpretation and materials science

In the previous section I discussed the importance of considering research questions in terms of certain narrative scales. This process involves three things:

1 Framing a set of interpretative questions and setting out to answer them by working with artefactual data which are firmly related to context.
2 Examining this data using analytical procedures with enough resolution to distinguish between the contextual differences in artefacts.
3 This procedure should also be reflexive in its approach: working back and forth between research questions, site and artefact.

In order to examine what this interpretative approach to materials science might resemble, I will consider the work of Peter Schmidt (1996, 1997), since his studies encompass many of the approaches to archaeological science advocated above. Schmidt is interested in studying the nature of iron technology in East Africa. His stated aim is to 'recuperate

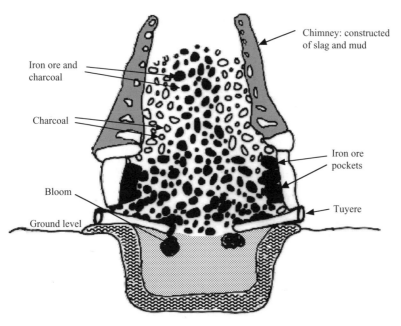

Chimney: constructed
of slag and mud

Iron ore and
charcoal

Charcoal

Iron ore
pockets

Bloom

Tuyere

Ground level

Figure 4.3 A schematic view of the Haya furnace

the history of African iron technology' (Schmidt 1997, 1). This is because Africa has long been viewed through the lens of primitivism. For
Europeans, Africans lacked history. Europe was the home of the technologically advanced and literate, while Africa was inhabited by the technologically inferior and illiterate. Such views often manifest themselves
in depictions of the development of iron technology, which usually use
prehistoric Europe as their model. Due to this impoverished view of iron
technology Schmidt (1996) was interested in examining the technology of
iron smelting and investigating the use of a technological process known
as *preheating*. This process involved heating gases running through the
tuyeres into the furnace, which enabled a higher reducing temperature to
be achieved during smelting and produced a higher yield of pure metal
(Fig. 4.3). The very existence of this process was contested by a number
of people on the grounds that the process had not developed in Europe
until the Industrial Revolution. At the outset Schmidt's aims were to
investigate this particular smelting technology as a means of contesting
the colonialist bias through which much African technology is viewed.
His approach to this problem include ethnoarchaeological documentation, thin-section analysis of slags and blooms, and an analysis of the

performance characteristics of *tuyeres* using a thermocouple during use and through visual examination after use.

Schmidt approached a number of retired Haya smelters and blacksmiths who inhabit the region around the western edge of Lake Victoria, Tanzania to reproduce furnaces in the present that allowed the performance characteristics of both furnace and *tuyere* to be determined. The investigative procedure itself was not linear in its aims and outcomes. The creation of furnaces and the production of iron blooms were fraught with problems from a number of quarters: social, ritual and technological. Schmidt's account draws together each element of the procedure and allowed him to establish the veracity of the preheating process, using temperature measurement of the *tuyeres* and thin-section investigation of the slags and iron blooms.

From this analysis the existence of the preheating technology was confirmed. The confirmation procedure involved a cohesive alliance between the scientific examination of the furnace components and the products of the furnace with the experimental and ritual procedures and oral testimonies of the local iron smelters. This then led Schmidt to investigate the time-depth of this technology through the excavation of ancient smelting and forging sites. This exercise established that smelting technologies of this kind potentially dated to the second century AD, confirming the technological process of preheating to be a process that predated European expansion by at least a millennium.

This investigation of the antiquity of East African iron smelting processes is admirable in itself since it provides a firm platform from which to challenge Eurocentric beliefs concerning the technological abilities of non-Europeans (see Harding 1991, 191–218). But Schmidt goes beyond this to examine how iron production relates to ideological beliefs and the construction of local histories. His observations of smelting and forging encompass both the 'functional' dimensions – the shape of the furnace, the position of the *tuyeres*, the temperature of the furnace and the physical and chemical characteristic of the iron blooms – and the 'ritual' dimensions, such as the songs performed while smelting, the deposition of smelting charms beneath the furnace, the construction of spirit houses, the observation of taboos, etc.

As in many parts of Africa, the symbolism of iron production here is associated with sex and fecundity. It is men who undertake iron production and they must abstain from intercourse during the smelting process. In Buhaya, the area studied by Schmidt, the technological process of production bears many similarities to reproduction and birth. More widespread practices also make this explicit connection. For example Herbert's (1993) study of iron smelting in West Africa notes how the kiln is modelled both conceptually and physically as a female figure; the furnace is fed with charcoal and iron ore, it excretes slag and gives birth to an iron bloom. The sequence of activities relates the production process to the biological process undergone in human birth.

The presence of the phallic-shaped *tuyeres* and the use of bellows to force air into the furnace complete the sexual metaphors that pertain to Haya iron production. Sex is considered to be 'hot' – like iron production. Therefore an important requisite for fertilisation is that the phallic *tuyeres* should be hot; for this reason they are inserted deep within the furnace, preheating air as it enters the furnace and enabling higher temperatures to be reached. An understanding of the coherence between the symbolic and physical elements of action clarifies how it is that the preheating process came into existence. Without an understanding of the symbolism surrounding iron production, any elucidation of the preheating process would have been technologically one-sided – and would have taken little account of the social.

Such an analysis allows us to gain a detailed understanding of how a particular non-European technology was developed and used within a distinct world of cultural meaning. Furthermore, it enabled Schmidt to investigate the manner by which iron production was tied to both the mythology and kingship ideology of the region. Forging was an important element of the inauguration of kings since iron, like the power of the king, was related to fecundity. What is more the association between a mythological iron tower and the inauguration of a king of some historical importance was demonstrated to have a concrete relationship to an important iron production centre. This analysis strengthens our understanding of the time-depth of oral histories in the area.

This discussion highlights the use of a gamut of materials science techniques from the domains of engineering, chemistry and physics within a research framework derived from social anthropology or interpretative archaeology. The critical point I wish to draw out is that the examination of East African iron technology began with a significant question – can we use a scientific examination of technology to rewrite the conventional colonialist histories of Africa? During the investigation, the data derived from detailed microscale scientific analysis were allied with an investigation of symbolism that not only explicated certain problems inherent in our understanding of the nature of belief systems and history but also clarified our understanding of the technological process itself. The mode of investigation moved from the microscale to examine the macroscale historical processes and, having done this, returned to explicate the microscale. This form of investigation enables us to envisage how it is that we may proceed with laboratory-based scientific analysis while also retaining an eye on the historical and cultural context of the objects and samples that we analyse. Such a process encompasses a shift between scales and also employs a reflexive approach, since it works back and forth between European and non-European understandings in order to create a cohesive and holistic interpretation.

Having examined a case study that emphasises the alliance between materials science and material culture studies, I now wish to extend this investigation in order to examine how we might use a specific kind of microscale analysis, the scale of the human life cycle, as a means of understanding the production, use and deposition of material culture. I will also explore how, within this framework of analysis, we can employ materials science techniques to open up our understanding of these processes.

5 Material culture and materials science: a biography of things

Introducing a biographical perspective

One of the major points to emerge from our discussion of scales of analysis is that modes of analysis that only attend to large-scale structures have little to tell us about how people lived and structured their lives on a daily basis. In order to understand these issues, we have to consider temporal and spatial scales of a more limited nature and duration, and work from these to consider how activities performed at these smaller scales transform larger-scale structures. What we are interested in, then, is how material culture is used to create and maintain meaningful social relations, relations that affirm the definition of identity and belonging at individual, local and wider scales.

One scale of analysis that provides a useful starting point is the human life span (Gilchrist 2000, 325). The narrative structure of human life cycles provides an extremely broad framework determined by biographically important events such as birth, life and death by which people make sense of their lives. Much of the literature concerning the way in which artefacts are invested with meaning focuses on their *biographical* relationship to human beings.

The notion of biography has arisen out of our understanding of the perception of objects in gift-based economies (see Mauss 1925 for his classic delineation of the notion of 'the gift'). Gifts, unlike commodities, are exchanged as a means of establishing relationships between people. Gifts are not simply conceived of as objects distinct from people (a notion that is critical to commodity-based exchange systems). Instead, things are often considered to possess some of the qualities of people. If objects can be thought of as having some of the qualities of people, then it seems reasonable that objects have lives that conform to the same structure as those of people: they are born, they live and they die. Just as we might think of objects as intervening in human lives and becoming 'animate' in the process (see chapter 2), likewise in many societies objects may be thought of as sharing aspects of human lives, and thereby becoming imbued with biographical status.

A useful distinction between the concept of 'biography' and that of 'use-life' has recently been made by Gosden and Marshall (1999, 169). Use-life is often framed from a materialist perspective: artefacts are created, they have a finite use-life, they become worn and are discarded. The concept of biography, while embracing the insights that a use-life perspective brings to artefact analysis, also encompasses the idea that objects are used to construct and maintain social identities. This point has been reiterated by Janet Hoskins (1998), who examines the way in which objects are not only socially identified with particular people, but also used to describe and relate their life histories. She is interested in the way in which artefacts are used by people as a means of making meaning of their lives. All in all, the concept of artefact biographies is a useful metaphor for thinking about the way in which people and artefacts are mutually related over time. This concept is especially useful for thinking about how it is that social identities are expressed through the medium of artefacts over different stages of the their use-lives.

How are we to examine this concept archaeologically? First and foremost we are aided in this project by the notion of 'contextual archaeology' (Barrett 1987; Hodder 1986; Shanks and Tilley 1987). This allows us to consider the possibility that the meanings associated with an artefact are not fixed; rather, they are transformed or altered according to the context within which the artefact is situated. This means that we are able to examine how an artefact may change its meaning over the course of its life as it shifts from one context to another. However, we also need to be aware that the notion of artefact biographies is not to suggest that objects can be read as ciphers for the human life cycle. Rather the notion of biography encompasses the idea that objects are utilised to express differing modes of identity at different points in their own lives, while various objects may themselves be used to express varied kinds of identity over the course of the lives of human beings (Sofaer-Derevenski 2000).

Thomas (1996) adopted this approach in his examination of the differing character of deposits from the British later Neolithic. For Thomas, artefacts are used as active components in the process of constructing different identities, and identities are constructed through the juxtaposition and manipulation of sets of artefacts. Tilley's (1996) account of object use and deposition in the early-middle Neolithic of southern Scandinavia lays more emphasis on the symbolic identities of artefacts at various stages of their lives and examines the way artefacts, in particular axes and pots, are perceived in relation to each other. This account re-emphasises the point that different types of artefact are materially distinctive and may be employed in the construction of different, but related, kinds of cultural biography. Sofaer-Derevenski (2000) has clearly delineated the mutual relationship between objects and identities, in her examination of the significance of copper technologies (beads and arm–rings) to the categorisation of gendered individuals at various points over the course of their lives in the late Neolithic and Copper Age of the Carpathian Basin.

It is important to reiterate that if we are to examine the nature of the relationship between people and things over the course of an artefact's life, we need to consider not only aspects such as exchange or deposition but also production and use. In other words, we need to emphasise the *entire life* of an artefact as the object of analysis. In doing this we should also be aware that when we are considering whole classes of artefacts, we operate at a scale of analysis which may transcend individual biographies to construct instead an image of the ideal career of an object (Tilley 1996, 248). While the concept of biography is a useful way of understanding the use-life of a single artefact, we may also examine the nature of artefact biographies at much larger temporal and spatial scales. Such an approach informed Bradley's (1990) examination of the nature of depositional practices from the Neolithic to Iron Age at a pan-European scale. The biographical approach to artefacts informs our understanding of the 'cultural life of things' at a number of scales of analysis.

I will now look at how social and cultural identities are expressed at various stages of an artefact's life, through the technology of production, through use and consumption and through exchange and deposition. But more importantly, I will examine how these issues might be clarified and given more resolution through the application of a series of techniques from the field of materials science. Tite (1999) has usefully examined some of these issues in relation to the 'use-life' of ceramics; here I wish to broaden the discussion to include other types of archaeological material. As Kingery (1996, 185) notes, the physical narrative of artefact production, use and discard is enmeshed with the narrative of the utilitarian, spiritual, emotional, creative and aesthetic life of artefacts. However, he argues that much materials science begins with production and works towards discard, while many interpretative accounts operate in the opposite direction. In this chapter it is essential that we align our studies and articulate the materials science perspective with a biographical approach to artefacts.

Making material culture: artefact production
and landscape

A number of studies of the procurement of materials have provided a useful framework within which to examine the way that resource procurement relates to environmental factors (Arnold 1985; Torrence 1986). These broadly ecological approaches (see Matson 1965 for original formulation of concept of artefacts and ecology) describe the parameters within which people procure and use resources. Here the environment is seen to have a crucial effect on the organisation and scale of production, on distribution networks, etc. While these approaches are important in delineating the possibilities and constraints available to people within differing kinds of environment, I believe that we need to consider not only the environmental factors but also the cultural perceptions of that environment prior to the procurement of resources. Site-catchment approaches such as ceramic ecology (Matson 1965) operate within a paradigm that views space as neutral and homogenous. Moreover, the environment may be treated with a degree of economic rationality, as an abstract framework within which human communities act.

But there are other ways of conceptualising landscape and environment. We may consider the natural world to be appropriated socially and culturally. As a component of the classified and lived human world landscapes are heterogeneous, and various features of the human environment will possess a multitude of different meanings. Such an approach embraces an understanding of human experience as being intimately involved in the process of actively interpreting, classifying, and being in, the material world (Ashmore and Knapp 1999; Thomas 1996; Tilley 1994). Within this interpretative framework the initial appropriation of natural products used in the technological processes of production is an active part of this classification process. If we are to understand in more detail how the natural world may be appropriated in the construction of material culture, it is essential to look in more detail at the issue of *place*.

Places are an important component of the socially classified landscape. Through the alteration and inhabitation of specific places, people are implicated in the land (Gow 1995), and as such different places are imbued with meaning. What is more, through the history of inhabitation, places also become identified with particular people (Weiner 1991). This understanding of place, which views places to be bound up with the history and identity of people, also proposes that the inhabitation of place is characterised by particular memories. For instance, Casey (1987) notes the way in which memories are place-specific. Activities conducted within a particular place are an important part of the act of remembrance. This

perspective is particularly relevant to the way in which we view the procurement and use of materials for the production of material culture.
Since landscapes are made up of different kinds of place, each associated with different memories and identities, the use and incorporation of
materials derived from different places is an important means by which,
through production, the identity of material culture may be initiated.
Indeed, the incorporation of materials from a series of different places
may be an important means of expressing particular types of identity
through production (Munn 1986; Battaglia 1991; Tilley 1999).

The use of specific materials from culturally significant places is one
means by which the power of place is grounded (Chapman 2000a, 25).
This is because, by virtue of their material constituents, artefacts carry
the social and cultural significance of particular places beyond the confines of a single zone of cultural significance. Although physically suitable
materials are necessary for the construction of artefacts, physical properties need not be the only thing to structure the use of materials in cultural
production (Tacon 1991). The production of material culture involves a
process of acquiring the physically and culturally appropriate materials
for the task, which may in itself involve a process of exchange between
social groups, possibly between boundaries defined by age, gender or
kinship (Mackenzie 1991; Tacon 1991). These approaches to landscape
need not require the abandonment of the broad frameworks established
by an ecological approach to the procurement of resources. Rather, we
simply need to note that the selection of these resources will be determined by their cultural classification. I believe that this approach allows
us to consider the procurement process with a more fine-grained degree
of subtlety.

Interestingly, Arnold has examined the nature of the categories involved in the procurement and use of pottery temper, the raw materials
of pottery production, amongst the Ticul of Yucatan, from an 'emic'
perspective (Arnold 1971). His 'ethnomineralogical' approach was concerned with defining and relating archaeologically observable data with
native categories. Importantly, while physical attributes such as colour
and hardness were seen as important, one of the key means of categorising material was by source (*ibid.*, 27). Both the material (clay) and the
source were bound up in a single idea of place that defined how the clay
was to be employed in the manufacture of pottery. Other archaeologists
have recognised the importance of place-specific identities to the manufacture of material culture. For instance, the physical location of stone axe
quarries has been recognised to be of great significance to the subsequent
distribution of their products (Bradley and Edmonds 1993; Cooney and
Mandall 1998). Similarly, the location of copper mines has also been

viewed to be critical to understanding their social role within the wider landscape (O'Brien 1994, 1999).

A variety of analytical techniques may be applied to answer the question of place-specific artefact provenance, ranging from simple geological provenance techniques such as petrology, used in the case of stone tools and ceramics (e.g. Clough and Cummins 1979; Cooney and Mandall 1998; Peacock 1969; Rice 1987), to geochemical techniques such as isotopic analysis, in the case of metals (Gale and Stos-Gale 1992). However we may also apply a number of chemical characterisation techniques which range from optical emission spectroscopy (OES), used in early obsidian characterisation studies (Renfrew, Cann and Dixon 1966; Williams-Thorpe 1995), to techniques such as XRF, ICPS and NAA, used in the analysis of materials such as ceramics (Neff 1992), metals and stone.

When considering the issue of provenance, we must again be aware of the issue of scale. Here we have to consider both the resolution of various techniques, and the survey and sampling procedure prior to analysis. For example, obsidian characterisation has been extremely successful using fairly low-resolution procedures such as OES. Broad sampling procedures coupled with OES have enabled researchers to establish exchange patterns across the eastern Mediterranean. The use of NAA at a later stage enabled increased resolution of specific obsidian sources (Aspinall, Feather and Renfrew 1972). Much of the subsequent analysis of the patterns of exchange determined from these analyses has been firmly placed within a macroscale narrative of contact and supply zones for obsidian procurement and exchange (Renfrew, Dixon and Cann 1968). Attempts to understand the localised procurement of obsidian at places such as Melos similarly subscribed to analysis within this broad framework (Torrence 1986). If we wish to obtain a more detailed understanding of obsidian procurement and distribution, then we are required to undertake detailed field sampling methods (Hughes 1994) coupled with high-resolution analytical techniques. This form of analysis linked with a *microscale* examination of technology and production (see Dimitriadis and Skourtopoulou forthcoming) should provide an increased understanding of the social relations involved in more extensive exchange.

Similar problems of resolution have been encountered in the isotopic analysis of bronze. Much work has been undertaken in refining the resolution of the analysis of lead isotopes in bronze in order to provide an increased resolution for the source of copper (Gale and Stos-Gale 1992), but the ability of this technique to provide precise information on the sources of copper has been questioned (Budd *et al.* 1995). As argued previously, an integrated combination of techniques is required in order to gain clear resolution. For example, the work of Joel, Taylor, Ixer and Goodway (1995) combines the use of lead isotope analysis with ore petrography to provide a distinct signature for the metal sources of the copper mines of the Great Orme, Wales. Similarly, Mandal (1997) has shown how the combination of petrology and XRF has distinguished the products of two stone axe quarries in northeast Ireland.

Studies that utilise a combination of techniques coupled with fine-grained field-based sampling procedures should allow us to construct detailed narratives concerning the place-specific origin of artefacts. Such analytical rigour enables us to tie together information concerning the analysis of materials with a concomitant level of detail concerning the provenance of materials. This detail then enables us to discuss the significance of the source of materials and the social relations involved in their extraction with far more clarity (for such an attempt in relation to stone axes see Cooney and Mandal 1998; Cooney 1999). Similarly, techniques of sampling which pay attention to the exigencies of local geology have also provided a detailed understanding of the source of clays used in regional potting traditions (see Howard 1981; Cleal 1996).

If we are to answer questions regarding the microscale significance of materials, then wherever possible we are also required to undertake detailed regional surveys in order to obtain compositionally different materials from a variety of locations around the landscape. It is only by attending to the twin problems of resolution of analysis and resolution of sampling that we will be able to distinguish the distinct locales from which materials are obtained. By attending to these problems of analysis, we can consider the social significance of the locations from which these materials are derived at a greater level of interpretative sophistication.

Shaping technology: production and materials science

As observed in chapter 1, the study of technology and production in archaeology has traditionally been a focus of study for materials scientists – it is considered to be one of the primary subject areas in which science has a clear and obvious role to play (Sillar and Tite 2000). Nevertheless, studies of technology and production have fairly recently come under the critical attention of anthropologists and interpretative archaeologists, as well as historians of science and technology (Callon 1991; Bijker, Hughes and Pinch 1987; Lemonnier 1992; Pfaffenberger 1988).

These studies have questioned the linear evolutionary narrative prevalent in many studies of technology. As we well know, the notion of the progressive nature of technology is one of the prime structuring principles of Western capitalism. As such, technology is often treated as an extra-societal force that acts independently of human beings. However if we are to fully understand technology and its effects on society we need to place human beings back into the picture (Pfaffenberger 1992; Latour 1993; Dobres 2000). One of the simple points that arise from this theoretical reorientation is the realisation that technologies are created through intentional human action.

Technologies are created by techniques of the body. As Mauss (1935) noted, these techniques are first and foremost cultural; moreover, they are also culturally specific. The creation of new technologies therefore requires a cultural choice (Lemonnier 1993). There is never simply one way to execute a technical action; there are many possible ways. What is more, each choice in technical production is linked to the next by its outcome. We are therefore able to distinguish a series of interlocking technical actions, *chaînes opératoires* or operational sequences, that go to make up technologies and through which we are able to examine the trajectories by which different cultural actions are executed on materials. In short, different cultural choices 'shape' technologies in different ways. Given this approach we need not view techniques as something to which meaning is added on at a later stage, but rather see techniques as complex phenomena that encapsulate symbolic considerations from their inception (Dobres 2000).

Technologies, therefore, weave together the material, social and symbolic dimensions of human life. We need not view culture as a determining factor over the constraints of the material world. Rather we need to remember that, as with our analysis of science, our task is to examine the creative alliances made between people and the material world; we should think of technologies as the mode by which humans act through material means. By studying technologies we simultaneously investigate how it is that people make things work for them and how things act to structure subsequent human action. It is through this process of interaction that technologies may be considered to create different categories of person (Dobres 2000). At a basic level, personal identities are instantiated through their association with particular kinds of activity; however, we also need to realise that the structures by which technologies are organised also serve to structure the nature of interaction and the nature of a person's identity. Pfaffenberger (1999) discusses this point with regard to the organisation of the production of canoes and yam-houses in two cultural contexts in Melanesia and the organisation of tin mining in nineteenth-century Britain. He notes that it is not so much the artefact created, but the experience of making the artefacts that conditions or disciplines people. I will take this point up further, later in this chapter.

There are a number of points we need to consider in relation to technology and materials science. First, materials science may be useful in determining artefact composition, the sequence of artefact production and the mechanical performance of artefacts. Determinations of the composition of artefacts may also reveal considerable details about the techniques involved in production, and the mechanical abilities of material culture. For example, elemental analysis of metals enables us to determine the precise smelting technology used in winning metal (Budd, Gale, Pollard, Thomas and Williams 1992); similarly, techniques such as petrology enable us to determine the composition of pottery and therefore the choices made in production. What is more, studies of firing temperature and atmosphere, whether through thermoluminescence studies or simple observation of colour changes in native clays (Matson 1968), enable us to discuss the parameters of choice and functionality in the production. Techniques aimed at defining the composition of *parts* of an artefact, for example glazes on pottery (e.g. Mason and Tite 1997) or the hafting adhesive for flint sickles (e.g. Endlicher and Tillman 1997), also have an important function in determining the sequence of steps required to achieve these effects.

We may also wish to employ materials science techniques in order to reveal the sequences involved in the production of artefacts. For example, xeroradiography is useful in ceramic analysis (Carr 1990) as a means of understanding the techniques involved in ceramic production such as coiling, slab building, etc. Similar analytical techniques may disclose production techniques involved in the production of metalwork, such as welding (Craddock 1995, 7; Killick 1996).

As Killick (1996) notes, the techniques involved in the production of artefacts may be elucidated using image intensification methods, such as light microscopy and scanning electron microscopy (SEM). Such techniques of identification have been routinely used to examine the working of metals and of other materials such as stone. Furthermore, techniques such as SEM, coupled with elemental detectors such as energy dispersive analysis by x-ray (EDAX), have the added advantage of enabling the composition of artefacts to be determined at the trace level.

Other materials science techniques aimed at determining the mechanical properties of objects enable us to assess the relationship between the material and non-material properties of artefacts. Measurements of tensile strength developed in engineering may allow us to understand to what extent mechanical properties were a consideration in the production of stone axes (Bradley *et al.* 1992). Similar approaches to the assessment of thermal shock resistance (Schiffer 1988; Skibo 1993) in pottery may also enable us to determine to what extent this was an important factor during production.

In these enquiries we need to be especially aware of the mode by which our materials analysis coheres with our theoretical framework. There is a tendency for many materials scientists to adhere to an evolutionary view of technological progress. For example, Craddock's (1995) account of early metal mining and production is situated very clearly within the discourse of social evolution. Smelting and mining techniques are consistently referred to as either primitive or advanced. In these kinds of narratives we must take into account the view raised in the previous discussion. Techniques and operational sequences are not simply progressive in order, but are determined by the cultural outlook of those employing them. It is critically important that account is taken of the coherence between the techniques employed and the symbolic system within which they are situated. This is well illustrated in the example described by Schmidt discussed in the previous chapter. In a similar vein Hosler (1993) has discussed the importance of cosmological ideas related to creativity and to solar and lunar deities in influencing the production technologies in historic west Mexico. She notes the use of alloying to create shimmering colours, and the significance of the kinds of objects made of metal – especially bells and rattles, which are associated with the creative power of thunder and rain. Lechtman (1984), too, has noted that in order to produce metals of certain colours, the Peruvian Mochica developed a complex set of alloying techniques. These techniques were developed so that the critical ingredient, usually gold or silver, was incorporated within the body of the metal. This was because of the belief that the 'essence of the object, must also be inside it. The object is not that object unless it contains within it the essential quality' (Lechtman 1984, 30). Saunders (1999, 246–7) underlines the culturally specific nature of these metallurgical concepts in his discussion of the exchange of precious metals between native Americans and Europeans. He discusses the way in which gold was impregnated with copper amongst a number of peoples in historic Mesoamerica. Due to their luminosity, both metals were related to the power of the sun and each metal was considered to have been embellished by this alloying process. However, alloyed gold caused considerable consternation to Spanish traders, who considered it to be adulterated or impure. This example forces us to reflect on the cultural specificity of technologies and provides an important warning against the simple rationalist description of technological histories. We need to be aware of the likelihood of culturally specific technologies in both historic contexts, such as those discussed above, and prehistoric contexts. Indeed Hamilton (1991) has successfully demonstrated the specificity of differing traditions of copper metallurgy in prehistoric Europe using proton-induced x-ray emission spectroscopy (PIXE).

The social organisation of production

If we take on board the notion that technologies are humanly related through webs of interaction, as mediums by which the social, symbolic and material are interwoven and used as a means of defining or maintaining different social identities, then we need to consider how technologies are produced and reproduced. How are the webs of interaction between the social and material created? Here we need to consider the social relations involved in production. When considering this issue, we again need to be aware of the scale of analysis at which we operate, since it is at the local level of the interaction between people and things in technical production that microscale analysis comes into its own. As Dobres and Hoffman (1994, 213) note, a microscale approach enables us to 'model the dynamic social processes involved in ongoing, day-to-day technological endeavours, and to consider the differential participation of the actors and groups involved'.

In the domain of ceramics studies a number of innovative archaeological studies were undertaken to examine the proposition that the patterns observed in the production of material culture relate to particular sets of social relations (Deetz 1968; Hill 1970; Longacre 1981, 1985). These studies were concerned with examining how the production of ceramics may be related to particular sections of a social group. Specific characteristics of ceramics were mapped both spatially and temporally, enabling a concomitant mapping of social groupings. For instance, Deetz (1968) was concerned to suggest that material culture quantified in such a way enabled particular kinship configurations to be mapped spatially, while the rules of descent associated with such kinship groups could also be determined through the study of the patterning of material culture characteristics through time. This approach was realised in its most detailed form in Hill's study of Broken K Pueblo, Arizona (1970). Here, through the quantification of specific design features on pottery and the observation of the patterning of these design features throughout the settlement, Hill asserted that the communal organisation of pottery production was related to two moieties, with matrilineal descent rules, through the transmission of knowledge from mother to daughter.

More recently, Arnold (1989) has investigated learning networks through ethnoarchaeological fieldwork. Realising that there are problems with modelling descent and residence groups from material culture patterns, he sets out to demonstrate that a kinship model of learning can account for the transmission of ceramic style. While he demonstrates that residence and kinship groups may be one means by which pottery styles may be transmitted, he suggests a dichotomy between the fabrication of pottery – which involves the long-term learning of particular motor habits – and the decoration of pottery, which is derived from cognitive knowledge. This conclusion is useful in indicating that the production of material culture may be transmitted through kin-based learning networks. However, it does not explain why the transmission of knowledge associated with the production of material culture is the same from one generation to another. It is necessary to explain both the maintenance and change of material forms.

There are, of course, problems with these approaches in that they perceive an unproblematic relationship between material culture patterning and social organisation (Allen and Richardson 1971). If we are to employ some of these insights we need to consider two issues. First, how are we to conceive of learning networks; and second, how can we examine them using materials science? Learning involves the social demonstration of bodily techniques related to the working of specific materials (Dobres 1995, 2000). Connerton (1989) argues that because social knowledge is embodied, the production process is one means by which memories are evoked and channelled. Since the physical form of artefacts embodies the techniques of previous generations, the repetitive production of artefacts therefore involves a process of recall that draws on existent artefacts as a template. So, the act of production may involve drawing relations of affinity with objects associated with past kin or lineage members, or it may involve a change or alteration in the production techniques associated with past kin members.

Social relations are also constructed through acts of production. This is an especially important consideration where an artefact is multi-authored, since there may be a tension in what is being expressed by each author (Mackenzie 1991). The production of artefacts is thus a powerful means for expressing specific social relations and, as Munn (1986, 141) notes in relation to the construction of canoes on Gawa, the use of materials considered to be symbolically male and female may be perceived to materially objectify specific social relations. It is the social decision to alter or maintain the techniques of artefact production that lies at the heart of learning networks. It is the operation of this process that is archaeologically visible in patterns of similarity and difference, as noted by Deetz (1968), rather than the simple transmission of styles (Wobst 1977). Rather than viewing artefact patterning as the simple and uncontentious result of residence pattern and descent rules, the production of artefacts may be used to express a number of different possible relationships.

Materials science has an obvious role to play here since the distinction between the composition and construction of artefacts may be refined through materials science analysis. In order to provide adequately detailed data concerning the distinction between artefacts as discussed above, we need to consider both the resolution of our sampling strategies as well the resolution of our characterisation techniques. If we are to answer questions regarding the spatial and temporal differences in the composition of artefacts, and thence social organisation, our sampling strategies must again be conducted at the microscale level in relation to intra-site contexts.

Exchange, consumption and materials science

So far we have considered the way in which social networks shape the alliances made between people and things – in this sense people are made by the technological conditions in which they operate. I will develop this idea by suggesting that we also need to be aware of the modes by which artefacts shape social relations. One of the more important ways in which artefacts shape social relations is through their mobility, and this mobility enables social influences to be extended spatially and temporally (Battaglia 1991; Gell 1998; Strathern 1998). If we are to consider the influence of artefacts in the creation and maintenance of social relations, then we need to consider the processes of exchange and consumption.

I will begin with the issue of exchange. Traditional accounts of exchange within archaeology have tended to operate within macroscale frameworks. According to these macroscale perspectives, formal typologies for exchange were established and attempts were made to link these types to particular distributional patterns of artefacts in the 'archaeological record'. These patterns were then, in turn, used to define ideal social types (Sahlins 1972). For example, a strong correlation was made between the exploitation of certain types of resources, the exchange of these resources and the development of ranked societies (Renfrew and Shennan 1982).

There are considerable problems with the development of typologies related to mechanisms of exchange. The least of these is that it is difficult to distinguish from the evidence of patterns in the archaeological record alone between one mechanism of exchange and another. Another problem is that the creation of types of exchange relies heavily upon Western concepts of utility and economy. An alternative approach would be to note that 'exchange in non-western societies is really a form of diplomacy, and for this reason it cannot be understood in purely "economic" terms' (Bradley and Edmonds 1993, 11–17). Exchange here is concerned with the 'creation', protection and manipulation of social relationships' (*ibid.*, 12). So instead of considering exchange wholly in terms of the transaction of socially neutral commodities, we also need to consider exchange in terms of the transaction of socially valued gifts.

But what do we mean when we talk about consumption? As Gosden (1999, 163) succinctly puts it, consumption is the process of 'using things in social acts'. The notion of consumption captures the point that the way in which we consume need not relate to ideas of rationality and necessity (Douglas and Isherwood 1979), but may be viewed as an active means of creating cultural order and of defining oneself. The process of consumption is therefore bound up with the construction and display of particular kinds of social and cultural identities (Friedman 1994; Miller 1995). In essence, consumption is a creative process that is determined both by the cultural perceptions of the consuming group and by the kinds of identities that consumers wish to construct for themselves.

This perception of consumption was pioneered by the work of Mary Douglas, who examined the way in which meals were used as a form of cultural expression (Douglas 1984). The important components of this expressive activity concerned what was consumed, the mode by which it is consumed and with whom (Douglas 1973). Meals, for instance, may be seen as structured activities that express ideas of cosmology, identity and specific types of social relations (Deetz 1977; Johnson 1994, 1995; Orlove 1994) on a number of planes. Our focus on food suggests a degree of finality, but in fact food is only one substance that may be used as an expressive medium of communication – many other forms of artefacts are also used. For example, in an archaeological context a number of authors have considered the deposition and destruction of stone (Thomas 1996; Tilley 1996), bronze (Barrett and Needham 1988) or iron (Bradley 1990) artefacts as mediums for display and consumption. If we are to distinguish the cultural specificity of acts of consumption, then we need to consider the *type of artefacts* consumed and the *manner* in which they are consumed. When we discuss consumption, then, we are not simply considering the use and discard of objects. Rather the involvement of an artefact in specific consumption practices is a critical element of that artefact's biography; it determines how the artefact is culturally perceived and socially deployed. Artefacts may be consumed in many different ways, and in different contexts, over the course of their lives.

Importantly, when we consider consumption processes, we need to remember that in many pre-industrial societies there is a close relationship between production and consumption (Longacre 1981). The choices made in production are related to the way in which the artefacts are consumed. More importantly, if we are to consider the role of materials science in consumption studies, the way in which objects are categorised structures the way in which they are consumed. So one way of 'getting at' the issue of consumption archaeologically is to look at the differences in the construction and subsequent use of artefacts in different contexts.

When we consider consumption, we are required to consider the physical dimensions of artefact function, but crucially we also need to be aware that, like technology, the notion of 'function' is socially constructed. The relationship between form and function is not determined by universal rules of common sense; it is embedded within culturally specific symbolic structures. There is a whole series of physical criteria by which artefacts may be categorised and consumed, including form, colour, texture, hardness, etc. However, we need not assume that the consumption of artefacts is dependent on universal notions of functionality and performance. As Miller's (1985) study of pottery production in Central India demonstrates, the consumption of pottery is structured by a series of variables such as colour and morphology and their association with structuring principles such as caste, gender and the structured consumption of food. Rather than a simplistic correlation between form and function, material culture may be categorised according to a complex cultural framework that involves the categorisation of material according to a series of differing symbolic dimensions. As Miller (1985, 53) notes, the simple correlation of certain vessel features with function is confounded by the use of the same vessel form for entirely different functions both within and between social groups. Several dimensions of the artefact will be drawn on for distinct cultural events. The categorisation of vessels in use is therefore context specific. This study indicates that we are required not only to consider the mechanical and physical properties of artefacts, but also to tie this consideration to an understanding of context.

If we are to consider issues of consumption from the perspective of materials science, I believe we need to commence with a formal view of functionality. Here the use-life perspective comes into its own; many studies of the functional aspects of artefacts have been undertaken, and we need to think in terms of which dimensions, physical qualities and properties of artefacts will be important. For example, studies of ceramic function have been useful in drawing out the importance of discussing factors such as thermal shock resistance (Schiffer 1988) and the mechanical properties of ceramic wares in terms of distinct functional capabilities (Rye 1980; Schiffer 1988; Skibo 1993). Our attention should also be drawn to fundamental differences in artefact construction, such as volume (Barrett 1980; Woodward 1995; Woodward and Blinkhorn 1997). Aspects of the physical properties of objects, such as colour, may be considered more fully through a clear understanding of the nature of these properties in relation to modes of production (see Andrews 1997). Furthermore, at this scale of analysis it is also useful to consider each artefact as a component of a wider assemblage. Although this is fraught with problems – how are we able to determine if we have a 'complete' assemblage (DeBoer and Lathrap 1979) – we are able to distinguish between the broad differences in the *use* characteristics of different components of artefact assemblages.

In terms of ceramics, simple macroscopic analysis of use-wear may reveal information concerning consumption practices (Skibo 1993). Moreover techniques such as GC/MS are able to provide a reasonable degree of resolution in terms of ceramic use (Dudd *et al.* 1999; Evershed *et al.* 1990; Pollard and Heron 1996). For stone tools, microwear techniques will also provide information concerning usage, while similar microscopic techniques enable us to distinguish wear patterns in the use of metal tools. Importantly many of these techniques enable us to intersect with the domains of expertise associated with other archaeological scientists, especially plant macrofossil specialists and faunal specialists (Meadows 1997). For example, Meadows (1997) uses the spatial distinctions in different kinds of faunal remains and associated artefacts from the Late Iron Age and Early Roman period at Barton Court Farm, Oxfordshire, UK to provide an integrative account of changing consumption practices associated with the process of 'Romanisation'. This study highlights the critical point that, in order to consider the social nature of consumption, it is essential to take account of the spatial and temporal distinctions pertaining to artefact use on a given site. This allows us to understand how consumption practices are culturally performed.

In order to consider consumption practices at an intra-site level, we again need to consider techniques that will provide a fair degree of resolution in terms of the characteristic properties of artefacts. Given that we are able to resolve and describe differences within a site from this perspective, it should be possible to consider how we might relate studies of consumption practices at the local scale with a concern for exchange practices at a wider geographical level. As noted previously, our ability to characterise artefacts in terms of wide-scale exchange practices is fairly well refined. If we wish to consider exchange in terms of the consumption practices that motivate exchange relations, we need to set our consideration of the intra-site characteristics of artefacts alongside a wider scale of analysis. The issues of exchange and consumption neatly illustrate the problems of macroscale and microscale analysis. Rather than creating all-encompassing, rigid typologies of exchange patterns at the macroscale level, Bradley and Edmonds (1993) propose that we examine broad patterns of exchange alongside the microscale contexts of localised consumption practices (see Hodder 1982b). They argue that we need to

be aware that we are not able to understand either wider exchange or localised consumption practices without an awareness of the reciprocal relationship of the other. We are required to oscillate between an awareness of
exhange at the macroscale level and an awarness of specific consumption
practices at the microscale level if we are to understand the nuances and
interrelationships of either practice. For instance, Bradley and Edmonds'
(1993) analysis of stone axe consumption and exchange practices in
Neolithic Britain operates at local, regional and national scales, since the
data provided by their work at the site of production in the Lake District
were complemented by an examination of exchange and consumption
patterns in northern England, which works with the detailed petrological
data compiled in Britain since the beginning of the twentieth century.

In essence, we need to set our detailed understanding of localised consumption against our knowledge of larger-scale exchange patterns and
continue to tack back and forth between the kind of information provided
by local contexts of interaction and that provided by wide-scale exchange
studies. In each case we are required to provide an adequate characterisation of artefacts at each scale of analysis. Studies that consider both local
and wider scales of analysis should operate with comparable techniques
of analysis. However, such studies may favour a multiscale contextual
approach to sampling, one which seeks simultaneously to examine distinct local contexts of difference, in which the sampling of artefacts is
extremely detailed, and distinctions of difference at much larger regional
scales, in which the sampling of artefacts is reasonably coarse.

Fragmentation: the science of deposition

As noted at the beginning of this chapter, our accounts of the life of an
artefact necessarily work backwards from the final stage of the life of the
artefact – its discard. It is a truism that it is at the end of an artefact's life
that the artefact becomes most archaeologically visible. Throughout this
chapter we have examined the relationship between the various stages of
the life of an artefact and the scales used in its analysis from a materials
science perspective. Given the critical importance of deposition to our
understanding and analysis of the life of an artefact, I will commence
by considering how we characterise archaeological deposits. As indicated
in the opening chapter, the characterisation of archaeological deposits is
subject to debate. From a rationalist perspective, deposits consist of the
traces of past physical processes. However an alternative perspective is to
view the deposits as structured, a concept predicated upon the idea of
the archaeological record as the result of intentional action. Structured
deposition was initially correlated with structured activity such as ritual

(Richards and Thomas 1984), in part since many structured deposits appeared to be on sites of a non-functional or ritual nature. However we limit ourselves if we simply equate structure with ritual, and the lack of structure with non-ritual activity. A more developed view may be that no deposits of an anthropogenic nature can be dismissed as simple casual discard, given that all forms of depositional activity are of a cultural nature and therefore are informed by culturally specific systems of logic. We need to move beyond the simple recognition of differential patterning in artefact assemblages (Brown 1991; Cleal 1991; Pollard 1992, 1995) to consider how these deposits may once have been deployed in the construction and expression of social relations.

Critically, Hoffman (1999) notes that differing modes of destruction or discard may be considered to be important ways by which social groups both define themselves and create social relations. He notes examples in contemporary contexts – such as graffiti – and in prehistoric contexts – the breakage of metals – as two differing cultural modes expressing both the definition and the creation of social identities. The recognition of the deliberate breakage of objects prior to deposition has been noted for some time. For example, in the ceramic ethnographies of Africa (Barley 1995; Sterner 1989) and in the deposits within the facade of Danish and Swedish passage graves (Tilley 1984, 1996; Shanks and Tilley 1987) acts of breakage seem to be both periodic and deliberate. Here processes of destruction may be understood according to a number of aspects associated with the biography of an artefact. The artefact, like any animate life form, may be considered to contain 'spirit', and therefore its corporeal form is destroyed at the end of its use-life. Alternatively, the destruction of commodities acquired through exchange may be one means of gaining social prestige which may occur through a number of mechanisms, notably through the staging of feasts or as a votive deposition. Or the destruction and deposition of objects may be linked to the activities with which artefacts are related, for instance mortuary rituals. There are, therefore, a series of socialised activities that may result in the destruction and deposition of material (Bradley 1985, 1990), as opposed to the simple causative principles of wear or accident (Arnold 1991; DeBoer and Lathrap 1979; Nelson 1991; Schiffer 1976). We might consider acts of destruction or deposition within the broader parameters of consumption practices, and these kinds of activities should be considered as achieving similar social ends.

John Chapman (2000b) has recently taken this point further in his investigation of depositional practices in Eastern European prehistory. He considers artefact depositional practices in terms of states of fragmentation, wholeness, juxtaposition and accumulation. He proposes that we might consider the social relations represented by depositional practices in terms of fragmentation and accumulation. He suggests that the fragmentation of objects, the accumulation of sets of objects and the recomposition of fragmented objects are critical to the creation of social relations, since the act of breaking and sharing material culture establishes affiliation between people. Similarly the act of accumulating objects and the act of creating composites out of distinct fragments harnesses the relations established in sharing, through cementing and articulating together shared social bonds, and thereby re-articulates a new set of social relations. Depositional practices may therefore involve very complex acts in which social identities are clearly signalled.

So if we embrace the view that depositional practices are the result of intentional and meaningful activity, how are we to relate this to a materials science perspective? Are we to abandon the view of the archaeological record as physical trace? It is important to realise that while a contextual or structured approach to the archaeological record may allow us to discuss how artefacts were employed to construct and live in past social worlds, a notable failing of such an approach is the tendency to overlook the material qualities of past material culture. We need to develop an approach that views the material properties of artefacts to be critical elements in enabling us understand the taphonomic nature of the site. We also need to be aware that the formation processes involved in the creation of the site were the result of culturally specific depositional practices.

First, if we are to examine the meaningful nature of artefact deposition, we need to consider the mechanical properties of different materials (Cotterall and Kamminga 1990). This enables us to consider the attrition of artefacts at both pre- and post-deposition stages (Schiffer 1976). Microscopic analyses of artefacts enable us to consider the level of wear on artefacts and so allow us to consider the processes involved in the destruction of artefacts prior to deposition. For example, we have to consider questions such as are the edges of artefacts worn, suggesting pre-depositional wear, or are their edges freshly broken, suggesting deliberate destruction prior to deposition? If this information is combined with simple metrical analysis of artefact size (Bradley and Fulford 1980; Schiffer 1976), and knowledge of the likely mechanical breakage patterns of distinct materials, an analysis of this nature will allow us to consider the detailed contextual differences in the nature of depositional practices.

One further process involved in analysing the practices that lead to the creation of on-site deposits is the investigation of artefact refitting patterns (Lindauer 1992). This is obviously easier with certain classes of artefact than others. However, the task of refitting may also be aided by characterisation studies. If we have an adequate characterisation of the distinct composition of an artefact, then the process of refitting may be clarified. For instance, the relationship between fragments of stone tools and pottery may be clarified by petrological or elemental analyses. Again, a combination of approaches that attend to the fine-grained analysis of artefacts alongside a materials science approach should provide fruitful results.

Conclusion

A biographical approach to artefacts allows us to chart the trajectories of an artefact's life from the raw materials of production through to its final deposition. However, it is important to remember that biographies are fluid. What I have presented here is simply a broad narrative structure – we must not forget that as an artefact progresses through its life, it is likely to change its meaning and status. Attention to its material status at various stages of its life, through the application of materials science techniques, will enable us to draw out this fluidity. As we shift away from a view of the object as a static entity and begin to consider how we can chart its changing trajectory as it moves from context to context, we are required to engage with this idea using the imaginative application of materials science techniques. In the following two chapters I will demonstrate how such an approach to materials science and artefact biographies might be applied.

6   A biography of ceramics in Neolithic Orkney

The next two chapters provide an extended case study that illustrates some of the ways in which we might articulate the methodologies of materials science with the concerns of interpretative archaeology. Before commencing with this, I want to reiterate a point that recurs throughout this volume: we are required to consider the interpretative framework within which we operate prior to undertaking our analyses. Dobres articulates this well with regard to technological studies when she argues that 'explicit consideration of the sociopolitical nature of technologies cannot be done *after* the material facts are settled; one cannot simply insert symbolism, questions of value, or the dynamics of social differentiation into a pre-existing materialist pot that, by definition, discounts or downplays them as constitutive elements'. She then goes on to point out, 'These intangible processes clearly play a structural role in shaping and changing technologies...and if we are to understand how they did so in the past, they must be *central* to our conceptual frameworks rather than added after the facts are in' (Dobres 2000, 118, original emphasis).

In this chapter and the next, I will present an analysis in which concerns of a theoretical nature play a central role in determining what and how material is analysed and how this analysis ultimately relates to wider theoretical concerns. My case study focuses on the analysis of a pottery assemblage from the later Neolithic settlement site of Barnhouse, Orkney, Scotland. Before examining the details of the case study, I will situate the analysis within the broader framework of Neolithic studies.

Problems in Neolithic archaeology

Traditionally the onset of the Neolithic is characterised by a number of significant events. These include the change from a shifting hunter-gatherer economy to an economy based on sedentary agriculture and the adoption of a suite of novel forms of material culture, including pottery and polished stone tools and the construction of substantial stone, timber or earth monuments. Although the term 'Neolithic' has undergone considerable alteration and redefinition (Thomas 1993), until recently the role of the economy was considered to be critical to the process of becoming Neolithic (Higgs and Jarman 1972). The use of new forms of material culture was assumed to be allied to this economic change, with pottery and polished stone axes viewed as consequences of the processes of sedentism and deforestation that arose from an economy based on agriculture. Monuments too were assumed to be financed by agricultural surplus (Case 1969; Sherratt 1990).

However, this view of economic primacy has increasingly been criticised. For instance, Thomas (1991, 7–8) argues for the inseparability of issues of economy with the social changes that constitute the Neolithic. He considers the Neolithic to be a historical process bound up with a changing set of relationships that occurred both between people, and between people and their environment (see also Hodder 1990). This point is echoed by Whittle, who notes that the Neolithic in Europe was based 'on a set of beliefs, values and ideals' (1996, 355). He goes on to say that these beliefs concern 'the place of people in the scheme of things, descent, origins and time, and about relations between people' (*ibid.*). We might reverse the equation then and suggest that we view the Neolithic not as a social effect brought on by the adoption of agriculture, but as an effect of changing social relations and beliefs which made the idea of agriculture possible. This proposal has been substantiated by careful examination of the chronological sequence relating to the adoption of agriculture and the construction of monuments.

In many areas of Neolithic Europe the chronological evidence suggests that monuments are found alongside agriculture or that monuments actually precede agriculture (Bradley 1993), so reversing the traditional causal emphasis. Rather than viewing monuments as a by-product of agriculture, we may view them as central to the process of becoming Neolithic. If we are to consider the Neolithic as a process that engendered an alteration of beliefs and social relations then monument construction appears to be a critical element in this process. Monuments evoke an altered conception of both time and place; they embody an alteration of the natural world, and their construction involves the creation of a new kind of place in the landscape which, by their very nature, they endure. This perception of the world may be allied to the perceptions required of the agricultural regime, but there is no necessary relationship. The relationship between food production and monumentality is therefore complex.

Curiously, although the adoption of novel artefacts at one stage defined the Neolithic, recent assessments of the period have emphasised either agriculture or monumentality. As I have argued above, both of these aspects of the Neolithic are critical to our understanding of the period. However, we have seen less emphasis placed on the significance of material culture in the process of becoming Neolithic. I would argue that a reconsideration of the role of material culture is essential if we consider this process to be bound up with the reconfiguration of the relationship between people and the world they occupy. As we have seen in the previous chapter, material culture is central to the construction and maintenance of social relations. An examination of the manner in which material culture is employed during the Neolithic should enable us to understand in more detail how relations between people and their world are configured during this period.

Importantly, while monuments altered the experience of time and place, the creation of monuments will also have drawn on the culturally categorised landscape. Plants, animals, and other elements of the landscape will be meaningful components of the culturally classified landscape prior to monument construction (Jones 1998, forthcoming a). If we are to understand the Neolithic as a series of changing relationships between people and the natural world, then we are required to take into account not only the temporal and spatial experience invested by monuments. We also need to consider the temporal and spatial experience associated with plants and animals and with the production, use and deposition of artefacts. The aim, then, is to examine one aspect of the Neolithic, in this case pottery, as a means of illuminating the complex relationships that existed between material culture and agriculture and monuments. Each of these elements forms the conditions through which the Neolithic was constructed and lived. What interests us here is how each element was deployed in the process of constructing and living in the Neolithic.

Pots and people

The typological classification of pottery remains the primary tool for archaeologists seeking to understand the chronology of a given site. Pots have consistently been employed by archaeologists as a fine-grained indicator of the presence of specific cultural groups. Archaeologically, pots appear to equal people. However this relationship requires further examination. We need to carefully assess what relationship exists between pottery and people, and ask why pottery is assumed to be such a precise indicator of cultural groups. While an interpretative analysis of a pottery assemblage comprises the core of this case study, the study has involved the use of a series of scientific analytical techniques in order to characterise the nature of the pottery assemblage. The specific techniques of thin-section petrology and Gas Chromatography coupled with Mass

Spectrometry have been drawn on in order to examine and define the relationship between pottery, social practices and social identity.

Typologically, pots have been traditionally studied as objects divorced from their cultural context. This is a general problem of artefact analysis. Pots are used for the storage, preparation, cooking and consumption of food, amongst other things, and it is essential to view pots not simply as passive decontextualised sherds, but as actively produced and used according to the culturally specific motivations of people. In order to do this it is essential to study not just individual aspects of pots such as their function (Braun 1983); production (Wardle 1992); use (Evershed *et al.* 1995) or deposition (Richards and Thomas 1984), but beyond this to realise that all of the above aspects are important. Pots are at all times linked with each field of activity, since pots are made by people who are embedded within a particular social structure and cultural framework. Just as the processes of production, use and deposition of pots are linked, so the functional (Rice 1996) and symbolic (Hodder 1982c; Tilley 1984) or metaphorical (Gosselain 1999) aspects of pottery cannot be separated (see Boast 1998).

Given the assumed status of pots in relation *to* people and in order to fully understand how this relationship is brought about, it is essential to examine the way in which pots are produced, used and deposited *by* people. Here it is important to expand the way in which we might consider these practices. Rather than examining these activities as ciphers for static social identities, I prefer to consider identities to be created through practice, a process in which the performance of social practices in distinctive ways is productive of different kinds of subjects or people (see Butler 1990; Strathern 1988). This perspective allows us to move away from an equation that simply relates specific forms of material culture with specific kinds of identity, and towards an examination of the way in which identities are instantiated by the contextual relationship of artefacts associated with different practices (see Jones 1997, 106–44). An excellent example of this approach to material culture is Mackenzie's (1991) analysis of the gendered identities associated with the production of woven bags in Papua New Guinea. Here bags are made by women and embellished by men, so the bags are 'androgynous' – they are associated with both men and women. Yet as objects they serve to materialise the complex construction of gender relations in this area.

The aim then is to examine how social relationships are expressed through the practices associated with the production, use and deposition of Later Neolithic Grooved ware pottery, and how social identities are formed out of these relationships. This approach allows us to conceptualise how identities might shift over time as artefacts are transferred from one context to another and enter into fresh contextual relationships with other artefacts. It is the dynamic associated with the creation of fresh or novel contextual relationships over time that allows us to see how – through contextual juxtaposition – artefacts are used to express a range of different kinds of social identities (for example see Thomas 1996, 141–83).

Introducing Grooved ware

Grooved ware is a class of Later Neolithic pottery whose distribution spreads from the Orkney Isles in the north of Scotland to southern England. Many Grooved ware assemblages derive from 'ritual' sites such as henges or structured deposits within pit clusters found throughout mainland Britain. The defining characteristic of Grooved ware is its unusual decoration, which lends the pottery its name. It has long been noted that these decorative motifs are analogous to many other forms of later Neolithic material culture (see Fig. 6.1) especially passage grave art (Bradley 1984, 1989; Bradley and Chapman 1986; Cleal 1991; Piggott 1954; Shee Twohig 1981; Wainwright and Longworth 1971), the art found on objects such as the Folkton drums (Kinnes and Longworth 1985), the Garboldisham macehead (Edwardson 1965) and the carved stone balls of northern Scotland (Edmonds 1992; Marshall 1977).

Due to its unusual decoration and its association with apparently non-domestic contexts, Grooved ware has been characterised as an 'exotic' (Bradley 1984; Cleal 1991) or 'ritual' (Richards and Thomas 1984) ceramic. Meanwhile, other aspects of Grooved ware, such as its function, have largely been ignored (see Cleal 1992 for a general discussion of studies of function in relation to British Neolithic ceramics). This state of affairs is due, in part, to the fact that many studies of this class of pottery have emphasised its distribution in the southern half of Britain, where it is more usually found on 'ritual' sites. This is somewhat paradoxical since the earliest radiocarbon dates are derived from the Orkney Isles (see Bradley 1984). While Grooved ware in the rest of Britain and Ireland is typically associated with non-domestic and non-mortuary contexts, in Orkney the pottery is primarily found in settlements, as well as in sites that might be considered to be more overtly related to 'ritual' activities, such as passage graves and henges.

Grooved ware and Neolithic Orkney

The Orkney Isles are situated ten miles north of the Scottish mainland (Fig. 6.2). The archipelago comprises around seventy islands of variable size. The isles are situated at latitude 59° north, in the North Atlantic

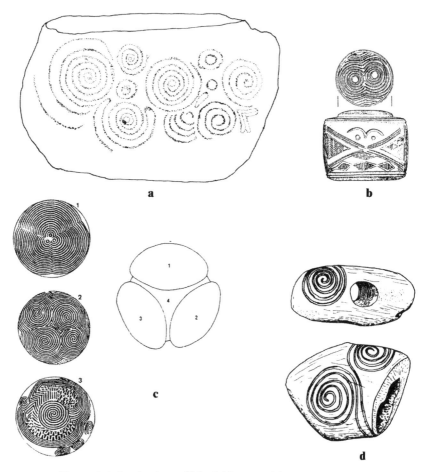

Figure 6.1 A selection of Neolithic material culture exhibiting similar curvilinear motifs

Ocean, and this northerly location provides them with contrasting light conditions over much of the year. In the summer months, the hours of daylight are numerous, with only around two to four hours of darkness; in the winter months this is reversed and the hours of darkness are numerous, and only two to four hours of daylight are experienced. This situation is important for understanding a variety of aspects of Later Neolithic life (Richards 1990a).

The topography of the islands provides a contrast between the land and the sky, while the treeless nature of the landscape means that the sky is also an ever-present feature of the Orcadian horizon. All these aspects

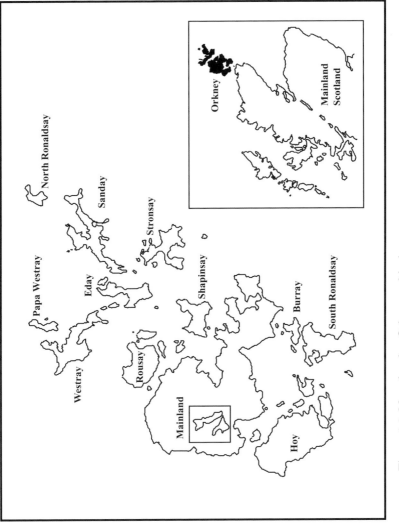

Figure 6.2 Map showing Orkney archipelago

go to make up a picture of a fertile but dramatic landscape, unchanged in terms of vegetation since the Later Neolithic, and dominated by coastal stacks of rock and lowland lochs. Geologically the islands are comprised almost entirely of Middle and Upper Old Red Sandstone. The sandstone bedrock laminates into easily worked slabs that comprise much of the building stone used during the Neolithic. Probably the most important geological features of the islands, in relation to this study, are the intrusive igneous dykes that outcrop intermittently around the inland and coastal shores of the islands (Mykura 1976).

The Later Neolithic period in Orkney is characterised by a series of stone-built architectural forms, including settlements, passage graves and henges. Interestingly each of these is constructed with a similar emphasis on circular space. Richards (1990a) has noted that the circular form of the Later Neolithic house is organised according to a cruciform axis. The house is focused around a central hearth, with a 'dresser' or set of shelves towards the rear of the house, and 'box-beds' or stone boxes situated either side of the hearth, with the entrance itself completing the cross-shaped arrangement of space (Fig. 6.3). For Richards, the consistency of this arrangement is related to specific cosmological principles

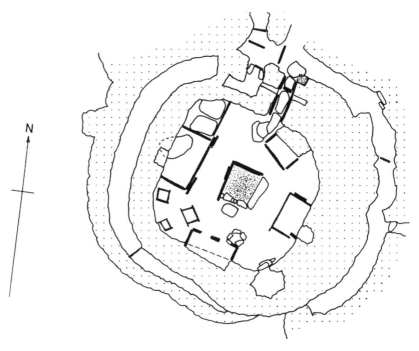

Figure 6.3 The spatial layout of the Later Neolithic house in Orkney

of classification. Not only are hearths arranged in order to face specific cardinal points, related to events of calendrical significance, especially the midwinter and midsummer sunrise and sunset, but most of the houses at Barnhouse, Skara Brae and Rinyo lie on a northwest/southeast axis. This arrangement of space, as well as having an underlying symbolic logic related to ideas of concentricity and circularity, applies not only to the house, but also extends to other monumental constructions such as henges and passage graves (Hodder 1982d; Richards 1993a), as well as the landscape itself (Richards 1996).

It is notable, then, that a number of homologies exist between the construction of houses and other monument forms (Fig. 6.4). Passage graves are constructed with a central chamber with a series of side cells exiting this space, and an extensive passage exiting the central chamber enabling access to the exterior of the monument. Henges, such as the examples at the Ring of Brodgar and the Stones of Stenness, are defined by a circular bank and ditch which surround a circle of monoliths. In the case of the Stones of Stenness, the relationship between house and henge is emphasised by the construction of a large hearth in the centre of the monument (Richards 1993a). Each of these architectural constructions is related through similar principles of order. Moreover, each form of architecture provides the context for the use and deposition of Grooved ware pottery. If we are to understand how the biography of Grooved ware unfolds in Later Neolithic Orkney, we are required to begin with an examination of both the house and the settlement.

Orkney constitutes one of the few areas of Europe with substantial up-standing evidence for Neolithic habitation. Although houses are stone-built, the occupation sequences on many Orcadian Neolithic settlement sites provides evidence of continuous episodes of building and rebuilding. Neolithic settlements in Orkney often have a tell-like form with long sequences of occupation throughout the Neolithic. Due to this occupational history, and due to the practice of depositing midden material in close proximity to the house and within the wall core of the house, archaeologists have been able to establish pottery sequences for much of the Orkney Neolithic. The primary sequence was established by Gordon Childe (1931, 130–2) after his excavation of the celebrated site of Skara Brae:

Class A Relief/applied decoration; A1 simple applied cordons; A2 cordons applied with slip. A1 was found in all phases, A2 was found only in phase 2.
Class B Relief decoration augmented with incisions on grooves. Does not occur beyond phase 2.
Class C Grooved decoration incised into slipped surface. Found in phases 1 and 2.

This broad scheme, based on differences in the technique of decoration, with incised or grooved decoration at the beginning of the sequence

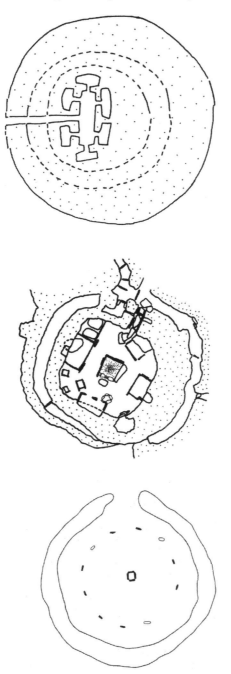

Figure 6.4 The spatial homology between passage grave, house and henge

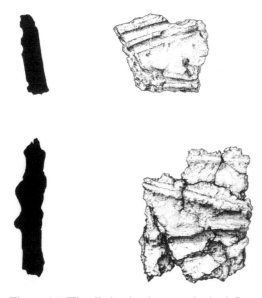

Figure 6.5 The distinction between incised Grooved ware and applied Grooved ware

followed by applied cordons (Fig. 6.5), accords with more refined sequences for Orkney Grooved ware (Hunter and MacSween 1991). Later Neolithic settlements therefore provide well-stratified pottery sequences, enabling us to examine the changing nature of social practices over time. Moreover, the high density of well-preserved settlements across Orkney also enables us to examine the nature of interactions between contemporary settlements within the islands.

The principal aim in this study was to examine the nature of the biography of Grooved ware as it was constructed through social practices in different kinds of context, such as the settlement, henge and passage grave. A further aim was to examine the way in which – at a regional scale – such biographies were related to the construction of settlement histories. In order to achieve these aims, a detailed study was made of a large Grooved ware assemblage from the settlement site of Barnhouse.

Introducing Barnhouse

The Barnhouse settlement itself is situated on a promontory in the centre of Mainland Orkney (Richards forthcoming). This area is topographically low lying, and forms the centre of a natural bowl bounded by two lochs and surrounding hills. It is located in the centre of a remarkable concentration of Neolithic monuments (Fig. 6.6). Within sight of the settlement

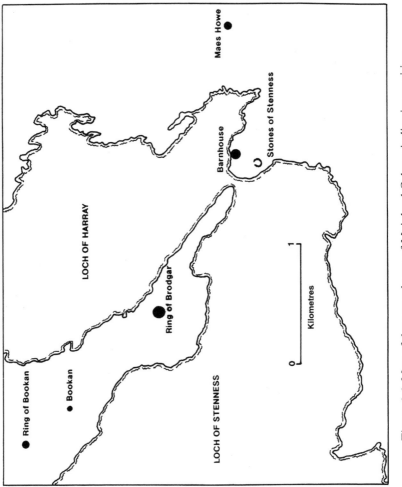

Figure 6.6 Map of the central area of Mainland Orkney indicating position of principal monuments

to the east is the passage grave of Maes Howe, and the Stones of Stenness henge is located some 150 m away. Also visible from Barnhouse is the earlier Neolithic chambered tomb at Unstan. Nearby lies the immense henge and stone circle, the Ring of Brodgar, and some distance north of this is the Ring of Bookan, a probable passage grave, as well as the chambered tomb of Bookan. On the farm of Bookan, to the northeast of Brodgar, there is also a possible Later Neolithic settlement represented by a rich artefact scatter (Callander 1931).

Since the construction of houses in Orcadian Neolithic settlement sites is fluid, it is difficult to divide the site into phases, although various constructional episodes can be isolated. The initial stage of construction involved laying a complex system of drains. Despite the apparently mundane nature of this activity, it would seem that this initiated and solidified the spatial structure of the settlement. Two discrete systems of drains are arranged in two concentric arcs. The inner arc of drains connects house 6 as well as later houses 1, 11 and 12 in the centre of the settlement. The second arc of drains connects houses 2, 3, 5 and 9.

The spatial arrangement of the settlement therefore consisted of two concentric arcs of houses surrounding a central space. This central area is important for our considerations of the spatial organisation of pottery production. In the earliest phase of settlement around seven houses were built, including houses 2, 3, 5, 6, 7, 9 and 10, followed by houses 11 and 12 (Fig. 6.7). Most houses appear to have been, at some time, demolished and then built over, in approximately the same position and orientation. This is particularly clear in the case of structures such as house 5, rebuilt over four times. What is most notable is that both houses 2 and 3 appear to continue in use through much of the life of the settlement, and the architecture of these houses conforms with excavated examples from the earliest levels of Rinyo and Skara Brae (Childe 1931; Childe and Grant 1939).

Not all houses at Barnhouse are constructed in precisely the same way. The architecture of house 2 draws on an arrangement of space similar to other Later Neolithic houses; however, the house also has a double cruciform arrangement with a total of six recesses, an architectural form that recalls the plan of the passage grave at Quanterness (Renfrew 1979). House 2 stands out from the rest of the settlement and, as we shall see, the activities conducted within it mark it out as unusual.

The final use of the Barnhouse settlement is marked by the construction of a monumental building, structure 8. This building was constructed south of the main area of settlement and consisted of an external clay platform on which a large square building was constructed (see Figs. 6.7 and 6.19). The platform contained a series of hearths and was surrounded

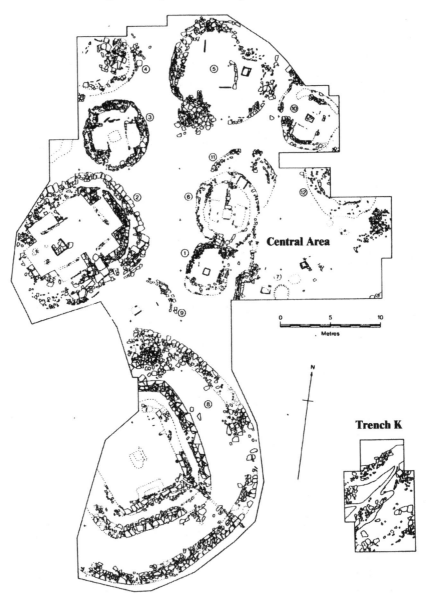

Figure 6.7 Plan of the Later Neolithic settlement at Barnhouse

by a stone wall, and the central building was entered through an elaborate porch. This building draws on the spatial arrangement of other Later Neolithic houses, having a large central hearth and dresser, while also having similarities to the architecture of the passage grave (with an external platform) and henge (a large central hearth and porch-like entrance).

The occupation of the site spans a four-hundred-year period as estimated by calibrated radiocarbon dates. The earliest calibrated dates for the settlement are 3600–3110 BC and 3500–3100 BC, while the latest dates are 3270–2920 BC and 3090–2910 BC.

With this detailed chronology it is possible to examine the changing production and use of Grooved ware in relation to different houses and at different stages during the life of the settlement. While the first two phases of building associated with the settlement are fairly fluid, the construction of structure 8 marks the final phase of occupation, and it is possible to contrast the Grooved ware associated with this later building with that from the earlier houses. Like other Later Neolithic settlements, the earlier phases of building are predominantly associated with Grooved ware decorated by incision, while the later phases of occupation are generally associated with Grooved ware decorated by cordon.

Analysing the Barnhouse Grooved ware

As noted earlier, my interest in the Barnhouse Grooved ware assemblage relates to the way in which social identities were instantiated during episodes of procurement, production, use and deposition. I was also interested in the way in which these activities helped to shape certain social identities both within the settlement and beyond. Here I will describe how the interpretative approaches taken to the examination of this pottery assemblage were allied with specific methodological objectives.

My initial examination of the Barnhouse Grooved ware assemblage was concerned with the macroscopic characterisation of the pottery. As indicated in chapter 3, traditional accounts of pottery from many British prehistoric sites commence with an attempt to characterise pottery assemblages with the ultimate aim of relating the pottery with other similar assemblages. This practice is, of course, an artefact of earlier culture-historical approaches allied to an interest in the use of artefacts as a dating mechanism. I found this pursuit to be largely fruitless with regard to my investigation of pottery and social identity, since the ultimate product of such an activity is a static catalogue of annotated sherds. A number of 'diagnostic attributes' of pottery are traditionally recruited for this task, the most obvious being decorative motifs, decorative technique, and rim and base morphology. However, my interests related to the active construction and use of pottery. While decoration and rim and base morphology are crucial elements of pottery characterisations, I was equally concerned to consider the fabric of the assemblage since this allowed me to consider differences in the choices made in production technologies (see Cleal 1996; Sillar and Tite 2000). Rather than placing emphasis on the traditional diagnostic attributes of pottery, I wished to examine the individual components of the pottery assemblage in terms of a range of variables, which emphasised not only their morphological differences but also their functional differences (Braun 1983; Cleal 1992).

I was interested in considering each component as part of a functioning pottery assemblage. As both Miller (1985) and Boast (1990, 181–2) have indicated, categories of pottery are created through the manipulation of various 'dimensions of variability'. Such 'dimensions of variability' may include fabric, wall thickness, decorative motifs, decorative scheme, etc. It is the variation in these 'dimensions of variability' which distinguish one category of vessel from another. The aim, then, was to distinguish the various dimensions along which Grooved ware vessels varied, and thereby characterise the differences that constitute the various categories of Grooved ware at Barnhouse.

In order to consider the dimensions along which these individual components varied, I needed to examine a range of attributes. While these included morphological variables, I was also concerned to examine distinctions in other attributes related more closely to the performance characteristics of pottery (Schiffer and Skibo 1987), including volume (Woodward 1996), fabric (Cleal 1996), use-wear (Skibo 1993), sooting (Hally 1983) and organic residues (Evershed et al. 1992). This perspective, which has seen less emphasis in the context of British ceramic studies, led me to examine the internal differences in the pottery assemblage.

Having examined the different categories in the assemblage, my analysis was directed towards the construction and use of these different categories of pottery in relation to the different contexts within the settlement. Here my theoretical influence was twofold. First, I was struck by ideas promoted by the early generation of processualists concerning the construction of kinship networks from material culture patterns. While I found these ideas appealing, they carried with them the problems associated with treating the archaeological record as a direct and unmediated record of past events (see Patrik 1985 and Barrett 1994, 2000 for critical discussions). While influenced by these approaches to artefact patterning, I preferred the approach adopted by Dobres (1995, 2000) and Jones (1997) concerning the relationship between the practical organisation of production and the more subtle expression of social differences. I also took on board the relationships established by Arnold (1989) between learning networks, motor habit and identity. Adoption of these perspectives led to the petrological examination of a representative sample of pottery from each house at Barnhouse. Rather than concerning myself with problems of supralocality (*contra* Sheridan 1991), I was more concerned with the internal constitution of the assemblage and with the relationship between differences in the assemblage and different procurement strategies (see Howard 1981). I therefore applied a microscale approach that took account both of differences in the assemblage and of differences in context in the sampling procedure.

This microscale approach to sampling enabled me to define differences in the primary tempering strategies from different contexts in the site. These differences led me to consider the relationship between the use of these resources and the significance of the locality of these resources in the lived landscape. Here the framework developed by Arnold (1985) relating to the influence of resource availability on procurement strategies was critical. However, discussions concerning the significance of the cultural categorisation of the landscape (Tilley 1994) and the relationship between place and identity (Casey 1987; Gow 1995) influenced my approach to the magnetometer survey of the area surrounding the Barnhouse settlement and my subsequent survey of the environs of Quanterness passage grave.

Having examined the distinctions between place, production and identity, I was concerned to examine the distinctions between the use of different categories of the assemblage in relation to context. Here at a primary level I was interested in the kinds of arguments concerning food and consumption developed within anthropology (Douglas 1966, 1973; Lévi-Strauss 1970). However, after Friedman (1994) and Miller (1995), I was also interested in the role that consumption practices play in the construction of identities (see Orlove 1994 for a good example). It was this influence that led to the selection of specific categories of pottery (related to the overall demography of pots in each house) from specific contexts for Gas Chromatography/Mass Spectrometry (GC/MS) analysis. For this reason more samples were taken from the more frequent medium-size vessels than from the small or large vessels. Analysis here was meant to be representative of the excavated assemblage from each house. This analysis cohered with the known information derived from faunal and botanical studies from Barnhouse and other sites in Orkney. This allowed me to construct GC/MS standards for different species against which to match the Grooved ware data, but moreover it allowed me to articulate the analysis of food and Grooved ware with a contextual study of animal and plant deposition (Jones 1998, 1999).

The combined data derived from each of these forms of analysis enabled me to construct biographical trajectories for distinct categories of pots from their place of production, through use, and to relate both of these factors to their place and manner of deposition. My concern with the examination of the biographical process of artefacts was primarily related to recent discussions in anthropology (Battaglia 1991; Thomas 1991; Weiner 1990) and archaeology (Dobres 1995; Edmonds 1995; Thomas 1996; Tilley 1996). My interest in biography led to a more detailed microscale approach to petrological sampling, and it was the specificity of tempering strategies defined by petrological analysis that allowed me to work back from pots deposited within settlement middens, henge ditches and passage graves to define their place of origin.

The Barnhouse Grooved ware

The Barnhouse Grooved ware mainly varied in size and capacity. Morphologically, the same broad 'bucket' shape was employed at different scales. While a continuum in size was observed, three broad clusters of pottery size could be discerned: large, medium and small. These vessel sizes were defined by distinctions in three main 'dimensions of variability', including fabric, wall thickness and decoration. In characterising vessels of different categories, I will consider the process of production as a *chaîne opératoire* or a series of interconnected technical choices (see Sillar and Tite 2000), analogous in many ways to the hierarchical design decisions discussed by Friedrich (1970) and Plog (1980). The point here is that each category is made up of a series of technical decisions related together in a hierarchical or ordered sequence.

The primary factor that distinguishes vessels of different size categories is the manner in which pots were tempered. Fabrics can be broadly grouped into the following categories:

> **Fabric A** Rock-tempered with a frequency of inclusions between 10–30 per cent.
> **Fabric B** Rock-tempered with a frequency of inclusions of 50 per cent or more.
> **Fabric B1** Rock-tempered with a frequency of inclusions of 50 per cent or more, also tempered with approximately 10 per cent shell (observed as voids).
> **Fabric C** Shell-tempered with a frequency of inclusions of 10–30 per cent (these are observed as voids since the shell has decayed in acidic soil conditions).
> **Fabric D** Untempered, only non-plastics include naturally rounded quartz inclusions.
> **Fabric E** Untempered.

Primary variation therefore depends on the type of temper used: shell, rock or no temper. There is also further variation depending on the frequency of the tempering agent. Vessels tempered with rock vary according to the frequency of temper: for fabric A, 10–30 per cent; for fabric B and B1, 50 per cent. Although fabrics D and E remain untempered, the presence or absence of natural non-plastics within the clay also distinguishes them. Shell-tempered vessels are again distinguished by this variable: fabric C vessels are distinguished by the high frequency of shell inclusions; and fabric B1 is tempered with a lower frequency of shell along with a high frequency of rock.

The reasons for this variation were initially difficult to understand; however, if we compare temper frequency in terms of fabric, against wall thickness, then we see that variation in temper depends on the size of vessel constructed (Fig. 6.8). Fabrics A and B include vessels tempered with rock inclusions; vessels of fabric A are 10–15 mm in wall thickness;

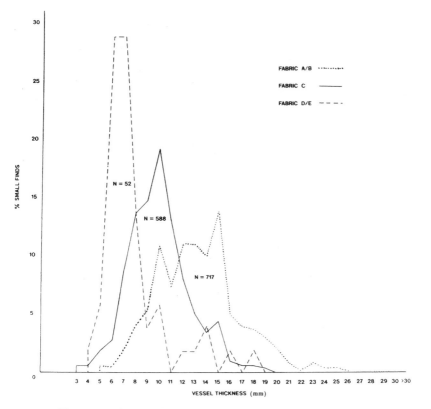

Figure 6.8 Graph of fabric plotted against wall thickness

while vessels of fabric B are typically over 20 mm in wall thickness. Shell-tempered vessels of fabric C are 7–15 mm in wall thickness, while those of fabric B1 are typically at the extreme end of the scale being over 25 mm in wall thickness. Fabrics D and E are essentially part of a continuum ranging from 5–9 mm thickness, with Fabric D occupying the upper end of the scale, fabric E the lower. At the outset then vessels are distinguished by fabric and wall width. These variables are related to the three distinct sizes of Grooved ware vessel from Barnhouse. Since Grooved ware vessels are similar in shape, these variables also provide an index of vessel volume:

1 **Large vessels** (Fabric A, B and B1): Vessels with a wall thickness of 16–30 mm and a volume of 10,000–35,000 cc.
2 **Medium vessels** (Fabric A and C): Vessels with a wall thickness of 9–15 mm and a volume of 2,000–8,000 cc.
3 **Small vessels** (Fabric C, D and E): Vessels with a wall thickness of 5 to 9 mm and a volume of 2,000–3,000 cc.

The next major variable is decoration. We observe differences in the nature of vessels of each size with a *hierarchy* of decoration; large vessels are simply decorated with a single incision or cordon; medium-size vessels are decorated with three curvilinear incisions or with a cordon that is altered in a serpentine pattern; and the small vessels are decorated with curvilinear incisions or serpentine cordons. However, with the small vessels we also witness the addition of passage grave art motifs such as rings of dots or rosettes. While we can observe differences in decorative technique and the use of simple decorative elements or motifs, we also note differences in decorative *scheme* on vessels of different sizes. It would also seem that certain decorative schemes are restricted to different categories of vessel (see Figs. 6.9, 6.10, 6.11 and 6.12).

In the later phases of settlement, associated with structure 8, we see a simpler decorative scheme employed. Large vessels are decorated by simple cordon. Medium-size vessels are decorated with a scheme that involves the repetition of incisions. The incisions are used either deeply or lightly on the surface of the vessel and cover the whole surface to give an all-over incised appearance (see Fig. 6.20).

Production and procurement at Barnhouse

Having characterised the nature of the pottery assemblage at Barnhouse, I will consider the nature of production strategies in relation to issues

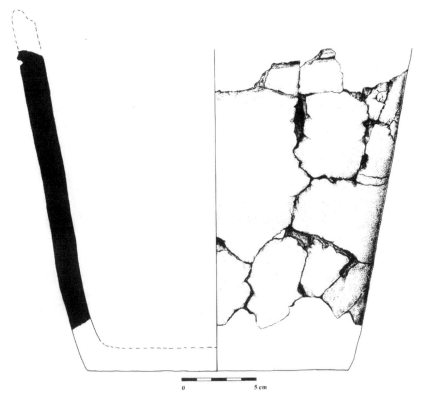

Figure 6.9 Large Grooved ware vessel from Barnhouse

of social identity. The primary step in this analysis involved examining the contextual differences in pottery. First, I examined the 'demography' of vessels in each of the houses at Barnhouse. This indicated regularity in the frequencies of vessels of each category (see Foster 1960). The 'population' of vessels for each house consisted of a single large vessel, around fifteen medium-size vessels, and one or two small vessels. What is more, the decoration on vessels from all houses in the earliest phase of settlement was identical. Each house was using vessels that were decorated using the curvilinear or serpentine decorative scheme for medium vessels and the complex decorative scheme with the addition of dot motifs for small vessels. This immediately provoked questions concerning the relationship between production and social identity. Was pottery produced at the level of the household or was the mode of production more communal in nature?

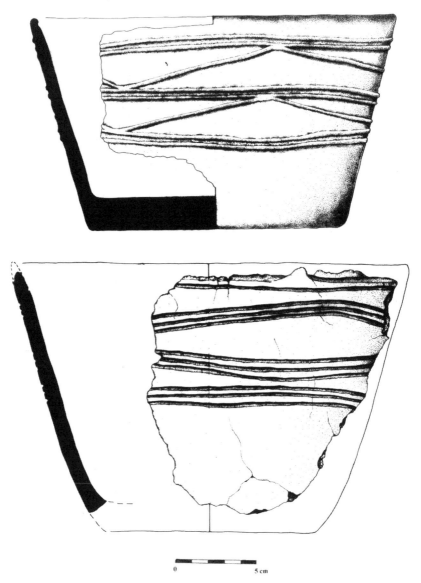

Figure 6.10 Two medium-size vessels from Barnhouse with character-istic decorative schemes

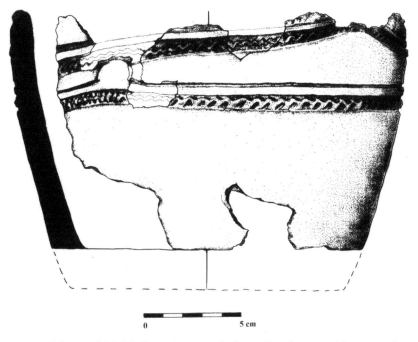

Figure 6.11 Medium-size vessel from Barnhouse with serpentine applied cordons

I began investigating the problem of production by examining the deposits in the central activity area (Fig 6.13). The definition of pottery production sites in British prehistory is notoriously difficult. In order to define a pottery production site, Wardle (1992) lists a series of attributes such as the presence of wasters, artefacts used in production, raw materials, structural evidence for the curing/mining of clay and the presence of distinctive manufacturing assemblages. According to these criteria, the central area at Barnhouse bore all the hallmarks of a pottery production site. The deposits in this area were focused around a large stone slab with a high magnetic susceptibility reading. In close proximity to this stone was a clay-filled pit. Around the stone there were spreads of ash and burnt bone, pieces of pumice, polished pebbles and large numbers of pottery sherds. These sherds consisted of wasters, broken during firing, and abraded sherds. Radiocarbon dates from this area indicated the area was used throughout the occupation of the earlier houses. However an examination of the fabric of the sherds from this area found that 89 per cent were shell-tempered (fabric C). If this was a production site, then activity at this site did not account for the production of all vessels.

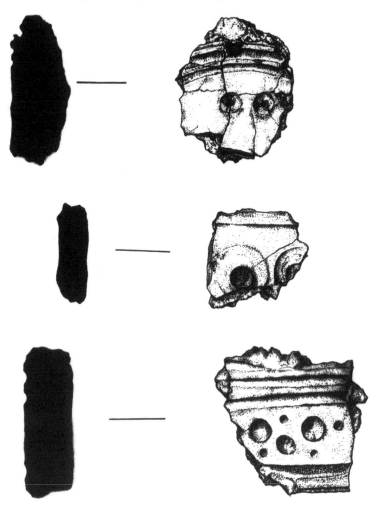

Figure 6.12 Sherds from small vessels from Barnhouse with passage grave art motifs

Analysis of over 180 petrological thin-sections of Grooved ware vessels from individual houses at Barnhouse showed that the stone and shell used to temper pottery was employed in a number of specific ways. Those houses situated at the centre of the settlement, houses 1, 6, 11 and 12, only contained pottery tempered with *shell*. This was in stark contrast to the houses at the periphery of the settlement, houses 2, 3, 5 and 9, that employed *rock* temper (see Fig. 6.14). So, pots of *different fabric* were

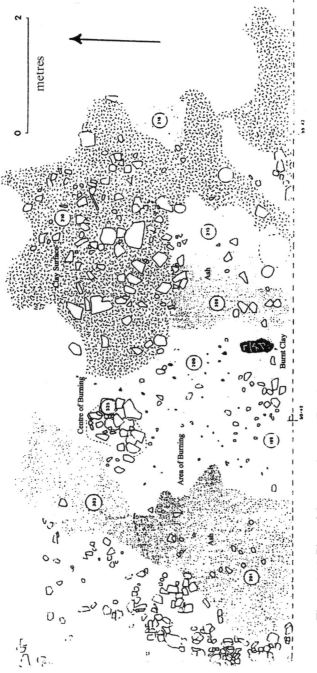

Figure 6.13 Plan of the central area at Barnhouse

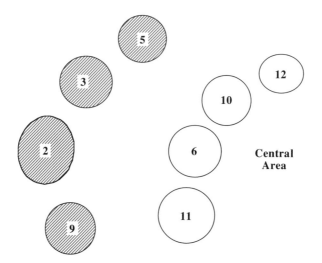

Figure 6.14 Schematic diagram indicating the distinction in the use of temper between inner houses and peripheral houses at Barnhouse

related to *different houses*. At a more detailed level, petrological examination of the pottery from the peripheral houses – those using rock temper – indicated that each house was employing its own specific temper 'recipe' of sandstone and rocks from igneous dykes (Table 6.1). This suggests that in these houses pottery production was a household-based activity.

Having observed the use of distinct tempering strategies or temper 'recipes' in the houses at the periphery of the settlement, it remained to examine the provenance of these rock sources. A provenancing project was undertaken in the environs of Barnhouse. The rocks used in the

Table 6.1 *Presence/absence of tempering agents in different houses at Barnhouse*

	House 2	House 3	House 5	Structure 8
Sandstone	Yes	Yes	Yes	Yes
Siltstone	Yes	Yes	No	Yes
Mudstone	Yes	Yes	No	No
Dyke rock source 1	No	No	Yes	Yes
Dyke rock source 2	Yes	Yes	Yes	Yes
Dyke rock source 3	Yes	Yes	Yes	Yes
Dyke rock source 4	No	Yes	No	Yes
Dyke rock source 5	No	Yes	No	No
Dyke rock source 6	No	No	No	Yes

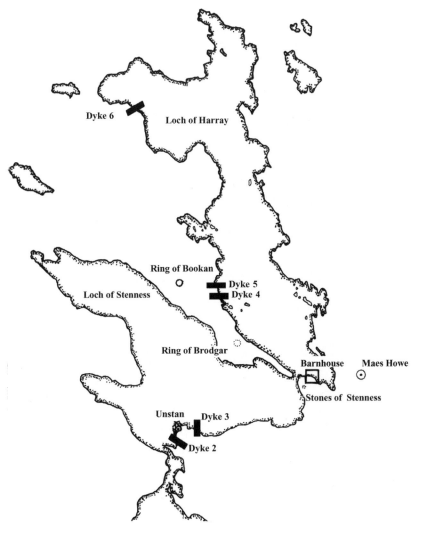

Figure 6.15 The location of dyke rock sources in the Barnhouse environs

Barnhouse pottery were predominately from localised igneous dykes that outcropped at discrete points on the loch (or lake) edge. The provenance project indicated that the sources of the rocks used in each household were located less than 1 km by foot or boat from the settlement (Arnold 1985, 45–6); a more detailed analysis of their source location indicated that they were derived from a number of significant places (Fig. 6.15).

Two sources were located in proximity to the earlier Neolithic chambered tomb at Unstan, while another was located in proximity with the Later Neolithic artefact scatter at Bookan (Calder 1931), which is likely to represent another contemporary settlement site. In one instance, then, stone was related to a place of the dead, likely to be associated with the identity of a specific ancestral group; in the other instance, stone was linked with the identities of the members of another settlement. In both of these cases, people are implicated in the land through rights of access to, or ownership of, resources.

Crucially, it was not simply individual rock sources that were employed in tempering vessels. Rather, rock sources from different locations in the landscape were *combined together* in specific 'recipes' in the production of vessels within individual houses (see Table 6.1). This suggests that the act of combination itself was constitutive of the expression of social identity and provided a metaphor for the creation of links between different households and communities. This is most obvious when we examine the Grooved ware from structure 8, which represents the latest phase of occupation at Barnhouse. The pottery associated with this house contained all those rock sources that had previously been employed in each of the earlier houses (Table 6.1). The production of Grooved ware in relation to this later house would appear to represent the notion of communal production and sharing in a very concrete manner.

As noted above, each house in the settlement utilised a similar suite of vessels, and although shell-tempered pottery was a component of the houses at the settlement's periphery, no rock-tempered vessels were found in the houses at the centre of the settlement. Despite the distinction between the organisation of production related to shell-tempered and rock-tempered vessels, and the distinctions related to different households, each house decorated their pottery in *precisely the same way*. Importantly, the common decorative scheme used on small (Fig. 6.12) and medium-size (Fig. 6.11) Grooved ware vessels suggests the expression of communal identity. This practice is not unique to Barnhouse; in fact, during the *earliest phases* of the Later Neolithic it would appear that each settlement in Orkney was decorating pottery according to a settlement-specific scheme. Although the primary production of pottery involved the complex articulation of identities through the medium of tempering strategies, it is important to note that through the subsequent process of slipping, burnishing and decorating vessels the social relations involved in primary production become hidden. The memory of these relations is embedded in the fabric of the pot.

Social relations are therefore inscribed on the surface of the vessel. Pottery decoration involves an active process in which similarity and difference are articulated through the medium of particular decorative schemes. Through materials and techniques the technology of pottery production at Barnhouse involves the complex articulation of notions of identity. The production process is twofold, and two distinct 'layers' of memory are bound up in primary and secondary production. The memory associated with primary production remains hidden and must be retained and transmitted from one individual to another through teaching and learning (see Arnold 1989), while the memory associated with secondary production is highly visible and is communicated by visual observation. The hidden aspect of memory is associated with the dyke rocks whose location is highly localised within the landscape, while the visible aspects of memory are linked to the decorative motifs displayed on the surface of the pot.

The consumption of Grooved ware at Barnhouse

The next stage of my analysis focused on the manner in which different categories of pottery were related to different consumption practices. In order to understand the nature of consumption practices across the settlement, a number of samples of pottery of each category were analysed using the technique of Gas Chromatography/Mass Spectrometry. Most of these samples were derived from the houses, from midden deposits close to the houses and from the central area.

Residue analysis relies on the identification of specific biochemical compounds, and in the case of the Barnhouse assemblage, the lipid or fat group was considered to be the most amenable to preservation. Once lipids migrate into the ceramic matrix of a vessel due to their hydrophobic properties they are retained (for further details see Evershed et al. 1990, 1992; Jones 1986). The identified residues are generally in the form of fatty acids, the basic 'building block' by which more complex lipids are made up. The diagenesis of complex fats to fatty acids occurs as the result both of cooking and of natural decay over time (Evershed et al. 1992, 203). The identification of specific fatty acids is feasible and may provide a signature, or 'taxonomic marker' indicating the species origin of the food. In order to provide a set of standards for identification, I analysed the food remains from contemporary settlement sites in Orkney. This allowed me to define a series of possible food species. Samples from each of these species, both plant and animal, were then analysed using GC/MS, and these provided known standards by which to compare the samples derived from the Grooved ware.

A total of forty-five sherds were examined, and most of them showed positive evidence of use. The results are presented below, and in each case

Table 6.2 *Simplified results of GC examination of sherds from large Grooved ware vessels at Barnhouse*

	Large vessels	
Sherd number	Context	Contents
SF 1554	House 3, ash dump	Milk
SF 1564	House 3, ash dump	Wheat/barley
SF 1586	House 3, ash dump	Unidentified plant material
SF 1589	House 3, ash dump	Bark resins, milk
SF 1685	House 2, NW alcove	No evidence for fatty acids
SF 1812	House 3, ash dump	Milk
SF 1827	House 3, ash dump	Wheat/barley
SF 2000	House 3, below dresser	Barley only
SF 4227	Structure 8, exterior ditch	Wheat/barley, milk
SF 4246	Structure 8, exterior ditch	Unidentified plant material
SF 5053	Structure 8, platform	Unknown
SF 5299	Structure 8, platform	Milk
SF 5618	Structure 8, ditch	Milk
SF 5662	Dump near central area	Milk
SF 6218	Dump near central area	Milk and unidentified sugar
SF 1839	Structure 8, interior	Barley only
(Complete vessel)	(set into floor)	

a simplified list of the food type found in each sherd is presented (Tables 6.2, 6.3 and 6.4). This is not the context for the discussion of the precise details of analysis, since more detailed discussions may be found in Jones (1997) and Jones *et al.* (forthcoming). Here I simply want to discuss the integration of these results with the wider analysis.

Overall the use of Grooved ware at Barnhouse is both complex and structured. Large vessels appear to form a coherent group of vessels (Table 6.2). The major food found within these large vessels is dry food such as barley, although they also appear to be used for the temporary storage of milk. The use of medium-size vessels is more problematic. Many vessels seem to contain milk, and these are vessels of both fabric A and C; however, it would also seem that cattle meat is consumed within vessels of this size (Table 6.3). Plant material is also obviously utilised in these vessels, but its origins are difficult to determine. Given the fact that the small vessels were sampled from three quite different contexts, these vessels would appear to be clearly and singularly associated with barley (Table 6.4).

In order to draw out how these foods were prepared and utilised, a further stage of analysis examined the presence or absence of sooting as an index of cooking (Hally 1983). The pattern for the site as a whole indicates that sooting predominates on sherds of fabric C. However sooting

Table 6.3 *Simplified results of GC examination of sherds from medium Grooved ware vessels at Barnhouse*

	Medium vessels	
Sherd number	Context	Content
SF 10	Ash dump house 2	Cattle stomach
SF 165	Old land surface	Unidentified plant
SF 1080	Old land surface	Milk
SF 1577	Old land surface	Unidentified plant
SF 1650	Pit in W recess house 2	Unknown
SF 1655	Ash around E hearth house 2	Cattle meat
SF 1665	Hearth fill W hearth house 2	Cattle meat, milk
SF 1829	Ash dump house 3	Milk
SF 2032	Old land surface	Milk
SF 2522/1905	Occupation deposits house 3	Unknown
SF 2547/3477	Occupation deposits house 3	Milk
SF 2578	Occupation deposits house 3	Unknown
SF 3727	Occupation deposits house 6	Unknown
SF 5511	Occupation structure 8 platform	Unidentified plant
SF 5587	Occupation structure 8 platform	Unidentified plant
SF 5607	Occupation structure 8 platform	Unknown
SF 5697	Ash spread central area	Milk, wheat/barley
SF 5855	Occupation structure 8 interior	Unknown

is concentrated on medium-size vessels of fabrics A and C for the sherds analysed from the houses at Barnhouse. On a more detailed contextual level, it would appear that medium-size vessels of fabric A are preferentially utilised for cooking in certain houses, such as house 2 or 5.

Notably there is a distinction between the absence of soot on large vessels of fabrics A and B through the early phases of settlement at Barnhouse, and the presence of soot on large vessels of fabrics A and B in the structure 8 platform. This suggests a shift in social practices, since although the 'grammar' of the assemblage remains the same in structure 8, with the production of large, medium and small vessels, the 'vocabulary' of

Table 6.4 *Simplified results of GC examination of sherds from small Grooved ware vessels at Barnhouse*

	Small vessels	
Sherd number	Context	Content
SF 1667	Fill of cut in W recess deposits house 2	Possibly barley
SF 1890	Secondary occupation house 3	Barley
SF 4263	Dump of material in ditch near structure 8	Barley

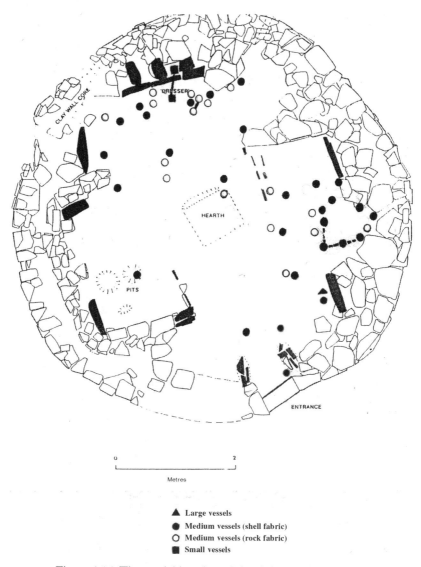

Figure 6.16 The spatial location of sherds in a typical house at
Barnhouse

use has changed, and large vessels are now used for cooking activities.
There is no sooting on small vessels of fabrics C, D or E.

An analysis of the location of sherds within a number of houses at Barnhouse (Fig. 6.16) indicates regularities between Grooved ware categories

and certain locations in the house. Large vessels are often placed at the back or the periphery of the house, either beneath dressers or in box-beds. Small vessels are found at the periphery and around the central hearth. Medium-size vessels are found most frequently around the hearth, although they are also stored in the right hand box-bed (Fig. 6.16). In general the most highly decorated vessels are concentrated around the central hearth, and those vessels with simple decoration are placed at the periphery.

Production and consumption in house 2

Although broad regularities occur within each house, we also observe contextual differences between houses at Barnhouse. In terms of spatial layout, house 2 is rather different to the other houses and the use of Grooved ware is more complex (Fig. 6.17). The range of decoration on vessels in this structure is greater than the other houses, and we observe the occurrence of different decorative schemes (see Fig. 6.18).

Furthermore, as noted earlier, the temper of this pottery is dominated by the use of sandstone and mudstone. The results from the GC/MS residue analysis indicate that this is the only house to be associated with the use of cattle meat. Everything would seem to mark out activities within house 2 as different.

The eastern hearth area in house 2 stands out due to its size and complexity. High phosphate readings to the south and east of this hearth indicate that ash was raked out to the left-hand side in this direction. This ash area was the only location to contain barley chaff (Hinton forthcoming). It would seem that the secondary processing of cereals occurred around this hearth. The localised nature of this activity suggests a number of things. First, the processing of cereals may have been subject to prescriptive rules, resulting in this activity being spatially demarcated. Given that the GC/MS analysis suggests the storage of barley in other houses, it is possible that subsequent to dehusking barley may have been redistributed between houses from this location. While the eastern hearth was marked out by the kinds of activities carried out around it, how does this relate to Grooved ware? The vessels found in this focal area are distinctively decorated. All of them are medium size and are a mixture of fabrics A and C. GC/MS analysis of two fabric A vessels indicates that they contained cattle meat.

A number of questions about the use of house 2 are raised by the presence of a sherd in house 2 that conjoins with a partner in the house 3 ash dump. It would appear that there was a degree of circulation of vessels between house 2 and the other houses – it seems likely that this sherd

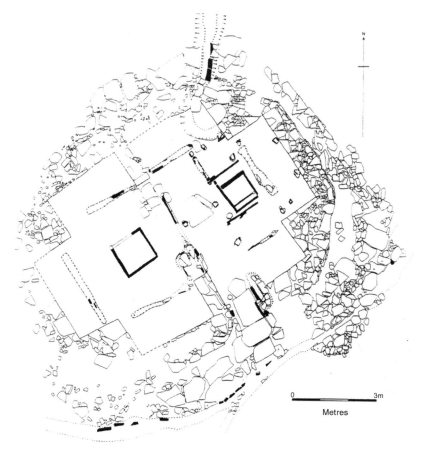

Figure 6.17 House 2, Barnhouse

was brought into house 2 from house 3. The evidence of the conjoined sherds and the distinctive production of the vessels in house 2 in terms of petrology and decoration suggest that they may have been made elsewhere for specific use in house 2.

The western room also contained a central hearth, while to the left of the hearth a small charred hollow may indicate the presence of an oven. Clay ovens were located in precisely this position in the Later Neolithic settlement at Rinyo, Rousay (Childe and Grant 1939). The western hearth contained sherds from three distinctively decorated medium and small vessels. The distinction between the hearths and the vessels in each room of this house suggests that food preparation activities took

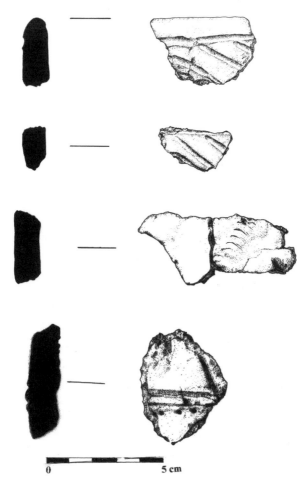

Figure 6.18 The Grooved ware from house 2, Barnhouse

place around the eastern hearth, while the cooking and consumption of foods, especially associated with small vessels, took place around the western hearth.

House 2 was also marked out as the focus for the specialised production of stone and flint tools (Clarke 1991; Middleton 1994). Two unfinished maceheads were found in the western area, while a lump of red and black banded mudstone was found in the west recess. It is precisely this material which is used to temper the Grooved ware in house 2, suggesting a link in the *chaîne opératoire* associated with stone tool and pottery production (Jones forthcoming b). In the eastern alcove next to the hearth, a complete polished stone chisel was deposited beneath the floor. A flake from a polished flint axe was found in the northwest alcove. The technological evidence from flint suggests that secondary core reduction sequences were undertaken in the western room. Flint and stone tools are produced in the western room and deposited in the eastern room. This represents the inversion of the cycle of activities suggested above for Grooved ware. In this house we observe two inter-linked activities: the first, associated with food, specifically barley and cattle meat, is conducted in a *less* secluded context to the east, while the second form of activity, associated with stone tool manufacture, occurs in a *more* secluded context to the west.

Consumption practices in structure 8

The latest phase of construction at Barnhouse was dominated by the monumental building, structure 8 (Fig. 6.19). An examination of the Grooved ware in the interior building and on the exterior platform indicate differences in the categories of vessels found in both areas (Fig. 6.20). The Grooved ware on the platform includes large vessels of fabrics A and B, and medium-size vessels of fabrics A and C. Most of the large vessels were burnished and a number were decorated with simple cordons. Many of these vessels were sooted and one example, on analysis by GC/MS, was found to contain cattle milk. Medium-size vessels were decorated with a simple all-over incised design.

It would seem that the large vessels were used for cooking foods, particularly cattle milk. The presence of sooting suggests that these large vessels were used for cooking, much as medium-size vessels were in the earlier period of occupation at Barnhouse. Unlike the earlier houses, these vessels were not positioned around the hearth but were placed around a series of stone boxes. Judging by the width of the sherds, these vessels were double the capacity of earlier cooking vessels. This suggests that the number of people involved in consumption activities was much greater in the case of structure 8.

By contrast, in the interior building we observe a quite different suite of vessels. The largest vessel, containing barley (based on GC/MS analysis), was buried up to the rim in the left-hand box-bed, a situation that parallels that of similar vessels in earlier houses and suggests a storage facility. Like those in earlier houses, medium and small vessels, decorated by all-over incision, were clustered around the hearth and dresser area.

Despite overall similarities with the earlier Grooved ware at Barnhouse, the Grooved ware within structure 8 was used differently. In the earliest phases at Barnhouse, medium-size shell-tempered vessels were used in the preparation and consumption of food, and medium-size rock-tempered vessels were used in the consumption of food. In structure

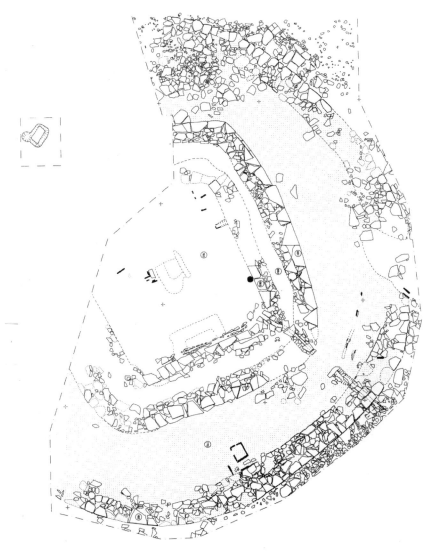

Figure 6.19 Plan of structure 8, Barnhouse

8 vessels were used according to a different grammatical structure. Although the use of medium and small vessels is broadly similar, the use of large vessels has changed. While large vessels were still used for storage in the interior of the building, they were also used for cooking food on the platform. The consumption practices and the concomitant categorisation of large vessels have therefore changed.

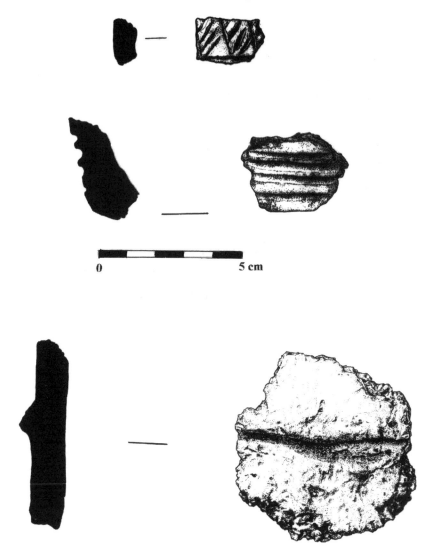

Figure 6.20 The Grooved ware from structure 8, Barnhouse

The death of Grooved ware at Barnhouse

I will now turn to depositional practices. Due to the distinctive petrological 'recipe' of pottery from each of the peripheral houses, I was able to relate the sherds from midden deposits with each house in terms of their

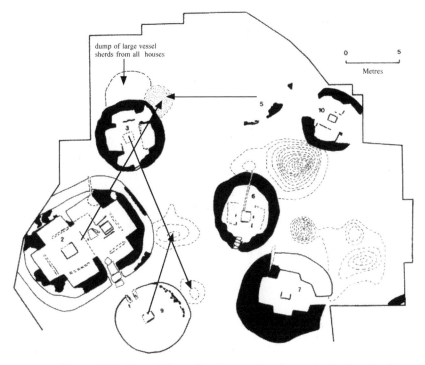

Figure 6.21 Plan of the early phase at Barnhouse indicating the depositional relationships between individual houses and middens

petrology. This evidence was combined with that for conjoined sherds to build up a picture of the patterns of deposition over the site as a whole (see Fig. 6.21).

I will begin with the earlier houses by examining the dumps associated with the peripheral houses. Each of these is a mixture of ash and fragmented animal bone along with large deposits of Grooved ware. Analysis of the dumps of pottery next to houses 2, 3 and 9 indicated that while each dump consisted of shell- and rock-tempered pottery, the petrology of sherds within these dumps suggested a complex set of depositional practices (Fig. 6.21). For example, a sherd from house 9 was located in the house 2 dump, two sherds from house 3 were located in the house 9 dump, sherds from house 2 and 5 were found in the house 3 dump. Meanwhile large vessels dominate the dump of pottery behind house 3, and petrological examination of these vessels indicates that they are derived from *all of the earlier houses* in the settlement. Analysis of each of the dumps located next to the peripheral houses suggests a difference in the relative quantities of shell- and rock-tempered pottery. What is more, the numbers of shell-tempered vessels in each dump seemed to depend upon the proximity of the dump to the central firing area. The house 9 dump, closest to the central area, contains more shell-tempered pottery, while the house 3 dumps located furthest from the central area contain a greater proportion of rock-tempered pottery.

There were large deposits of pottery in the central area which, as argued above, were likely to be associated with the production of shell-tempered pottery. Within this spread of material a large number of pits contained sherds from abraded shell-tempered pots. GC/MS analysis suggested that some of these vessels had been used to contain cattle milk. These pots were sooted and had undergone a fair degree of use prior to deposition. A spatial analysis of a further spread of medium-size vessels located behind house 6 indicated that the deposition of rock-tempered vessels decreased away from the central area.

It is evident that there is a fair degree of selective deposition occurring, with certain dumps of material having multiple sources. The most obvious pattern relates to the spatial structure of the deposits. The shell-tempered pottery in the central area appeared to be redeposited after some period of use. It would seem then that the central area is the most appropriate location for the deposition of shell-tempered vessels. Most interesting is the steadily increasing proportion of rock-tempered vessels as we progress away from the central area. The house 9 dump has a large number of shell-tempered vessels, while the house 3 dump contains few.

It is notable that the location of the dumps in relation to houses 2, 3 and 9 describes an arc of deposits circling the central area (Fig. 6.22). Crucially, the spatial patterning of deposits mirrors the spatial layout of the settlement itself. While it would appear that the deposition of different categories of vessels also echoes the concentric patterns for the distribution of different categories of vessel within the houses, what is also interesting is the deposition of large vessels behind house 3, which in the earlier phases of settlement would have been at the periphery of the settlement. It would seem then that the deposition of large vessels occurred at the edge of the settlement.

Finally, when we examine the spatial structure of deposits associated with the later use of structure 8, we observe that deposition also conforms to earlier patterns of concentricity and centrality. Medium-size vessels are placed in close proximity to structure 8, and large vessels are placed at the periphery within trench K.

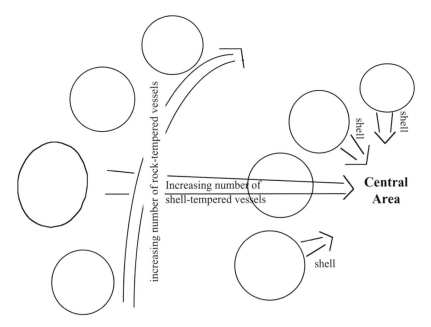

Figure 6.22 Schematic plan of Barnhouse indicating the relationships between shell-tempered pottery and the central area, and rock-tempered pottery and the periphery of the settlement

Conclusion

In this chapter we have followed the biographies of different categories of Grooved ware from their site of production, we have examined their role in differing consumption practices and finally we have observed their relationship to distinct modes of deposition. We have noted the way in which, at various stages of their lives, different categories of vessels are related to different contexts and thereby differing social identities. So far this analysis has concentrated on the biographies of vessels within the settlement site. In the next chapter I will expand the analysis to examine the relationship between the biography of the Barnhouse Grooved ware and Grooved ware deposited in other locations within the wider landscape.

While this analysis is conducted at a microscale intra-site level, in the next chapter I will examine the relationship between the practices related to Grooved ware and the wider apprehension of plants and animals. Moreover I will examine how the culturally informed practices relating to

Grooved ware biographies inter-relate with the specific mode of inhabitation of Later Neolithic settlements, and how the specific practice of living in these settlements help to constitute particular settlement histories. Finally, at a wider scale of analysis I will examine how an understanding of the detailed social practices associated with pottery enables us to gain a different viewpoint of the emergence of agriculture.

7 Making people and things in the Neolithic: pots, food and history

In the previous chapter I described the interpretative framework and analytical methodology I employed to examine the production, use and deposition of Grooved ware in the Later Neolithic settlement site of Barnhouse, Orkney. The analysis suggested that the 'lives' of different categories of pottery take quite different forms. Their production is associated with different areas of the settlement, while their use and deposition are framed by their association with different kinds of activity, different foods and different social occasions. The biographies of different categories of vessels are therefore associated with different, but overlapping, social identities. In this chapter I will delineate these biographies and outline their significance in relation to other sites in Later Neolithic Orkney. Following this I will examine the nature of the cultural metaphors that motivate the construction of these biographies and how these intersect with food technologies. I will then open out the discussion to examine how the social practices associated with food and pottery production are bound up with long-term settlement histories, and finally I will discuss the role of pottery and food in terms of our understanding of changing social relations during the Neolithic.

The biography of Grooved ware at Barnhouse

It is important to reiterate the distinction between the production of rock- and shell-tempered vessels. In the previous chapter I suggested that the production of shell-tempered vessels is undertaken communally in the space at the centre of the settlement, while rock-tempered vessels are produced by specific individual households. So not only are the raw materials of production procured from specific places, but their deployment in the production process is also related to specific places within the settlement. Such a distinction suggests that the precise place and manner of production are critical to the way in which vessels are used and perceived, and that the use of vessels will be related to either specific households or specific individuals within households. Finally, the manner in which vessels are deposited is guided by the duality between the identity of each vessel during production and its identity through use. I will now sketch a biographical outline for each category of vessel.

1 The large vessels at Barnhouse are produced communally in the central area and by individual households. In use they are placed around the walls of houses, where their position probably remained fairly static. In support of this it is worth noting that one vessel was set into the floor in just such a position in structure 8. The immovability of this category of vessel is especially apparent if we examine the evidence from a number of other contemporary settlement sites. Within hut D at the site of Rinyo, Rousay Childe and Grant (1938, 24) noted that a large vessel had broken *in situ* within a stone alcove. Measurements of the dimensions of the alcove and the vessel indicate that the vessel was immovable from the alcove in which it was situated. Furthermore, when Childe (1928, 1929, 1931) excavated house 7, Skara Brae, there were a number of large Grooved ware vessels smashed *in situ* within small alcoves, or placed in the 'box-beds', while a further vessel was placed in close proximity to the rear 'dresser'. While not all of these vessels were immovable, they were too large to fit through the low doorway of the house. This suggests that large vessels were integral to the construction of the house.

The spatial position of these vessels suggests that they were hardly visible during their period of use; as the evidence from GC/MS suggests they contained either barley or cattle milk, they are best regarded as storage vessels. It is notable that each house had a single large vessel, whose use is likely to have been shared by the household. On discard large vessels at Barnhouse were placed in a peripheral location at the edge of the settlement at the back of house 3, conforming to the same peripheral position they occupied during use. The material within this dump was derived from a number of locations around the settlement. Thus, on deposition, large vessels were placed in a communal location. After deposition certain vessels may have been incorporated within the walls of later houses as foundation deposits.

2 The biographies of medium-size vessels are more complex, and I will describe them according to fabric. Medium-size *shell*-tempered vessels were produced and fired in the communal space at the centre of the settlement. They were used in a number of locations around the settlement: most were used in the houses that border the central area, although a number were used in the houses on the periphery of the settlement. In both locations their use was similar; that is, they were stored around the periphery of the house and were used for cooking

within the central hearth. Evidence from GC/MS suggests they were used to cook cattle milk products. A number of shell-tempered vessels may also have been used as serving vessels for the consumption of foodstuffs. The high frequency of these vessels within each individual house suggests that they were used as individual serving vessels.

The identity of these vessels depends on two factors: where they were used and where they were made. If used in the houses around the periphery of the settlement, then they were deposited amongst the ash dumps outside the house, although the composition of these dumps suggests that shell-tempered vessels were preferentially dumped closer to the central area. If used in the houses bordering the central area, they were deposited within the central area, in the location in which they were produced.

3 Medium-size *rock*-tempered vessels have quite different biographies. These vessels were produced according to specific temper 'recipes', which related them to specific houses. Despite the clear association with certain houses, it is difficult to determine exactly where they were fired. They were located in similar places to the shell-tempered vessels within houses – being stored around the periphery of the walls – and used within the central hearth. These vessels may have been used either as cooking or serving vessels. In house 2, a number were sooted, suggesting their use as cooking vessels. They were used to contain cattle milk products and, in the context of house 2, cattle meat. As with medium-size shell-tempered vessels, their frequency suggests that they were also employed as individual serving vessels. The deposition of these vessels depends on a number of factors. Through use, certain vessels were related to specific houses and as such they were deposited in exterior dumps outside these houses. However, if used for the consumption of cattle meat in house 2, they were dumped outside this house or house 3. The identity associated with their use and deposition is complex, since it is related to the use of vessels in specific houses, such as house 2, and to the consumption of certain substances, such as cattle meat.

4 Small vessels have simpler biographies. Depending on how they were tempered, they were produced either communally in the central area or individually in separate households. Their use was similar to medium-size vessels, since they were found in peripheral alcoves within the house and around the central hearth. However, unlike medium-size vessels, they contained barley, and as such can be considered as serving vessels. The low frequency of these vessels in each household suggests that these vessels were shared in use. If produced within the central area, they were redeposited in this location; if used within individual houses, they were deposited amongst the hearth ash outside the house.

Grooved ware and social identity at Barnhouse

Each house at Barnhouse has a broadly similar assemblage of pottery, with the major difference between them being the manner in which the pottery was tempered, although each category of Grooved ware was used in a different way. Large vessels were most closely linked to the household, since they remained static within the periphery of the house and were used by all members of the household. However, those vessels that were used on a daily basis around the central hearth – medium and small vessels – were decorated with decorative schemes that suggest a notion of communal settlement-specific identity. Importantly, it was these vessels that were used in cooking and consumption activities and were thereby involved in the routine negotiation and sedimentation of social identities.

Rather than perceiving identities as constants that are simply read from the surface of the vessel, we need to consider the dynamic involved in the negotiation of identities. Through decoration each category of vessel is bound up with one set of identities, while through use these identities may be evoked, reworked or contested. I noted that, due to their frequency in individual households, small vessels were likely to be used in acts of sharing. Therefore these vessels refer, via decoration, to the community as represented by the settlement, while, in use, they refer to a different aspect of community, represented by the household. Meanwhile, due to their frequency, medium-size vessels may have been used as individual serving vessels. Decoratively, these vessels refer to the community as represented by the settlement, but in use they also represent the individual. In each case we may consider the notion of community to be drawn on in acts of household or individual consumption. A number of identities may have been constructed through this dialectic – especially those concerning the place of individuals and households within the community.

Grooved ware and social identity in house 2

The activities taking place in house 2 appear to be linked to certain notions of community. It is unlikely that this house was inhabited on a full-time basis, and the activities conducted in house 2 may have involved the community as a whole. It is notable in this regard that house 2 was a focus for the processing and redistribution of barley. The Grooved ware from house 2 was unusual; first an extremely uniform temper 'recipe' composed of widely available sedimentary rocks was used in the production of the pottery. Despite the uniformity in the production process, the decoration on the Grooved ware from this house was unlike that from the rest of the site. Specific categories of vessel were also utilised for the consumption of cattle meat. Notably, consumption activities within house 2 were restricted and could only be witnessed by those within the western room of house 2. Given the nature of the food eaten and the form of decoration on the pots, we may consider these activities to be restricted to those of a specific identity, with possible exclusions according to age, gender or lineage. Given that the house was a focus for the production of stone tools that were of particular importance as exchange objects, we may also consider the confines of house 2 to be the focus of some form of small-scale exchange activities.

Grooved ware and social identity in structure 8

In the earliest phases at Barnhouse, vessels employed in the cooking and consumption of food were used around the central hearth and were decorated in a similar manner. As such I noted that their use involved the expression of the identities of individuals and households in relation to ideas of community. This practice contrasts with the use of vessels for cooking and consumption in structure 8. Here the activities of cooking and consumption were spatially separated. The activities that surround the production of Grooved ware and its use in the cooking and consumption of food have changed, and the identities involved in the use of these vessels has shifted. The scale of cooking around the structure 8 platform was considerable; the vessels employed for cooking were twice the volume of earlier cooking vessels. It seems reasonable to assume that, if structure 8 was a house, then the scale of everyday cooking and consumption practices had increased, suggesting a larger number of people included within the household.

Materially the large cooking vessels and medium-size and small serving vessels both represent similar production histories and similar communal notions of identity. However, while cooking was a highly visible activity that occurred on the platform, consumption was more restrictive and occurred around the central hearth in the building's interior. The association between the act of consumption and the use of the central hearth was retained, suggesting that the hearth remained a focus for social interaction. It would seem that in this later period there was less emphasis on utilising pottery to represent differences within the settlement; rather, we may simply be seeing large-scale consumption as a means of cementing social ties within the community. We need not necessarily see this change in consumption practices as reflecting changing kinship relations, but rather as a change in the way social relations are expressed and represented. Richards (1993a, 163) notes that structure 8 may be seen as a *representation* of a house. In a similar way the Grooved ware used within it may also be considered as representational. The uniform and conglomerate method of construction and decoration would appear to be referring to a new kind of identity, a more overarching notion of community.

The biography of Grooved ware beyond Barnhouse

It is notable that Grooved ware is found in two other major contexts in Later Neolithic Orkney – henges and passage graves. To begin with I would like to contrast the activities at two locations: the site of Barnhouse Odin and the Stones of Stenness. Both sites are within around 150 m of the Barnhouse settlement. The Barnhouse Odin site represents the remains of two standing stones situated some six metres apart, and has been recently described as a form of symbolic gateway, allowing access from the Brodgar complex into the Stenness complex (Richards 1996, 199). A large scooped hearth, associated with flint debris and undecorated sherds of medium-size shell-tempered Grooved ware, was situated on the southeastern side of the stones.

We observe an immediate contrast when we compare this material with that found in the henge at the Stones of Stenness (Ritchie 1976). At Stenness all of the Grooved ware was rock-tempered and most of it was decorated (Henshall and Savory 1976). Notably one vessel is decorated with precisely the same decorative scheme as the Barnhouse Grooved ware (Fig. 7.1). A petrological examination of the Stenness Grooved ware (Williams 1976) revealed that it was tempered with two different sorts

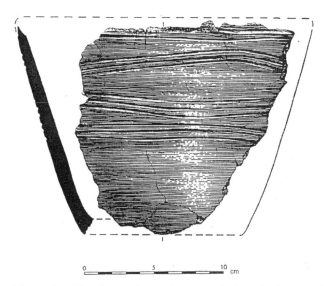

Figure 7.1 The Grooved ware from the ditch at the Stones of Stenness henge

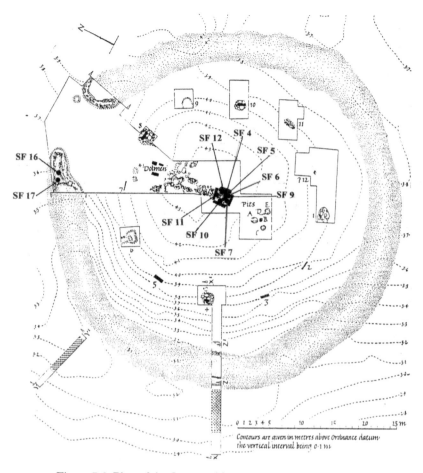

Figure 7.2 Plan of the Stones of Stenness henge indicating the position of Grooved ware sherds

of igneous and sedimentary rock. The first of these cannot be sourced, although it was used in a number of specific contexts at Barnhouse, especially house 2. The second is the source of rock used exclusively in house 5, Barnhouse. A total of twelve vessels are represented at Stenness, and these are mostly derived from the ashy fill of the central hearth and the western terminus of the rock cut ditch (Fig. 7.2). The radiocarbon dates for the use of the hearth are fairly late and are likely to date the final use of this feature. However the deposition of Grooved ware vessels in the primary fill of the ditch, vessels that are almost certainly provenanced from within the earliest houses at Barnhouse, suggests a degree of contemporary activity.

How was Grooved ware used in the henge, and what form did these activities take? In order to answer these questions, we need to consider the activities at Barnhouse Odin and Stenness together. At Barnhouse Odin large amounts of shell-tempered Grooved ware were mixed with ash and flint tools, but surprisingly little burnt bone. In contrast, it is notable that few flint tools were found within the henge. I believe that we are observing a distinction between activities inside and outside of the henge enclosure, with the butchery of animals and the cooking of food associated with shell-tempered Grooved ware taking place around the Barnhouse Odin hearth. The cooking process may then have been followed by the consumption of food around the large central hearth in the Stones of Stenness, with the subsequent deposition of food remains and pottery in the ditch. Interestingly, there were deposits of cattle, sheep and dog bones in the ditch and terminal of the henge (Clutton-Brock 1976, 35). What is also of interest with regard to the animal bones is the propensity of juveniles, suggesting that the animals had been slaughtered around late autumn or winter. Colin Richards (1993b, 238) has suggested that this may indicate activity around midwinter, a symbolically important point in the Orcadian year.

I now want to turn to the Quanterness passage grave (Fig. 7.3) to assess the nature of Grooved ware in this context. The passage grave

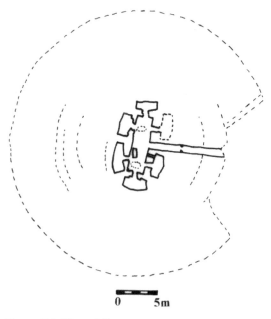

0   5m

Figure 7.3 Plan of Quanterness passage grave

Figure 7.4 Relationship between Quanterness passage grave and the Barnhouse settlement

at Quanterness (Renfrew 1979) is situated twelve miles distant from Barnhouse (Fig. 7.4). Excavation in the central chamber revealed a sequence of deposits of human remains initiated by deposits placed directly on the bedrock floor. This activity was followed by the construction of three cists cut into the floor deposits. Of these only two were excavated, cists A and B. Both cists contained a single inhumation: in cist A, an adult male between 30 to 40 years old was found. Cist A had subsequently been reopened, some time after, for the burial of a child and a female teenager. The deposits in cist B are more likely to be *in situ*. Further deposits of disarticulated human bone then covered the cists. Finally, a pit containing an adult male inhumation was cut into these upper deposits. The radiocarbon dates for the construction of this passage grave accord almost exactly with the Barnhouse settlement.

Although the deposits are disturbed (Barber 1988; Hingley 1996) we are not required to understand the spatial integrity of the twenty-two to thirty-four Grooved ware vessels (Henshall 1979, 75) deposited in this passage grave in order to understand the nature of deposition. However, as Renfrew (1979, 158) rightly notes, if the pottery was intermixed with bone prior to deposition, there would be less spatial differentiation between human bone and artefacts. Despite the disturbance of the contents of the passage grave, a Grooved ware sherd was found in a sealed context next to each individual in the cists and the inhumation in the pit. I contend that this repeated contextual association cannot be dismissed as coincidental or taphonomic.

One vessel from Quanterness (P2) was decorated with precisely the same curvilinear decorative scheme as the Barnhouse Grooved ware (Fig. 7.5). This was the only vessel from Quanterness to have been tempered with olivine-basalt (Williams 1979, 84), and examination of the thin-section (Jones 2000) revealed that it is from the same source of olivine-basalt that outcrops near the chambered tomb of Unstan in the loch of Stenness. It is this material that predominates as a tempering agent in the Grooved ware from houses 3 and 5, Barnhouse. Further examination of thin-sections from Quanterness revealed two sherds tempered with two different sources of igneous dyke material, again used preferentially in the Grooved ware from house 3 and house 5, repectively. More general examination of the thin-sections from Quanterness by Williams (1979, 96) indicates that at least twelve vessels from the site were not tempered with materials available in the local vicinity.

Given the specificity of the decorative schemes and the remarkable petrological concordance, it is suggested that at least three vessels from Quanterness were produced at Barnhouse. Notably, most of the sherds in Quanterness are derived from medium-size rock-tempered vessels. On this basis it seems likely that this category of vessel was especially appropriate for deposition in passage graves. It is difficult to determine whether the vessels placed within the passage grave were used beforehand or produced specifically for deposition within this context, but the presence of sooting on many of the vessels (Henshall 1979, 77) suggests they have been used elsewhere. At Barnhouse, this category of vessel was used for the consumption of specific foodstuffs, either cattle meat or milk.

What is the nature of the social practices surrounding the introduction of individual Grooved ware vessels into the passage grave? The inhabitants of a specific household at Barnhouse produced the vessel P2 deposited at Quanterness. My analysis of the production of Grooved ware at Barnhouse indicates that the manufacture of this vessel relates to individual households. Its use would have been fairly restricted during its

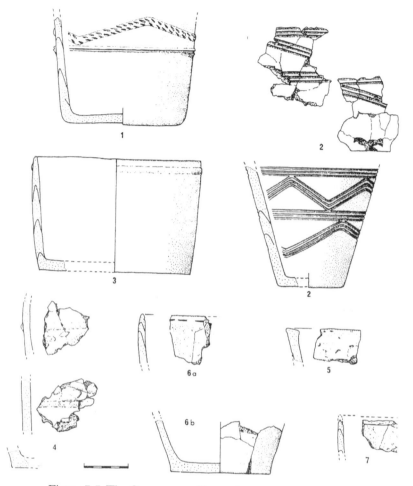

Figure 7.5 The Quanterness Grooved ware

use-life, with consumption confined to use around the central hearth of an individual house. Its use in a context beyond the settlement would suggest that a very specific aspect of its biographical identity was evoked in this context; an identity associated with kin relations between specific households in different settlements. A similar argument may be advanced for other vessels within Quanterness. Given the widespread provenance of pots within Quanterness, some form of exogamous kinship system connecting a number of geographically distinct groups is likely. The relationship between people and tombs is far more complex than the one-to-one relationship originally proposed by Renfrew (1979, 221). The dispersed nature of settlement is certain, but the complexities of the relationship between the passage grave and the settlements necessitate against a simple unitary or segmentary view of society. Rather, it is likely that a number of complex exogamous kinship relations, probably reckoned through marriage, were expressed over a wide area.

Things are bound up with the biography of people. The biography and memory associated with particular people and particular social groups are bound up in the production and use-life of the vessel. Thus, the use of an object so intimately connected to settlement-related notions of identity is especially appropriate in this context, since it is the memory of the relationship between one group and another that is being commemorated. The use of a vessel with a specific production history, decorative scheme and place of origin would have brought into focus, or presenced, the relationship between the deceased and those depositing the vessel in this context (see Chapman 2000b; Munn 1986).

Similarly, at the Stones of Stenness we see the use of at least one vessel that refers to Barnhouse due to its production history and decoration. Its presentation in a context outside the settlement must involve the representation of the notion of community, and the community of Barnhouse in particular. This is of interest if we consider that activities within the Stones of Stenness were visible to people beyond the community of Barnhouse. Precisely the same form of pottery is being used both in the intimate confines of the house at Barnhouse, and in the wider arena of the henge. This is especially interesting when we note that the architecture of the henge draws on the architecture of the house. This architecture is furthermore reproduced at a later date within the settlement, in the construction of structure 8.

Through the use of Grooved ware, which refers both to the house and to the community, the social relations of the household and members of the wider community were drawn on by those participating in the activities within the henge. This is an important point since we observe consumption and sharing associated with a vessel whose use would normally be restricted to the household. In a wider communal context, this act would have been essential to the creation of relations of affinity between the inhabitants of Barnhouse and those whose origins lay beyond the settlement.

It is important to note that in the case of the henge and the passage grave to the vessels used in each context were also associated with daily practices in the settlement. It is precisely because these vessels are associated with the quotidian that their use has impact outside the settlement. In the case of their use in mortuary practices in Quanterness, they stand for a

relationship between members of *one community and another* that are to be
dissolved or renegotiated on the death of an individual from one of these
communities. In the context of the Stones of Stenness, these vessels stand
for the community of Barnhouse, who are conducting activities within the
henge *on behalf* of the wider community. The significance of the vessels
is subtly transformed as they move from one context to another.

Food and consumption in Later Neolithic Orkney

So far I have analysed the 'grammatical structure' of the Barnhouse pottery assemblage. Broadly speaking, each category of vessel is employed
for the storage, cooking or consumption of specific foods. We have also
observed the way in which different categories of vessel are used in distinct
contexts inside and outside the settlement. In each case I have emphasised the nature of the identities expressed through the use of Grooved
ware in these contexts. Here I want to examine the way in which these
identities are emphasised not only by the biographical histories of individual pots, but because of the significance of the foodstuffs contained
within these pots. I want to elucidate the way in which the biographies associated with pottery are entangled with the biographies associated with
particular plants and animals as components of diet. As Samuel (1999)
notes, the use of plants and animals as foodstuffs involves a complex series
of stages in which they undergo a transformation in order to become food.
In the present discussion I want to examine how certain elements of the
chaînes opératoires associated with plants and animals, as food, intersect
with those of Grooved ware.

Most importantly, the use of plants and animals within the Barnhouse
Grooved ware appears to be selective. We only observe the storage and
consumption of barley and the cooking and consumption of cattle milk,
with cattle meat confined to consumption activities within house 2. I
believe that the selective use of these particular species is significant. If
we are to understand the significance of these foodstuffs in more detail,
we need to turn to the extensive faunal and botanical evidence from
Later Neolithic Orkney.

Let us begin by examining the evidence for the use of plant-based
foods. Most botanical material comes from the midden deposits associated with houses and settlements. Large amounts of carbonised grain
of barley (*Hordeum* sp.) were found in discrete deposits within the middens at Skara Brae, Tofts Ness and Pool (Bond 1994, 173–5; Clarke and
Sharples 1990, 73) along with crab apple (*Malus sylvestris*) pips in small
quantities (Camilla Dickson, pers. comm.). Other plant species found in
settlement sites include wheat (*Triticium* spp.), pignut (*Conopodium majus*)

and crowberry (*Empetrum nigrum*), hazel nuts (*Corylus*) and onion couch (*Arrhenatherum eliatus* ssp. *tuberosum*). Cereals such as *Triticium dicoccum* (emmer wheat), *Hordeum vulgare* (hulled six-row barley) and *Hordeum vulgare* var. *nudum* (naked six-row barley) grains were also deposited in mortuary contexts as at Isbister, South Ronaldsay (Lynch 1983, 174).

It is of interest then that of the wide range of wild and domestic plant species utilised in Later Neolithic Orkney, it was barley that was stored and consumed in Grooved ware pottery. I have discussed the significance of the association between cereals and pottery elsewhere (Jones 1999). There are a number of points concerning this discussion that are worth repeating here. The first point is that the production of large ceramic containers appears to facilitate the storage of cereals. This marks a significant break with previous periods where we observe little material evidence for the storage of cereals. With regard to the storage and consumption of cereals, it is notable that the large Grooved ware vessels used to store barley are located in the peripheral alcoves and dressers of Later Neolithic houses, while the consumption of barley occurs in small vessels decorated with passage grave art motifs. In both cases there is a striking relationship between the storage and consumption of cereals and the dead. First, there is a strong spatial homology between the location of the large storage vessels in the houses of the living and the storage of ancestral remains, especially skulls, in the peripheral alcoves of passage graves: the houses of the dead (Hodder 1992). Furthermore, the association between the decoration of small Grooved ware vessels and that of passage graves also provides a link with the dead. Finally we also observe the deposition of cereals in passage graves, as at Isbister, South Ronaldsay.

I have suggested that this association between cereal storage and consumption, pottery and the dead is best understood in terms of the creation and maintenance of memory (Jones 1999, 71–3). The cycles of growth, harvest and storage associated with cereals encourage an appreciation of the significance of memory. Furthermore these activities promote the remembrance of those previous generations involved in the production of crops (see Meillasoux 1972). It is for this reason that there is a close association between the storage of this ancestral resource, the storage of the dead in the passage grave, and the remembrance of the dead during consumption of cereals via the medium of the decoration on small Grooved ware vessels.

Having briefly examined the nature of plant use with regard to Grooved ware, I will now turn to examine Grooved ware and animals. I have argued elsewhere that the deposition of animal remains in Later Neolithic Orkney is selective. Animals are deposited in particular contexts, including chambered tombs and passage graves, henges and settlement middens. Settlement middens at Skara Brae provide the best evidence for the range of animal species, which includes cattle, sheep, pig, dog, whale and a number of bird and fish species (Noddle unpublished). However these animal species are not all deposited as the result of domestic consumption practices; certain species are selected for special treatment. Cattle skulls, whale skulls and long bones are found as structural elements embedded in the walls of the settlement. In the case of cattle, we also observe cattle bones embedded in the walls of passage graves (Sharples 1984). Other deposits include the 15 completely articulated red deer that were slaughtered and placed at the limit of the settlement at the Links of Noltland (Clarke and Sharples 1990), and the similar deposit found at Skara Brae (Richards forthcoming). The range of animal species deposited in settlements is paralleled in passage grave and chambered tomb contexts.

Spectacularly, we observe the deposition of at least 15 white-tailed sea eagles in the tomb located on the cliff edge at Isbister, South Ronaldsay (Hedges 1984). We also observe the deposition of around 14 and 36 red deer in the tombs located on the hill terrace at Knowe of Ramsay and Knowe of Yarso, Rousay (Callander and Grant 1935, 1936). Around 24 dog skulls were placed in the passage grave located on a hillside at Cuween Hill, Mainland Orkney (Charleson 1902) and around 16 sheep and lambs deposited in the tomb located on lower ground at Blackhammer, Rousay (Callander and Grant 1937). In summary, the process of deposition in various Later Neolithic depositional contexts is not arbitrary (see Table 7.1). It involves the selection of animal remains most appropriate to particular kinds of place, including both settlements located coastally and tombs situated in different locations within the lived landscape. I have argued elsewhere that the significance of this selective deposition relates to an association of particular species with certain habitats, with specific behavioural characteristics and according to their association with humans (Jones 1998).

For those animal species that are selected for special treatment, these species represent the most obvious characteristics of particular kinds of

Table 7.1 *Depositional contexts for animal species in Later Neolithic Orkney*

	Cow	Sheep	Pig	Dog	Deer	Whale	Birds	Eagle	Fish
Mortuary context	Yes	Yes	Yes	Yes	Yes	No	Yes	Yes	Yes
Settlement midden	Yes	Yes	Yes	Yes	Yes	Yes	Yes	No	Yes
Henge ditch	Yes	Yes	No	Yes	No	No	No	No	No

place and particular sorts of activity (Jones 1998). Sea eagles constitute the example of a bird *par excellence*, being the largest bird in Neolithic Orkney and the bird that is able to fly the highest. Whales are the largest sea mammals in Neolithic Orkney and constitute the most obvious aspects of the sea. Cattle are the largest domesticates, being of a similar size to the aurochs (Noddle 1983), while red deer are the largest non-domesticated land animal. Dogs, on the other hand, are the only domesticated carnivore and as such may serve to point up similarities between humans and themselves, since each eats the flesh of other animals. However, both dogs and cattle are associated with the settlement, while deer are associated with the hunt and are deposited on the margins of the settled landscape. Analysis of both deer and cattle skeletal elements suggest that cattle and deer were both important sources of meat (Barker 1984).

As a species cattle pre-eminently signify the life of the settlement. Cattle bones are closely associated with human bones in certain mortuary contexts, as at Isbister, and they are also embedded in the walls of both settlement and passage grave. They are therefore associated both with qualities of strength and protection and with the identities of specific individuals. Furthermore, the large size of Later Neolithic cattle in Orkney means that the slaughter of cattle would constitute a substantial provision of meat. It is worthwhile noting that it is sheep that dominate the faunal assemblages of the settlement, suggesting that sheep may form the bulk of the meat component of the diet, while cattle may be slaughtered on a more periodic basis. The periodicity of the pattern of slaughter is underlined by the high number of juveniles within both cattle and sheep assemblages, suggesting the slaughter of livestock in autumn. It is interesting, then, that the main cattle product to be found in the Barnhouse Grooved ware was cattle milk, which may be consumed on a periodic basis with no harm to the animal. The use of the more scarce resource of cattle meat was restricted to consumption within house 2.

Overall, it is interesting to note that while different categories of vessel were used together around the central hearth, they were used for the preparation and consumption of different kinds of food. Foods such as barley and milk were cooked within medium-size shell-tempered vessels, but were consumed in different categories of vessel. Barley was consumed in the smallest and most highly decorated vessels, while either cattle milk or meat was consumed within medium-size vessels, also highly decorated. The consumption of foods in a complex set of ceramics, and in specific restricted contexts, suggests that different foodstuffs may have been perceived hierarchically. Interestingly, quite different foods such as barley and milk are cooked in the same kind of vessel, but it is their consumption that is important and requires their division into separate categories of vessel. The use of ceramic containers like Grooved ware facilitates the separation and classification of foods. Concomitantly, this enables foods to become a useful tool for the mediation and expression of different aspects of identity in different social contexts. The relationship between the biography of certain vessels, their decoration and the substances consumed within them coheres in order to express subtle differences in the social identities of consumers.

We seem to observe a contrast between food that is associated with the community as a whole, such as barley and cattle milk, and foods that are associated with particular identities, such as cattle meat. This contrast allows us to understand how different foods are used in expressing different kinds of social identity. The consumption of barley is symbolically significant. This food is shared within the community but more importantly indicates a shared relationship between the living and the dead. On the other hand, the close association between cattle and people on death suggests that cattle may be associated with the self and the individual. As such, the consumption of the products of cattle in a number of different contexts is a powerful statement of the relationship between people. The sharing of cattle milk both within the community and in the context of activities in the henge and passage grave constitutes an important expression of social relations between communities. The consumption of cattle meat in the confines of house 2 constitutes an important means of defining the intimacy of relations between people.

People, pots and houses

Throughout this chapter I have demonstrated the link between particular categories of vessel and different kinds of social identity. Here I will clarify that link by examining the central metaphorical associations (see Gosselain 1999 for discussion of pots and metaphor) that relate different categories of vessel to different identities. This examination will enable us to elucidate how the production and use of Grooved ware is bound up with the social changes that take place over the life of the Barnhouse settlement and more generally within Neolithic Orkney as a whole. In this way I want to examine the subtle ways in which the biographies of various categories of Grooved ware are mediated by contextual associations with the house and the settlement.

Here I am concerned with examining the metaphorical relationship between pots and houses. I will begin this examination by considering the production process. Grooved ware is circular in shape, and the primary construction of a Grooved ware vessel begins by building a flat clay base.

The walls of the vessel are built using successive interlocking rings of clay. This primary construction process is analogous to the construction of a Later Neolithic house: first a clay floor is laid, and a low bank of clay is placed around the circumference of the house, while the walls are laid as successive interlocking rings of stone walling.

The Grooved ware vessel is strengthened using temper derived from specific sources related to the identity of particular people and ancestors, just as the walls of the houses are strengthened with midden material that is related to the identity of the previous inhabitants of the settlement. The exterior of the vessel is slipped in order to smooth the surface prior to firing. This allows a series of decorations to be placed onto the pots' surface. Again the exterior of the house is covered in a turf jacket, but the interior of the house may be decorated with a linear decoration similar to that found on the surface of some Grooved ware vessels. The pot is fired either within the centre of the settlement or outside this area, possibly within individual houses. The location of firing appears to structure the nature of the relationship between particular categories of vessel and the house. Just as the pot is warmed by fire to enable its transformation, the fire within the central hearth socially transforms the house (Richards 1990a).

Pots were used within houses in different ways. The large vessels, used for storage, were placed around the periphery of the house in alcoves, the 'dresser' or within pits. Medium- and small-size vessels were typically used around the central hearth. Most strikingly, pots were deposited in relation to houses, with those used around the hearth being deposited in close proximity to the house. Those made and used in the central area were deposited in this area, while those vessels most closely associated with the house, the large vessels, were placed at the periphery of the settlement. The social significance and identity of different categories of Grooved ware depended on their conceptual distance from the house. The whole field of activities associated with Grooved ware was based on the important metaphorical notion that pots and houses have properties in common and that each is naturally related to the other.

The relationship between different categories of pottery and houses is related more generally to the idea of mobility (see Battaglia 1991 for discussion of social mobility of people and things). The social mobility of different categories of vessel depends on the relationship of the category of vessel to the house. There are a number of attributes that define the social mobility of vessels: these include the vessel size; the materials used in production; the location of production; and the typical contents of the vessel. A further factor to consider is the decorative scheme, since this is drawn on in the differential contextual use of the vessel. Decoration is not confined to Grooved ware but found in a number of contexts during the Later Neolithic, including houses, passage graves, cist slabs, stone knives and carved stone balls. Much of this decoration consists of bounded linear motifs, although a number of passage graves are also decorated with curvilinear motifs. The presence of decoration on Grooved ware acts as an additional means of categorisation. Overall, as discussed previously, it is the specific biographies of Grooved ware vessels, coupled with their settlement-specific decorative schemes, that motivate their use outside the settlement in passage grave and henge contexts. It is the ability of Grooved ware to carry this place-specific meaning beyond the settlement that is crucial in these contexts.

Grooved ware and social change in Later Neolithic Orkney

The relationships between Grooved ware, houses and settlements are critical to our understanding of broader patterns of social change in Later Neolithic Orkney. Broadly speaking we observe three distinct changes occurring over the duration of the Later Neolithic:

1 As noted in the previous chapter, we observe a change in the decorative techniques (from incised to applied decoration) executed on Grooved ware vessels. This change in technique is associated with a change in the way in which decoration is related to settlement: in the earliest phases of the Later Neolithic, each settlement is deploying its own individual decorative scheme; by the later phases each settlement is deploying the same decorative scheme.

2 The earliest phases of the Later Neolithic are characterised by the construction of a series of monumental architectural constructions, including henges and passage graves (Richards 1998). In the later phases of the Later Neolithic these monuments fall out of use.

3 This shift in emphasis is also related to a change in house architecture and the nature of settlement. During the earlier phases of the Later Neolithic, settlements consist of free-standing houses; by the later phases we observe either the construction of monumental houses, such as structure 8, Barnhouse, or the nucleation of settlement in which house construction becomes conjoined, as at Skara Brae and the Links of Noltland.

In order to understand these changes in social practices, we need to consider the issue of social identity. Of particular importance here is the relationship between the expression and negotiation of identity in relation to consumption practices. There is a transformation in the social emphasis placed on the appropriate contexts for large-scale consumption during the Later Neolithic. In the earlier phases of the Later Neolithic, the large-scale communal consumption of food occurred in the context of henges and passage graves. By the later phases the emphasis had shifted to settlements as the contexts for large-scale consumptive practices, as we see in the form of the monumental structure 8 at Barnhouse. The changing contexts of consumption, along with the changing decorative motifs on Grooved ware, constitute an active expression of changing ideas of community. We observe a change from a more divisive form of social community, in which consumption occurred in visible public arenas such as the henge or the platform of the passage grave, to a more inclusive form of social community, in which consumption occurred within the settlement itself. This final expression of community was defined not only through the enactment of consumption practices within the settlement, but also through the production of similar forms of Grooved ware in each Later Neolithic community across Orkney. Finally, this inclusive notion of community is expressed in the architecture of house and settlement, where we observe a shift towards monumental houses or the nucleation of settlements. Importantly, the expression of these changing notions of identity emerges through the routine practices associated with the habitation of the settlement and the production and consumption of pottery.

Making people and things in the Neolithic

As I indicated in chapter 4, microscale studies also provide leverage with regard to problems of a macroscale nature. In the light of this I want to consider the analysis of the Barnhouse Grooved ware in relation to the general proposal by Julian Thomas that the Neolithic is the result of 'the wholesale transformation of social relations which results from adopting an integrated cultural system' (Thomas 1991, 13). Thomas qualifies this statement by suggesting that it is a recognition of the symbolic potentials of various elements such as domesticates, novel material culture and the construction of durable monuments which creates the Neolithic world. If we consider the historical phenomena we describe as the 'Neolithic' as occurring as the result of a reconfiguration of social relations, and a re-description of the relationship between people and their environment, then we need to consider both in what terms and through what medium these changes were defined. In particular it is important to highlight the coherence between the social relations expressed by people in their habitation and utilisation of the environment, and the relationship between material culture, food and the creation of new forms of social expression.

We have seen that within a single 'Grooved ware' settlement, the use of Grooved ware is complex. Different fabrics, volumes and decorative schemes distinguish different categories of pottery. 'Grooved ware' is therefore not a homogenous cultural label signified by the use of a specific class of pottery. Rather particular categories of 'Grooved ware' are both the medium and the outcome of particular ways of living. Here our attention is drawn to the close identification made between the expression of social identities and the articulation of an attachment to place and locality (see Lovell 1998). Certain pots are constructed from materials whose significance is specific to a place, while others are constructed within specific places, such as the house or the centre of the settlement, and other pots are also used or deposited in specific places. All of these apects of production and use simultaneously define and express a series of overlapping social identities. Moreover, at a regional scale the different Grooved ware biographies are related to the definition of the affinities and differences between different communities during the Later Neolithic. During the earlier phases of the Later Neolithic, we see certain categories of Grooved ware used to construct differences between communities, while towards the end of the Later Neolithic we see all settlements using the same category of Grooved ware to define a holistic sense of community.

The expression of place and locality is a critical component of being Neolithic (Whittle 1996, 355–71). These issues motivate not only the production and deposition of material culture, but inhabitation and sequences of settlement and the construction of chambered tombs and passage graves in which the dead are situated in place. While these aspects structure the temporal inhabitation of Neolithic lifeworlds, how are social relations maintained and expressed?

Here it is critical to consider the role of food consumption. Although subsistence has played a clear role in characterisations of the Neolithic, there have been fewer tendencies to examine the nature of the changing relations of consumption that, in part, motivated the alteration in subsistence practices. Where discussion has taken place, there is a tendency to relate consumption or feasting to the acquisition of status (Hayden 1990, 1996; Wiessner 1996), as part of a process of evolving social complexity. Within this framework the adoption and use of ceramics is seen to be a logical outcome of intensifying strategies in which groups wish to differentiate themselves. Instead we need to re-orientate our notions of how ceramics are socially deployed. The Barnhouse study suggests that pottery allows food to be cooked and consumed in more complex ways, and also enables the storage of foodstuffs. As I have argued elsewhere (Jones 1996, 1999), rather than viewing this as the inevitable outcome of the production and use of pottery, we need to realise that the production and use of pottery is related to specific ways of viewing the world. For

example, while storage is an expedient method of managing the problems of abundance and scarcity, it also marks a new way of organising
and engaging with issues of time and place (see Jones 1999). The activities of food production, consumption and storage in relation to ceramics
constitute new ways of engaging with and classifying the world. While I
have argued that the production and use of pottery is closely allied to the
expression of certain forms of social identity, the consumption of food
within ceramic containers also provides a new arena for the negotiation
of different kinds of social relations.

Although episodes of consumption in Neolithic Orkney can be characterised in terms of competitive feasting, it is important to note that
the commensal politics of consumption are not only confined to episodic
feasts but take place on a quotidian basis. Equally, as Falk (1994, 10–44)
argues, the meal acts as a mode of consumption at a number of ontolog-
ical levels. Food is incorporated into the body, just as the shared meal
itself embodies a process of incorporation in which individuals are incorporated into the group. Therefore social relations are expressed and
confirmed as much at the level of daily acts of consumption as on more
formalised occasions. The distinction between the preparation of food
outside and the consumption of food inside house 2 and structure 8,
Barnhouse might be described as diacritical feasting (Deitler 1996, 98)
intended to highlight and naturalise differences within groups. Similarly
the use of Barnhouse Grooved ware within the Stones of Stenness henge
for the consumption of food on behalf of the wider community might
be described as entrepreneurial (Deitler 1996, 92), in that those orches-
trating the feast will gain symbolic capital from the event. However we
also need to consider the relationship between community and household articulated by the use of medium and small vessels, and the relationship between stored produce and household articulated by the use
of large vessels at Barnhouse. The alteration in the terms in which social relations were expressed cannot be wholly reduced to aggrandising
strategies (Hayden 1996); rather, we must realise that such terms had
to be rethought before they could be expressed. Prior to their use in
defining differences between people, a re-evaluation of the relationship
between people and the foods that they ate was required to take place.
Foods were related to particular understandings of the world and as such
were also related to particular categories of person, or certain forms of
social occasion, as appears to be the case with cattle meat at Barnhouse,
house 2.

The process of re-evaluation undergone by foodstuffs also involves a
new definition of the relationship between people, between people and
place and their temporal habitation of the world. The practices of food

consumption are both medium and outcome for the expression of different kinds of communal identity. It is through the act of constructing social relationships through the medium of food consumption that we observe the changing production of pottery and changing definitions of settlement. It is through social practices such as these that people construct different ways of inhabiting the world. In short, then, we are able to observe that food, material culture and the construction of monuments are integrally related to the process of living in the Neolithic.

8   Before and after science

I will begin this final chapter by reiterating three theoretical propositions that I consider to be of signal importance to the motivation and structure of our practices as archaeologists:

1 Most importantly, knowledge does not arise from simple one-to-one observations and descriptions of pre-existing categories in the world. Instead knowledge is created from our engagement with the world through the construction of categories. These categories are then utilised as the means to interrogate and provide an understanding of that world.

2 If we accept the view that knowledge is constructed, we need to consider precisely how it is constructed. One of the ways in which we may understand the process of knowledge construction is through an analysis of the practices of particular groups of people. As I have already observed, distinct practices are associated with distinct groups of people or cultures.

3 It follows from the above two points that cultural knowledge is not a static or concrete entity that can be grasped 'out there' in the real world; instead people live within cultures, and they both use and alter cultural knowledge through practice. Culture is therefore a contingent process that must be continually performed if it is to be maintained. It is this point that I want to develop with regard to science and archaeological practice in the context of this chapter.

These viewpoints apply with as much force to the study of scientific practice as they do to the cultural practices of other peoples distant in place or time. This is the essence of the symmetrical approach of the anthropology of science – we apply the same principles to the examination of the beliefs and practices of other cultures as we do to our own (Latour 1993). In this chapter I will return to this problem in the light of the preceding chapters and conclude by emphasising the correlate of these perspectives to our analysis of archaeological knowledge, scientific or otherwise.

Science and history

The approaches to science and practice discussed throughout this volume may still occasion some problems for those practising science-based archaeology. As I noted in the opening chapters, we observe a radical disjunction between the views of the natural sciences and those of the social sciences. In the former view, the world is seen to be a static entity that can be adequately represented by scientific analysis. In the latter the world is seen to be a contingent or shifting entity which is imperfectly represented through the lens of culture. Moreover the approaches of the natural sciences are usually applied to the analysis of stable or concrete entities within the natural world, while the approaches of the social sciences are applied to the mutable worlds of culture and sociality. We therefore have a distinction between the static and stable representation of knowledge, on the one hand embodied by observable, demonstrable scientific facts, and on the other by the shifting theoretical perspectives of social knowledge. One obvious worrisome query might be that if we embrace a viewpoint that suggests that scientific practice is contingent and changeable then we may be in danger of losing sight of the concrete results of scientific analysis. Added to this is the worry that if we lose access to the reliable and observable results of our analyses, on what grounds are we able to claim knowledge of the past – again, the spectre of relativism arises.

I will address this point more generally later in this chapter. Here it is worth pointing out that this query appears to be especially pertinent in the context of archaeological enquiry. Archaeology is, of course, an unusual discipline since it employs the physical elements of the world (such as material culture, architecture, and faunal and botanical remains) as a means of studying the social world. Not only this – it also relies on the physical presence of the traces of past activity as a means of mediating between past and present (Barrett 1994, 2000). On the face of it, then, archaeology would seem to be furnished with an abundance of concrete physical evidence for the existence of past worlds. It is the critical importance attached to this concrete material evidence that I will explore through the remainder of this chapter. In particular I will examine the distinction made by many between the observable and concrete nature of the material evidence of the past, and the facts derived from the scientific analyses of this material evidence and the changeable nature of archaeological theory. The approach I want to develop here will attempt to overcome the problems related to the bifurcation between these two divergent approaches to knowledge by suggesting that we are required to embrace the concrete *and* contingent nature of both theory and data.

How are we to surmount the problems related to the distinction between the concrete nature of scientific facts and the shifting nature
of theoretical perspectives? One of the ways in which we may overcome
these difficulties is by examining the practice of science. This is precisely
the approach I have adopted throughout this volume. I noted that scientific facts are constructed and that scientific knowledge is subject to
a process in which particular narrative and rhetorical devices are used
to convey certain kinds of information in order to convince or persuade
their target audience (Harraway 1989; Knorr-Certina 1981; Latour and
Woolgar 1987). This point is important since it highlights the fact that
people are active in the process of creating knowledge. It follows that if
knowledge is actively constructed by people, then it is constructed in particular ways at particular times – in other words, knowledge of the world
is not static, it is historically contingent.

But if knowledge is historically contingent, how does this relate to
the apparently concrete nature of the world? Are we to return to the
problems related to incommensurable worlds of knowledge, as raised by
the approaches of Kuhn and Feyerabend? As we change our perspective
do we also inhabit different worlds? Or does the concrete world remain
the same while we simply change our perspectives on it? In both cases
problems arise because we tend to treat either the natural world or our
knowledge of it as static. In the first instance the notion of paradigms is
historically defined or bounded – knowledge is fixed in relation to specific
paradigms, and in order to overcome this problem the natural world is
required to change with the paradigm. In the second instance the natural
world is fixed and instead our perspectives on it change.

If we are to overcome these problems we need to investigate the nature
of practice in more detail. I have already noted that scientific analysis involves the construction of facts. But this situation is somewhat one-sided.
Problems arise when we oppose the constructive activity of science with
the static immutable nature of the 'real world'. However as I have pointed
out at various junctures throughout this volume, scientific activity does
not simply involve the intervention of the scientist in the natural world;
rather, it involves a process of active engagement with the world. The
world is not just made up of people; it is composed of people *and* things.
This perspective is critical to any attempt to overcome the difficulties that
arise between models of concrete scientific knowledge and changing interpretative models. In chapter 2, I introduced two critical concepts that
help us overcome these problems. The first was the notion that scientific
practice is characterised by a relationship between animating subjects
(people) and animated objects (technologies made up of machines and
instruments). The second important notion was that networks, composed
of both people and instruments, shaped scientific knowledge.

We need to reappraise these ideas here. While it is important to retain the notion that knowledge is constructed through the creation of associations between people and things, we need to question how this process operates. Should we consider scientific knowledge to be entirely constructed by scientists drawing together scientific facts, instruments and other people into networks of interpretation? The problem with this proposal is that it suggests that people are solely responsible for the worlds that they construct and live in.

Again we are faced with a dilemma, since an objective viewpoint suggests that the concrete nature of the world has an important part to play in the construction of reality. Yet, throughout this volume I have discussed the notion that objects – be they scientific instruments or otherwise – have a degree of agency, that they are animated since the intentions and motivations of their authors are embedded within them. If this is the case, might we be able to accord motivations and intentions to the material world?

Rather than considering scientific analysis to be solely related to the intentions, motivations and observations of scientists, following Pickering (1995, 9–21) an alternative perspective might be to suggest that the material world also operates with a degree of intentionality. This is because the material world simultaneously constrains and structures the observations, actions and intentions of the scientists observing it. As observers, our theories are required to be accommodated with regard to the form and structure of the material world. Therefore, while the material world may be observed and interpreted in a multiplicity of possible ways, interpretations are not wholly open-ended; the nature of the material world resists some kinds of interpretation while it provides the means for others.

It is a process of resistance (from the material world) and subsequent accommodation (from those making observations related to that world) that characterises the process of interpretation (Fig. 8.1). The process of accommodation is furthermore affected by both the theoretical and practical orientation of scientists, since the practical application of specific ideas or techniques 'frames' the material world and enables it to be observed in particular ways (Pickering 1995, 93–6). This allows us to understand the kind of process involved in formulating ideas, 'testing' these against our observations, and changing our ideas according to whether these appear to fit our initial observations.

This perspective encompasses both the notion of objectivity and that of relativism, since it proposes that the observations of scientists are always situated in specific concrete material conditions, and that these conditions affect the observations and construction of the theories of those scientists. However this perspective is provided with a historical dimension since it also grants the fact that the observations and theories of previous scientists determine those material conditions. To paraphrase Pickering (1995, 33):

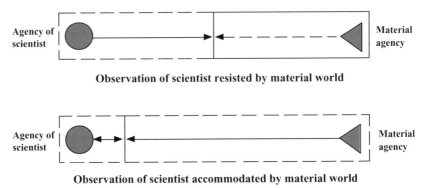

Figure 8.1 The relationship between the resistance and accommodation of material and human agency

'What counts as knowledge now is a function of the specific historical trajectory that practices have traced out in the past.' Although I do not have space to enter into this here, this notion serves equally well for scientific practices in relation to the material world and scientific practices in relation to the world of concepts or ideas (Pickering 1995, 68–147). Both ideas and the material world resist and structure the nature of our observations and theories. The most important thing about this proposal is that it circumvents the problem of opposing concrete observations and explanations based on scientific analysis with rapidly changing theoretical perspectives.

We can think about the operation of the relationship between the traditional distinctions between objective knowledge and subjective interpretation in terms of objective knowledge existing in time as a series of stable framed 'events' along a chain (Fig. 8.2). Each of these framed events would appear to maintain its stability due to our practical interaction with and observation of these events. Notably this is very different from claiming that we simply move from one form of truth to a better form of truth. Instead, referring back to the original argument concerning networks, what I am proposing here is that it is the interaction of people, instruments and theories that creates this stability. I am suggesting then that the change in the nature of objective (or representational) knowledge and theory emerges over time through practice: it is wrought by the interaction between the agency of people and that of the material world.

Science in context

The purpose of the foregoing discussion is to bring issues relating to the nature of observations and to the formulation of theories into focus

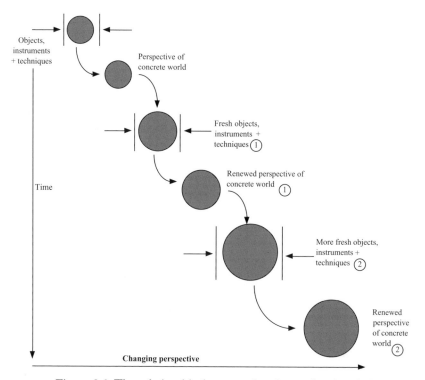

Figure 8.2 The relationship between the observational techniques of science and the representations of the concrete nature of the world by scientists

with regard to archaeological science and interpretative archaeology. Problematically, on the one hand we have theoretical archaeologists suggesting that archaeological scientists are operating in a theoretical vacuum (Thomas 1990), and on the other we observe the singular reluctance of archaeological scientists to engage in theoretical discussions based on the interpretation of their data. As Renfrew (1992) rightly points out, there is a tendency amongst archaeological scientists to place a heavy reliance on the truth and veracity of their data, over and above the more fleeting and less concrete interpretations of other archaeologists. In the preceding discussion I noted that both interpretations and concrete observations are mutually constituted; each is made stable by the other. Moreover an instability in either observation or interpretation serves to provide a point of resistance that may re-structure subsequent interpretations or observations.

I will illustrate this point with a case study derived from a recent article by Knapp (2000) concerning science-based archaeology and its application to the study of the metals trade in the Mediterranean. Knapp provides a neat discussion of the issues surrounding the application of lead isotope analysis (LIA) to the study of the trade in copper in the Late Bronze Age eastern Mediterranean. Broadly stated, a series of data for the isotopic ratios of lead in copper sources have been obtained from the oxhide ingots (so-called because of their distinctive shape) that characterise units of exchange in this area of the ancient world. Although the main function of LIA is to provide negative data – proving that particular ingots were not derived from certain sources – these data are remarkably consistent. Initial interpretation of this pattern of consistency suggested that all ingots from across this region must be derived from a single source in Cyprus (Gale and Stos-Gale 1987). Here the interpretation was situated within a framework that emphasised long distant exchange, and the notion of exchange relied heavily on conceptions borrowed from our understanding of capitalist economics. The interpretation was therefore constrained by the framework within which it was interpreted. However the results resisted a single analysis, and an alternative proposal for the data was put forward (Budd *et al.* 1996). These authors suggested that the data indicated processes of pooling copper from different sources or recycling of metal artefacts. Here the suggestion was based on technological knowledge related to metal production. This technologically derived interpretation, in turn, structured further interpretations regarding the status and organisation of both the extraction and distribution of metal in the eastern Mediterranean. As Knapp (2000, 45–7) notes, along with the evidence for non-Cypriot artefacts found on Cyprus, interpretations must focus on alternative gift-based models of exchange based on the maintenance of social relations rather than the simple supply and demand of commodities.

The notable point about this example is that although we can observe a historical shift in the state of our knowledge the data itself appears to remain static. Interpretations have altered as we progress through time, yet at the same time the objective data has remained the same – the interpretations are still made with recourse to the LIA data, alongside the evidence from the distribution of oxhide ingots and archaeological sites throughout the eastern Mediterranean. The stability of that data both materially and scientifically is maintained by our continued referral to it. Moreover, the increased stability of the data is maintained by recruiting other aspects of evidence alongside the original data. It is this that creates a more solid, more wholly satisfactory description of the evidence. A disequilibrium in the scientific status of this material may occur if further analysis, structured by renewed interpretation and using different techniques, or on different but complementary materials, were to be undertaken which contradicted or problematised the status of the primary data. It is under these conditions that we may speak of a different point being reached in the state of objective knowledge.

This case study demonstrates the mutual relationship between the analysis of scientific data and the interpretation of that data. As Knapp (2000, 47) observes, we cannot expect the results of scientific analytical techniques to be interpreted in the absence of any form of theoretical framework. Indeed as the case study demonstrates, the application of other theoretical perspectives has a profound effect on our understanding of the data. Moreover, it allows that data to be more firmly set within a constellation, or network, of other relevant evidence. It is the relationship between each of these elements, including theoretical orientations, data and further evidence, that characterises a network approach to interpretation.

It is precisely this approach that I adopted in my analysis of the Barnhouse pottery assemblage. Here again the specific scientific techniques used were motivated by particular theoretical presuppositions. These altered with the interpretation of the data generated by those presuppositions: the data both resisted and enabled particular lines of enquiry. These subsequent interpretations were also framed by further evidence, such as the specific architecture of the house, the nature of faunal and botanical evidence, the evidence from lithics, etc. Finally these interpretations were reflexive since they also altered assumptions concerning the nature of each of these aspects of the material evidence. This point serves to underline the important fact that interpretation is not simply derived from the relationship between theory and evidence; rather, it is derived from the relationship between theoretical considerations, scientific analysis and other strands of evidence. Interpretations arise through the tension created between each of these factors. It is for this reason that scientific analysis is required to be undertaken in context, since context is a critical component of this creative tension (Barrett 1987a).

In the opening chapter I noted that there was often a 'brick wall' between the interpretations of science-based archaeologists and interpretative archaeologists. Part of the problem arises because scientific data is perceived as objective and therefore bears a closer correspondence to the truth, while interpretative discussion is perceived as holding little relationship to the concrete nature of the material evidence. However the model proposed above allows both objective knowledge and contingent theory mutually to constitute each other. As an alternative, then, I want to propose that it is no longer viable for science-based archaeologists to forego interpretation. Equally it becomes imperative that interpretative archaeologists understand and contextualise the results of science-based archaeology.

Science, material culture, time and agency

I will now consider in more detail the relationship between the notion of scientific investigation proposed above and the nature of past material culture. In particular I will develop the view that there are considerable similarities between certain aspects of the philosophical framework out-lined above for examining the relationship between different orders of knowledge and certain proposals for the study of past societies through the medium of their material remains. Here I want to outline a frame-work for the analysis of both scientific and other broader archaeological practices, both in the present and in the interpretation of the practical action of people and societies in the past.

It is important to draw out two of the crucial considerations in the analysis of scientific practice. The first of these concerns the relationship of the practices of scientists to the concrete material conditions that they inhabit. I noted earlier that while these conditions affected the observa-tions of scientists, the nature of these conditions was ultimately deter-mined by prior scientific theories. The second important point concerns the nature of agency. Here I noted that logically scientific analysis of the material world was motivated by the intentions of scientists. However, I also noted that the generation of theories or instruments derived from those observations was, in part, determined by the resistance of the ma-terial world – interpretation was therefore a process of accommodating, or fitting, observations with the constraints of the material world. Pickering (1995, 20–1) describes this as a dialectical process in which the agency of people and things is, by turn, active or passive, as each accommodates to the other's intentions. The main point to note here is that although the material world is multi-dimensional, there are limits to the way in which it structures our observations.

This notion resonates with recent perspectives in anthropology and archaeology. Here a number of authors have underlined the notion that there is a critical relationship between people and things, and that ma-terial culture may be considered to possess a form of agency (Battaglia 1991; Gell 1998; Strathern 1985, 1998). Similarly, archaeologists have embraced the realisation that material culture serves to structure social relations (Hodder 1986). Barrett (1994, 2000) has provided this pro-posal with additional coherence by suggesting that we need to consider in more detail the nature of agency afforded by material culture. To sim-plify matters we may consider agency – the ability to act – to be made up of two components. The first is related to the intentions and motivations of human actors. The second relates to the material conditions in which those people act. Human actors are therefore only able to act within the framework of constraints and possibilities of the material world. As Gosden (1994, 77) notes: 'Material things have both enabling and constraining properties so far as human action is concerned.' So, in precisely the same way as discussed above, when we wish to consider the agency of the material world at the level of material culture, we also need to review the possibility that material culture may be understood to operate like other aspects of the material world. While the properties of material culture are multiple, the particular form and structure of material culture shape the way in which material culture is perceived, utilised and imbued with meaning (see Tilley 1999, chapters 2 and 8 with regard to the metaphorical properties of material culture). Moreover, just as the material conditions of the material world – as they are formed by previous scientific analyses – serve to structure the nature of future observations, so material culture can be understood as an historical phenomenon (Dobres 2000). As Gosden (1994, 77) again relates: 'History needs to be written not just to take account of how people operate in an environment, how culture shapes nature, but to look at how the transformed world is itself transforming.'

If we are to take this point further, we need some practical examples of material agency. A neat example is provided by Latour (1999, 186–7). He discusses the concrete speed bumps laid down in certain residential areas to limit the speed of passing traffic in order to reduce accidents. These simple lumps of concrete, often known as 'sleeping policemen', provide mute testimony to the concept of material agency. Latour describes them as the translated material form of the intentions and actions of road traffic officials. Rather than employing people or road signs in order to reduce traffic speed, the intentions of these officials are now articulated by concrete. These lumps of concrete – the congealed intentions of past human actors – have a material effect on the actions and intentions of vehicle drivers. This is a simple example of how the agency of people is mediated by material culture, since the 'sleeping policeman' created by the intentions of the traffic police have a clear material effect upon subsequent actors. However, as noted above, material agents have histories, and they are not only involved in constraining action, they also have the capacity to transform the social and material world.

My next example, derived from the analysis of the Barnhouse Grooved ware assemblage, will examine the historical and transformative nature of material agency. In the earlier phase of settlement large vessels were produced as storage containers for barley and other foodstuffs. In the later phases of settlement this function persisted, however large vessels of a similar form were now also used for large-scale consumption practices on the platform of structure 8. The intentions of the earlier inhabitants of Barnhouse were translated into clay in the form of large storage containers. The material agency of these vessels cohered in their large size, their capacity and their durability. The material existence of the large clay vessels structured their production by people in the later phase of settlement. However the agency of these vessels was not entirely constraining, it was also enabling, and while the later vessels took a similar form their capacity allowed them to be employed in quite different ways. What is more, the large capacity of these vessels meant that they could be used in the active construction of a more inclusive and holistic form of communal identity. The material agency of the object therefore structured new forms of sociality.

The crucial point here is that we are able to conceptualise the contingent nature of material agency with regards to scientific analysis and with regard to past social and cultural formations using the same broad theoretical framework. I believe that this perspective allows us to reconsider some of the problems that I have discussed throughout this volume, including the problematic nature of the 'archaeological record' and the problem of scales of analysis. Our problems with the concept of the 'archaeological record' arise because we consider past material remains as a form of *representation*, representing either past physical events, or past social, economic or symbolic formations (Barrett 2000, 63–5). Each of these viewpoints carries similar difficulties, since each leads us to map the record in terms of causal events. Either we adopt a taphonomic approach that attempts to uncover the physical processes that led to the formation of the traces we observe, or we read the record as if it crystallised past economic or social formations. In the first instance, archaeological scientists are concerned with charting the physical conditions that may be read off from the material traces of the past; in the second instance, interpretative archaeologists are concerned to read material traces as the effects of past social processes.

It is important to realise that the archaeological record is composed of objects and features that both existed in the past and exist for us in the present. As I noted in chapter 4, they may be considered as 'boundary objects' which provide fixed points of reference between the past and the present. At the practical level, the concept of artefacts and their contexts as boundary objects is useful when we are considering how the techniques of science-based archaeologists and interpretative archaeologists are articulated. However, I believe that the notion has wider application if we think of how these practices relate to our conceptualisation of the archaeological record. I think that we need to replace the concept of the record as a representation with the theory of contingency, objectivity and agency developed above. We might consider the material record to be provisionally stable; however, we need to remember that it was created under particular historical conditions.

We may consider past material culture to operate in both the past and the present with multiple levels, or scales, of agency. In the present we can consider it in physical terms – here we might think of the degrees of constraint and enablement conveyed by the physical properties of the object – the characterisation of these material properties using the techniques of materials science and environmental archaeology is critical. Second, given a characterisation of these properties, we may consider both the constraints and the possibilities open to those constructing their lives using those material properties. We are interested here in *how* material culture is used both to create and sustain certain kinds of social relations. Both of these considerations of the agency of material objects are reliant on the relationship between the agency of objects and that of people. On one hand, the observational techniques of scientists, or interpretative archaeologists placing material culture within interpretative frameworks in the present; on the other, the agency of past social groups in relation to the potentialities of the properties of material culture.

This approach to the archaeological record therefore embraces the notion of material culture as a 'boundary object' having physical presence in both the past and the present. However the approach I advocate here is concerned with translating between the dual – past and present – aspects of material culture. It would first examine how the physical nature of the object is structured in terms of its physical or material composition, and then consider how, at a different scale, this structure impacts upon the way in which that object intervened in the lives of people in the past – how the physical properties of that object enabled or constrained past social actions in terms of its physicality. This perspective requires a shift from a view of the archaeological record as a representation of past regularities – physical or social – towards an understanding of the record as traces of the potentialities of past material culture.

The implications of this approach to past material culture can be accommodated at multiple scales of analysis (Pickering 1995, 229–42). As noted above we may consider the potentialities of the material world in relation to our observations and frameworks whether that world is composed of quarks, lead isotopes, oxhide ingots, pots or warplanes. This means that we may apply this understanding to our present analysis of the microstructural and elemental properties of objects, while this approach may also be scaled up to consider the effect of material agency

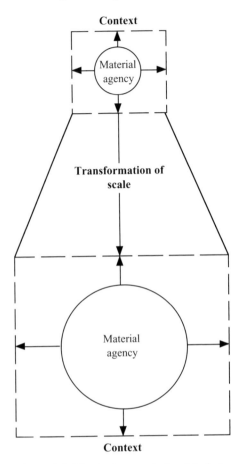

Figure 8.3 The intimate relationship between material agency and its context of influence depends upon the nature and extent of the scale of analysis

on large-scale social formations (see Fig. 8.3). Despite this, it does not mean that we are simply able to shift from one scale of analysis to another, from the microstructural properties of an object, for example, to an understanding of the relationship between material culture and social formations of differing sizes. This is one of the fallacies of approaches such as Social Darwinism, that attempt to understand the operations of society on the basis of the analysis of genetics. Instead we need to be aware that the process of transformation involves a shift from one scale of analysis to another (see Fig. 8.3). Equally we also need to be aware that the material agency of objects operates within different humanly constructed contexts. We might think of contexts in terms of geographic and historical frames of differing dimensions within which to observe the relationship between material agency and human agency. When we move from microscale analysis to macroscale and vice versa, we need to realise that the context of analysis also changes scale, since the parameters of our analysis are framed by context.

Relating to the past

I began this book by exploring the problematic relationship between the knowledge generated by scientific analysis and that generated by analysis in the social sciences. Throughout this book I have noted that attention to practice formed a critical method for shifting the focus of analysis from a priori epistemological distinctions to the active construction of knowledge. Moreover, as we have seen, a practice framework (see Dobres 2000) is of critical importance in the study of how scientific and archaeological practices generate knowledge through interaction with their subject matter. It furthermore allows us to begin to comprehend the relationship between people and the material world, both in the past and in the present. This shift in perspective marks a change from a framework dominated either by the analysis of human agency (social sciences), or by the analysis of the inanimate material world (natural sciences). The framework outlined earlier instead suggests that the agency of the material world and that of the human world can be seen as mutually related. Here it is worth making the point that archaeology, as the study of material culture, whether in the past or present, is centrally placed to play a critical role in the analysis of this relationship.

More important with regard to my central argument in this volume is the point that the elucidation of this relationship is not the sole domain of interpretative archaeology. Rather, since the study of archaeology involves the analysis of the material or physical remains of the past, the combination of the perspectives generated by scientific analysis in tandem with those generated by interpretative perspectives will pave the way to a greater understanding of this analysis. But in what terms should this dialogue take place? The philosopher Richard Rorty (1989) points out that the terms of our discussion tend to differ between those who believe that an accurate representation of the world through language is possible and those who think that the beliefs we state using language are contingent to our particular historical situation. As an alternative, he proposes that we describe our discussions in terms of 'conversation'. Here conversation is conceived as a discussion that is not bound to refer to the existence of objects in the external world, but rather to the relational nature of the terms of our argument (see also Rorty 1980). Moreover it is through conversation that we are able to redescribe the terms by which we come to view the world afresh. According to Rorty (1989), it is this process of redescription that affords practical, social and conceptual change. The present volume has aimed to be equally 'conversational' in its approach. I believe that it is the great strength of archaeology that archaeological practice encompasses both those with scientific and those with interpretative dispositions. I hope that the foregoing discussions equally stimulate conversation between the 'two cultures', from which it is hoped that we may begin a redescription of our practices which allow us to begin to think of ourselves as neither interpretative archaeologists nor science-based archaeologists, but simply as archaeologists.

References

Adams, M. and C. Brooke 1995 Unmanaging the past: truth, data and the human being, *Norwiegan Archaeological Review* 28 (2), 91–104.

Albarella, U. (ed.) forthcoming *Environmental archaeology: meaning and purpose.* British Archaeological Reports, Oxford.

Allen, W. M. and Richardson, J. B. 1971 The reconstruction of kinship from archaeological data: the concepts, the methods and the feasibility, *American Antiquity* 36, 41–53.

Allison, P. 1997 Why do excavation reports have finds catalogues?, in C. G. Cumberpatch and P. W. Blinkhorn (eds.) *Not so much a pot, more a way of life.* Oxbow monograph 83, Oxford, 77–85.

Anderson, S. and K. Boyle 1996 *Ritual treatment of human and animal remains.* Proceedings of the first osteoarchaeological research group. Oxbow, Oxford.

Andrews, K. 1997 From ceramic finishes to modes of production: Iron Age finewares from central France, in C. G. Cumberpatch and P. W. Blinkhorn (eds.) *Not so much a pot, more a way of life.* Oxbow Monograph 83, Oxford, 77–85.

Arnold, D. E. 1971 Ethnomineralogy of Ticul, Yucatan potters: etics and emics, *American Antiquity* 36, 20–40.

    1985 *Ceramic theory and cultural process.* Cambridge University Press, Cambridge.

    1989 Patterns of learning, residence and descent among potters in Ticul, Yucatan, Mexico, in S. Shennan (ed.) *Archaeological approaches to cultural identity.* Routledge, London, 174–84.

Arnold, D. E., H. Neff, R. L. Bishop and M. D. Glascock 1999 Testing interpretative assumptions of Neutron Activation Analysis: contemporary pottery in Yucatan 1964–1994, in E. S. Chilton (ed.) *Material meanings: critical approaches to the interpretation of material culture.* University of Utah Press, Salt Lake City, Utah.

Arnold, D. E., H. Neff and M. D. Glascock 2000 Testing assumptions of Neutron Activation Analysis: communities, workshops and paste preparation in Yucatan, Mexico, *Archaeometry* 42 (2), 1–16.

Arnold, P. J. 1991 *Domestic ceramic production and spatial organization.* Cambridge University Press, Cambridge.

Asad, T. 1986 The concept of cultural translation in British social anthropology, in J. Clifford and G. E. Marcus (eds.) *Writing culture: the poetics and politics of ethnography.* University of California Press, Berkeley, 141–65.

Ashmore, F. and A. B. Knapp 1999 *Archaeologies of landscape*. Blackwell, Oxford.

Aspinall, A., S. W. Feather and A. C. Renfrew 1972 Neutron activation analysis of Aegean obsidians, *Nature* 237, 333–4.

Barber, J. 1988 Isbister, Quanterness and the Point of Cott: the formulation and testing of some middle range theories, in J. C. Barrett and I. Kinnes (eds.) *The archaeology of context in the Neolithic and Bronze Age: recent trends*. Sheffield University Press, Sheffield, 57–62.

Barker, G. 1983 The animal bones, in J. W. Hedges (ed.) *Isbister: a chambered tomb in Orkney*. British Archaeological Reports 115, Oxford, 133–40.

Barley, N. 1995 *Smashing pots: feats of clay from Africa*. British Museum Press, London.

Barrett, J. C. 1980 The pottery of the later Bronze age in lowland England, *Proceedings of the Prehistoric Society* 46, 297–319.

1987a Contextual archaeology, *Antiquity* 61, 468–73.

1987b The Glastonbury Lake Village: models and source criticism, *Archaeological Journal* 144, 409–23.

1990 Archaeology in the Age of Uncertainty, *Scottish Archaeological Review* 7, (1990), 31–7.

1994 *Fragments from antiquity: an archaeology of social life in Britain, 2900–1200 BC*. Blackwell, Oxford.

1995 *Some challenges in contemporary archaeology*. Oxbow lecture 2. Oxbow, Oxford.

2000 A thesis on agency, in M.-A. Dobres, and J. Robb (eds.) *Agency in archaeology*. Routledge, London, 61–9.

Barrett, J. C. and R. Bradley 1991 Introduction, in J. C. Barrett, R. Bradley and M. Hall (eds.) *Papers on the prehistoric archaeology of Cranbourne Chase*. Oxbow Monograph 11, Oxford, 134–201.

Barrett, J. C. and S. Needham 1988 Production, accumulation and exchange: problems in the interpretation of Bronze Age bronze-work, in J. C. Barrett and I. Kinnes (eds.), *The archaeology of context in the Neolithic and Bronze Age: recent trends*. Department of Archaeology and Prehistory, Sheffield University, Sheffield, 127–40.

Barthes, R. 1977 The death of the author, in S. Heath (ed.), *Image-music-text: Roland Barthes selected essays*. Fontana, London, 142–9.

Barkan, E. and R. Bush 1995 *Prehistories of the future; the primitivist project and the culture of modernism*. Stanford University Press, Stanford.

Battaglia, D. 1991 *On the bones of the serpent*. Chicago University Press, Chicago.

Bayley, J. 1998 *Science in archaeology: an agenda for the future*. English Heritage, London.

Bender, B., S. Hamilton and C. Tilley 1997 Leskernick: stone worlds; alternative narratives; nested landscapes, *Proceedings of the Prehistoric Society* 63, 1997, 147–78.

Berger, P. L. and T. Luckmann 1966 *The social construction of reality: a treatise in the sociology of knowledge*. Doubleday, New York.

Bijker, W. E., T. P. Hughes and T. J. Pinch 1987 *The social construction of technological systems: new directions in the sociology and history of technology*. MIT Press, Cambridge, Mass.

Binford, L. R. 1962 Archaeology as anthropology, *American Antiquity* 28, 217–25.

1965 Archaeological systematics and the study of culture process, *American Antiquity*, 31 (2), 203–10.

1978 *Nunamiut ethnoarchaeology*. Academic Press, New York.

1982 Objectivity-explanation-archaeology 1981, in C. Renfrew, M. Rowlands and B. A. Segraves (eds.), *Theory and explanation in archaeology*. Academic Press, New York, 125–39.

1983a Objectivity, explanation, and archaeology 1981, in *Working at archaeology*. Academic Press, New York, 45–57.

1983b *Working at archaeology*. Academic Press, New York.

Binford, L. R. and S. R. Binford 1968 *New perspectives in archaeology*. Aldine, Chicago.

Bintliff, J. 1995 The contribution of an annalistes/structural history approach to archaeology, in J. Bintliff (ed.) *The Annales school and archaeology*. Leicester University Press, Leicester.

Blinkhorn, P. W. and C. G. Cumberpatch 1997 Introduction, in C. G. Cumberpatch and P. W. Blinkhorn (eds.) *Not so much a pot, more a way of life*. Oxbow Monograph 83, Oxford, 77–85.

Bloor, D. 1976 *Knowledge and social imagery*. Routledge and Kegan Paul, London.

Boast, R. 1990 The categorisation and design systematics of British beakers: a re-examination, Ph.D. thesis, Cambridge University.

1998 A small company of actors – a critique of style, *Journal of Material Culture* 2 (2), 173–98.

Boivin, N. 2000 Life rhythms and floor sequences: excavating time in rural Rajasthan and Neolithic Catalhöyuk, *World Archaeology* 31 (3), 367–88.

Bond, J. 1994 Change and continuity in an island system: the palaeoeconomy of Sanday, Orkney. Ph.D. thesis, Bradford University.

Bourdieu, P. 1977 *Outline of a theory of practice*. Cambridge University Press, Cambridge.

1990 *The logic of practice*. Polity Press, Cambridge.

Bradley, R. 1984 *The social foundations of prehistoric Britain*. London, Longman.

1985 *Consumption, change and the archaeological record*. Department of Archaeology Occasional Papers 13, Edinburgh University, Edinburgh.

1987 Against objectivity: an overview, in C. F. Gaffney and V. L. Gaffney (eds.) *Pragmatic archaeology: theory in crisis?* British Archaeological Reports: British Series 167, Oxford, 115–19.

1989 Death and entrances: a contextual analysis of megalithic art, *Current Anthropology* 30, 68–75.

1990 *The passage of arms*. Cambridge University Press, Cambridge.

1993 *Altering the Earth: the origins of monuments in Britain and Continental Europe*. Society of Antiquaries of Scotland Monograph series No. 8, Edinburgh.

1998 What do we want to know? Questions for archaeological science from the Mesolithic to the Iron Age, in J. Bayley (ed.) *Science in archaeology: an agenda for the future*. English Heritage, London, 63–9.

Bradley, R. and R. Chapman 1986 The nature and development of long-distance relations in later Neolithic Britain and Ireland, in C. Renfrew and J. Cherry (eds.) *Peer polity interaction*. Cambridge University Press, Cambridge, 127–36.

Bradley, R. and M. Edmonds 1993 *Interpreting the axe trade*. Cambridge University Press, Cambridge.

Bradley, R. and M. Fulford 1980 Sherd size in the analysis of occupation debris, *Bulletin Institute Archaeology* 17, 85–94.

Bradley, R., P. Meredith, J. Smith and M. Edmonds 1992 Rock physics and the Neolithic axe trade, *Archaeometry* 34 (2), 223–35.

Braudel, F. 1980 *On history*. Weidenfeld and Nicolson, London.

Braun, D. P. 1983 Pots as tools, in A. Keene and J. Moore (eds.) *Archaeological hammers and theories*. Academic Press, New York, 14–67.

Brown, A. 1991 Structured deposition and technological change among the flaked stone artefacts from Cranbourne Chase, in J. C. Barrett, R. Bradley and M. Hall (eds.) *Papers on the prehistoric archaeology of Cranbourne Chase*. Oxbow Monograph 11, Oxford, 101–34.

Budd, P., A. M. Pollard, B. Scaife and R. G. Thomas 1995 Oxhide ingots, recycling, and the Mediterranean metals trade, *Journal of Mediterranean Archaeology* 8, 1–32.

Budd, P., D. Gale, A. M. Pollard, R. G. Thomas and P. A Williams 1992 Evaluating lead isotope data: further observations, *Archaeometry* 35, 241–63.

Budd, P., R. Haggarty, A. M. Pollard, B. Scaife and R. G. Thomas 1996 Rethinking the quest for provenance, *Antiquity* 70, 168–74.

Butler, J. 1990 *Gender trouble: feminism and the subversion of identity*. Routledge, London.

Butler, S. 1995 Post-processual palynology, *Scottish Archaeological Review* 9/10, 15–25.

Callander, J. G. 1931 Notes on (1) certain prehistoric relics from Orkney and (2) Skara Brae: 'its culture and its period', *Proceedings of the Society of Antiquaries of Scotland* 65, 78–114.

Callander, J. G. and W. G. Grant 1935 A long stalled cairn, the Knowe of Yarso, in Rousay, Orkney, *Proceedings of the Society of Antiquaries of Scotland* 69, 325–51.

1936 A stalled chambered cairn, the Knowe of Ramsay, at Hullion, Rousay, Orkney, *Proceedings of the Society of Antiquaries of Scotland* 70, 407–19.

1937 Long stalled cairn at Blackhammer, Rousay, Orkney, *Proceedings of the Society of Antiquaries of Scotland* 7, 1, 297–308.

Callon, M. 1991 Techno-economic networks and irreversibility, in J. Law (ed.) *A sociology of monsters: essays on power, technology and domination*. Routledge, London, 132–65.

Callon, M., J. Law and A. Rip 1986 How to study the force of science, in M. Callon, J. Law and A. Rip (eds.) *Mapping the dynamics of science and technology*. Macmillan Press, London, 3–15.

Carr, C. 1990 Advances in ceramic radiography and analysis: applications and potentials, *Journal of Archaeological Science* 17 (1), 13–35.

Case, H. 1969 Neolithic explanations, *Antiquity* 43, 176–86.

Casey, E. S. 1987 *Remembering: a phenomenological study*. Indiana University Press, Bloomington, Ind.

Chadwick, A. 1998 Archaeology at the edge of chaos: further towards reflexive excavation methodologies, in *Assemblage* at *http://www.shef.ac.uk/~assem/3/*.

Challands, N., A. Cooper, D. Garrow, M. Knight and L. McFadyen 1998 Don't think – dig! Paper given at Theoretical Archaeology Group conference, Birmingham University, Birmingham, 16–18 December 1998.

Chaplin, R. E. 1971 *The study of animal bones from archaeological sites*. Seminar Press, London.

Chapman, J. 2000a Tension at funerals: social practices and the subversion of community structure in later Hungarian prehistory, in M.-A. Dobres and J. Robb (eds.) *Agency in archaeology*. Routledge, London, 169–96.

2000b *Fragmentation in archaeology*. Routledge, London.

Charleson, M. M. 1902 Notice of a chambered cairn in the parish of Firth, Orkney, *Proceedings of the Society of Antiquaries of Scotland* 36, 733–8.

Cherry, J. F. 1978 Questions of efficiency and integration in assemblage sampling, in J. F. Cherry (ed.) *Sampling in contemporary British archaeology* British Archaeological Reports: British Series 50, Oxford, 293–321.

Childe, V. G. 1929 Operations at Skara Brae during 1929, *Proceedings of the Society of Antiquaries of Scotland* 65 (1929–30), 158–91.

1931 *Skara Brae: a Pictish village in Orkney*. Kegan Paul, London.

1949 *Social worlds of knowledge*. Hobhouse memorial lecture. Geoffrey Cumberledge, London.

1956 *Piecing together the past: the interpretation of archaeological data*. Routledge and Kegan Paul, London.

Childe, V. G. and Grant, W. 1939 A Stone Age settlement at the Braes of Rinyo (First Report), *Proceedings of the Society of Antiquaries of Scotland* 73 (1938–9), 6–31.

Childe, V. G. and Paterson, J. W. 1928 Provisional report on the excavations at Skara Brae, and on finds from the 1927 and 1928 campaigns, *Proceedings of the Society of Antiquaries of Scotland* 64, 225–80.

Clarke, A. 1991 The Worked stone assemblage from Barnhouse, unpublished manuscript.

Clarke, D. L. 1973 Archaeology: the loss of innocence, *Antiquity* 47 (185), 6–18.

Clarke, D. V. and Sharples, N. 1990 Settlements and subsistence in the third millennium BC, in C. Renfrew (ed.) *The prehistory of Orkney*. Edinburgh University Press, Edinburgh, 54–82.

Cleal, R. 1991 Cranbourne Chase: the earlier prehistoric pottery, in J. C. Barrett, R. Bradley and M. Hall (eds.) *Papers on the prehistoric archaeology of Cranbourne Chase*. Oxbow Monograph 11, Oxford, 134–201.

1992 Significant form: ceramic styles in the earlier Neolithic of southern England in N. Sharples and A. Sheridan (eds.), *Vessels for the ancestors: essays on the Neolithic of Britain and Ireland*. Edinburgh University Press, Edinburgh, 286–305.

1996 Pottery fabrics in Wessex in the fourth to second millennia BC, in I. Kinnes and G. Varndell (eds.) *'Unbaked urns of rudely shape'*. Oxbow Monograph 55, Oxford, 185–95.

Clifford, J. 1994 *The predicament of culture: twentieth-century ethnography, literature and art*. Harvard University Press, Cambridge, Mass.

Clough, T. H. McK. and W. A. Cummins, 1979 *Stone axe studies.* Council for British Archaeology Report No. 23, London.

Clutton-Brock, J. 1976 Animal remains from the Stones of Stenness, in J. N. G. Ritchie (ed.) The Stones of Stenness, Orkney, *Proceedings of the Society of Antiquaries of Scotland* 107, 1–60.

Connerton, P. 1989 *How societies remember.* Cambridge University Press, Cambridge.

Cooney, G. 1999 *Landscapes of the Irish Neolithic.* Routledge, London.

Cooney, G. and S. Mandal 1998 *The Irish Stone Axe Project: Monograph 1.* Wordwell, Dublin.

Cotterell, B. and J. Kamminga 1990 *Mechanics of pre-industrial technology: an introduction to the mechanics of ancient and traditional materials culture.* Cambridge University Press, Cambridge.

Craddock, P. T. 1995 *Early metal mining and production.* Edinburgh University Press, Edinburgh.

De Boer, W. and D. W. Lathrap 1979 The making and breaking of Shipibo-Conibo ceramics in C. Kramer (ed.) *Ethnoarchaeology.* Academic Press, New York, 102–38.

Deetz, J. 1968 The inference of residence and descent rules from archaeological data in L. R. Binford and S. R. Binford (eds.) *New perspectives in archaeology.* Aldine, Chicago, 41–8.

1977 *In small things forgotten.* Natural History Press, New York.

Deitler, M. 1996 Feasts and commensal politics in the political economy: food, power, and status in Prehistoric Europe, in P. Wiessner and W. Schiefenhovel (eds.) *Food and the status quest.* Berghan, Providence, R. I., 87–125.

Dimbleby, G. W. 1985 *The palynology of archaeological sites.* Academic Press, London.

Dimitriadis, S. and K. Skourtopoulou forthcoming The petrographic examination of chipped stone materials from Sitagroi, in E. Elster and C. Renfrew (eds.) *Excavations at Sitagroi: a prehistoric village in northeastern Greece,* Vol. 2. McDonald Institute, Cambridge.

Dobres, M.-A. 1995 Gender and prehistoric technology: on the social agency of technical strategies, *World Archaeology* 27 (1), 25–49.

2000 *Technology and social agency.* Blackwell, Oxford.

Dobres, M.-A. and C. Hoffman 1994 Social agency and the dynamics of prehistoric technology, *Journal of Archaeological Method and Theory* 1 (3), 211–58.

Dobres, M.-A. and J. Robb 2000 *Agency in archaeology.* Routledge, London.

Douglas, M. 1966 *Purity and danger.* Blackwell, Oxford.

1973 Deciphering a meal, in M. Douglas (ed.) *Rules and meanings.* Routledge and Kegan Paul, London.

1984 Standard social uses of food: introduction, in M. Douglas (ed.) *Food in the social order.* Russell Sage Foundation, New York.

Drewett, P. L. 1999 *Field archaeology: an introduction.* University College London Press, London.

Dudd, S. N., R. P. Evershed and A. M. Gibson 1999 Evidence for varying patterns of exploitation of animal products in different prehistoric pottery traditions based on lipids preserved in surface and absorbed residues, *Journal of Archaeological Science* 26, 1473–82.

Dunnell, R. C. 1993 Why archaeologists don't care about archaeometry, *Archaeomaterials* 7, 161–5.

Eco, U. 1979 *A theory of semiotics*. Indiana University Press, Bloomington, Ind.

Edmonds, M. 1990 Science, technology and society, *Scottish Archaeological Review* 7, 23–31.

1992 'Their use is wholly unknown', in N. Sharples and A. Sheridan (eds.) *Vessels for the ancestors: essays on the Neolithic of Britain and Ireland*. Edinburgh University Press, Edinburgh, 179–93.

1995 *Stone tools and society*. Batsford, London.

Edwardson, A. R. 1965 A spirally decorated object from Garboldisham, *Antiquity* 39, 145.

Elkana, Y. 1981 A programmatic attempt at an anthropology of knowledge in Y. Elkana and E. Mendelsohn (eds.) *Sciences and cultures*. Sociology of the Sciences Yearbook 1981. D. Reidel Publishing Co, Dordrecht.

Embree, L. 1992 *Meta-archaeology*. Kluwer Academic Publishers, Dordrecht.

Endlicher, G. and A. Tillman 1997 Lime plaster as an adhesive for hafting eighteenth-dynasty flint sickles from Tell el Dab'a, eastern Nile Delta (Egypt), *Archaeometry* 39 (2), 333–43.

Eogan, G. 1986 *Knowth and the passage-tombs of Ireland*. Thames and Hudson, London.

Evans, C. 1998 Constructing houses and building context: Bersu's Manx round-house campaign, *Proceedings of the Prehistoric Society* 64, 183–201.

Evans, J. G. and T. P. O'Conner 1999 *Environmental Archaeology: principles and methods*. Sutton publishing, Stroud.

Evershed, R. P., C. Heron, and L. J. Goad 1990 Analysis of organic residues of archaeological origin by high-temperature gas chromatography and gas chromatography-mass spectrometry, *Analyst* 115, 1339–42.

Evershed, R. P., C. Heron, S. Charters and L. J. Goad 1992 The survival of food residues: new methods of analysis, interpretation and application, in A. M. Pollard (ed.) *New developments in archaeological science*. Proceedings of the British Academy 77. Oxford University Press, Oxford, 187–208.

Fabian, J. 1983 *Time and the other: how anthropology makes its object*. Columbia University Press, New York.

1991 *Time and the work of anthropology: critical essays 1971–1991*. Harwood, Reading.

Fahnestock, J. 1999 *Rhetorical figures in science*. Oxford University Press, Oxford.

Falk, P. 1994 *The consuming body*. Sage, London.

Feyerabend, P. 1975 *Against method*. Verso, London.

Foster, G. M. 1960 Life expectancy of utilitarian pottery in Tzintzuntzan, Michoacan, Mexico, *American Antiquity* 26, 205–14.

Fotiadis, M. 1994 What is archaeology's 'mitigated objectivism' mitigated by? Comments on Wylie, *American Antiquity* 59, 545–55.

Franklin, S. 1995 Science as culture, cultures of science, *Annual Review of Anthropology* 24, 163–84.

1997 *Embodied progress: a cultural account of assisted conception*. Routledge, London.

Friedman, J. 1994 *Consumption and identity.* Harwood Academic Publishers, Switzerland.

Friedrich, M. 1970 Design structure and social interaction: archaeological implications of an ethnographic analysis, *American Antiquity* 35 (1970), 332–43.

Gale, N. H. 1981 Mediterranean obsidian source characterisation by strontium isotope analysis, *Archaeometry* 23, 41–52.

Gale, N. H. and Z. A. Stos-Gale 1987 Oxhide ingots from Sardinia, Crete and Cyprus and the Bronze Age copper trade: new scientific evidence, in M. S. Balmuth (ed.) *Studies in Sardinian archaeology 3: Nuragic Sardinia and the Mycenean World.* British Archaeological Reports: International Series 387, Oxford, 135–78.

1992 Lead isotope studies in the Aegean (the British Academy Project), in A. M. Pollard (ed.) *New developments in archaeological science.* Proceedings of the British Academy 77. Oxford University Press, Oxford, 63–108.

Geertz, C. 1973 Thick description: towards an interpretative theory of culture, in C. Geertz (ed.) *The interpretation of cultures.* Fontana Press, London, 3–33.

1983 From the native's point of view: on the nature of anthropological understanding, in C. Geertz (ed.) *Local knowledge: further essays in interpretative anthropology.* Fontana Press, London, 55–73.

Gellner, E. 1982 What is structuralisme? in C. Renfrew, M. J. Rowlands and B. A. Segraves (eds.) *Theory and explanation in archaeology.* Academic Press, New York, 97–125.

Gell, A. 1998 *Art and agency: an anthropological theory.* Oxford University Press, Oxford.

1999 Strathernograms, or the semiotics of mixed metaphors, in E. Hirsch (ed.) *The art of anthropology.* London School of Economics Monographs on Social Anthropology 67. Athlone Press, London, 29–75.

Giddens, A. 1984 *The constitution of society: outline of a theory of structuration.* Polity Press, Cambridge.

Gilchrist, R. 2000 Archaeological biographies: realizing human lifecycles, -courses and -histories, *World Archaeology* 31 (3), 325–8.

Ginzburg, C. 1982 *The cheese and the worms: the cosmos of a sixteenth-century miller.* Penguin Press, London.

Gosden, C. 1994 *Social being and time.* Blackwell, Oxford.

1999 *Anthropology and archaeology: a changing relationship.* Routledge, London.

Gosden, C. and Y. Marshall 1999 The cultural biography of objects, *World Archaeology* 31 (2), 169–78.

Gosselain, O. 1999 In pots we trust: the processing of clay and symbols in Sub-Saharan Africa, *Journal of Material Culture* 4 (2), 205–31.

Gould, R. A. 1980 *Living archaeology.* Cambridge University Press, Cambridge.

Gow, P. 1995 Land, people and paper in Western Amazonia, in E. Hirsch and M. O'Hanlon (eds.) *The anthropology of landscape: perspectives on place and space.* Oxford University Press, Oxford, 43–63.

Gross, P. and N. Levitt 1994 *Higher superstition: the academic left and its quarrels with science.* Johns Hopkins University Press, Baltimore, Md.

Hacking, I. 1982 Language, truth and reason, in M. Hollis and S. Lukes (eds.) *Rationality and relativism.* Blackwell, Oxford, 48–67.

Hally, D. J. 1983 Use alteration of pottery vessel surfaces: an important source of evidence for the identification of vessel function, *North American Archaeology* 4 (1), 3–26.

Hamilton, E. 1991 Metallurgical analysis and the Bronze Age of Bohemia: or, are cultural alloys real?, *Archaeomaterials* 5, 75–89.

Haraway, D. 1989 *Primate visions: gender, race and nature in the world of modern science*. Routledge, London.

1991 *Simians, cyborgs and women: the reinvention of nature*. Routledge, London.

1997 *Modest_Witness @Second_Millenium.FemaleMan © _Meets_ OncoMouse^{TM}*. Routledge, London.

Harding, S. 1991 *Whose science? Whose knowledge? Thinking from women's lives*. Cornell University Press, Ithaca, N. Y.

Harris, E. C., M. R. Brown and G. J. Brown 1993 *Principles of archaeological stratigraphy*, second edition. Academic Press, London.

Hastorf, C. A. 1991 Gender, space and food in prehistory, in J. M. Gero and M. W. Conkey (eds.) *Engendering archaeology: women and prehistory*. Blackwell, Oxford, 132–59.

Hawkes, C. 1954 Archaeological theory and method: some suggestions from the Old World, *American Anthropologist* 56, 155–68.

Hayden, B. 1990 Nimrods, piscators, pluckers, and planters: the emergence of food production, *Journal of Anthropological Archaeology* 9, 31–69.

1996 Feasting in prehistoric Europe, in P. Wiessner and W. Schiefenhovel (eds.) *Food and the status quest*. Berghan, Providence, R. I., 127–49.

Hedges, J. 1984 *The tomb of the eagles*. John Murray, London.

Hempel, C. G. 1965 *Aspects of scientific explanation and other essays in the philosophy of science*. Free Press, New York.

Henshall, A. S. 1979 Artefacts from the Quanterness cairn, in C. Renfrew (ed.) *Investigations in Orkney*. Society of Antiquaries of London Monograph 38. London, 79–96.

Henshall, A. S. and L. Savory 1976 Small finds from the 1973–4 excavations, in J. N. G. Ritchie (ed.) The Stones of Stenness, Orkney, *Proceedings of the Society of Antiquaries of Scotland* 107, 1–60.

Herbert, E. 1993 *Iron, gender and power*. Indiana University Press, Bloomington, Ind.

Hesse, B. 1995 Husbandry, dietary taboos and the bones of the ancient Near East: zooarchaeology in the post-processual world, in D. B. Small (ed.) *Methods in the Mediterranean: historical and anthropological views on texts and archaeology*. Brill, Leiden, 197–232.

Higgs, E. 1975 *Paleoeconomy*. Cambridge University Press, Cambridge.

Higgs, E. and M. R. Jarman 1975 Paleoeconomy, in E. Higgs (ed.) *Paleoeconomy*. Cambridge University Press, Cambridge, 1–8.

Hill, J. 1970 *Broken K Peublo: prehistoric social organization in the American Southwest*. Anthropological papers of the University of Arizona 18. University of Arizona Press, Tucson, Ariz.

Hill, J. D. 1995 *Ritual and rubbish in the Iron Age of Wessex: a study in the formation of a specific archaeological record*. British Archaeological Reports: British Series 242, Oxford.

Hingley, R. 1996 Ancestors and identity in the later prehistory of Atlantic Scotland: the reuse and reinvention of Neolithic monuments and material culture, *World Archaeology* 28, 231–43.

Hinton, P. 1995 Plant macrofossil report from Barnhouse Orkney, unpublished manuscript.

Hodder, I. 1982a *Symbolic and structural archaeology*. Cambridge University Press, Cambridge.

1982b Toward a contextual approach to prehistoric exchange, in J. E. Ericson and T. K. Earle (eds.) *Contexts for prehistoric exchange*. Academic Press, New York, 199–209.

1982c Sequences of structural change in the Dutch Neolithic, in I. Hodder (ed.) *Symbolic and structural archaeology*. Cambridge University Press, Cambridge, 162–79.

1982d *Symbols in action*. Cambridge University Press, Cambridge.

1986 *Reading the past*. Cambridge University Press, Cambridge.

1989 Writing archaeology: site reports in context, *Antiquity* 63, 268–74.

1990 *The domestication of Europe*. Blackwell, Oxford.

1992 *Theory and practice in archaeology*. Routledge, London.

1996 *On the surface: Catalhöyuk 1993–95*. McDonald Institute Monographs, Cambridge.

1999 *The archaeological process: an introduction*. Routledge, London.

Hoffman, C. 1999 Intentional damage as technological agency: breaking metals in Late Prehistoric Mallorca, Spain, in M.-A. Dobres and C. Hoffman (eds.) *The social dynamics of technology: practice, politics and world views*. Smithsonian Institution Press, Washington, DC, 103–24.

Hollis, M. 1982 The social destruction of reality, in M. Hollis and S. Lukes (eds.) *Rationality and relativism*. Blackwell, Oxford, 67–87.

Hoskins, J. 1998 *Biographical objects*. Routledge, London.

Hosler, D. 1993 *The sound and colour of power: the sacred metallurgical technology of Ancient West Mexico*. MIT Press, Cambridge, Mass.

Howard, H. 1981 In the wake of distribution: towards an integrated approach to ceramic studies in prehistoric Britain in H. Howard and E. Morris (eds.) *Production and distribution: a ceramic viewpoint*. British Archaeological Reports: British series. 120, Oxford, 1–53.

Hughes, M. J., M. R. Cowell and D. R. Hook 1991 *Neutron activation and plasma emission spectrometric analysis in archaeology*. British Museum occasional paper 82, British Museum Press, London.

Hughes, R. E. 1994 Intrasource chemical variability of artefact-quality obsidians from the Casa Diablo area, California, *Journal of Archaeological Science* 21, 263–71.

Hughes, T. P. 1983 *Networks of power*. Johns Hopkins University Press, Baltimore, Md.

Hunter, J. and A. MacSween 1991 A sequence for the Orcadian Neolithic, *Antiquity* 65, 911–14.

Ingold, T. 1993 The temporality of landscape, *World Archaeology* 25 (2), 152–74.

1996 Human worlds are culturally constructed 'against the motion', in T. Ingold (ed.) *Key debates in anthropology*. Routledge, London, 112–18.

Jarman, M., G. Bailey, and H. Jarman 1982 *Early European agriculture*. Cambridge University Press, Cambridge.

Joel, E.C., J. J. Taylor, R. A. Ixer, and M. Goodway 1995 Lead isotope analysis and the Great Orme mine, in A. Sinclair, E. Slater and J. Gowlett (eds.) *Archaeological sciences 1995: proceedings of a conference on the application of scientific techniques to the study of archaeology*. Oxbow Monograph 64, Oxford, 123–32.

Johnson, M. 1989 Conceptions of agency in archaeological interpretation, *Journal of Anthropological Archaeology* 8 (2), 189–211.

1993 Notes towards an archaeology of capitalism, in C. Tilley (ed.) *Interpretative archaeology*. Berg, Oxford, 327–56.

1996 *An archaeology of capitalism*. Blackwell, Oxford.

Jones, A. 1996 Food for thought: material culture and the transformation in food use from the Mesolithic to Neolithic, in T. Pollard and A. Morrison (eds.) *The early prehistory of Scotland*. Edinburgh University Press, Edinburgh, 291–301.

1997 A biography of ceramics: food and culture in Late Neolithic Orkney, Ph.D. thesis. Glasgow University, Glasgow.

1998 Where eagles dare: landscape, animals and the Neolithic of Orkney, *Journal of Material Culture* 3 (3), 301–24.

1999 The world on a plate: ceramics, food technology and cosmology in Neolithic Orkney, *World Archaeology* 31 (1), 55–78.

2000 Life after death: monuments, material culture and social change in Neolithic Orkney, in A. Ritchie (ed.) *Neolithic Orkney in its European Context*. McDonald Institute Monographs, Cambridge, 127–38.

forthcoming (a) Relics of life and memorials of the dead: natural histories and social identities in Neolithic Orkney in J. C. Barrett and B. Boyd (eds.) *Making landscape: beyond the nature/culture dichotomy*. Blackwell, Oxford.

forthcoming (b) Polished performances: transforming stone, clay and people in the Neolithic of Northern Scotland in B. Boyd and B. Sillar (eds.) *Embedded technologies*. Routledge, London.

Jones, A., R. E. Jones and J. Coles forthcoming The results of residue analysis using GC/MS on the Barnhouse Grooved ware assemblage, in C. Richards (ed.) *Dwelling amongst the monuments: excavations at Barnhouse and Maes Howe, Orkney*. McDonald Institute Monographs, Cambridge.

Jones, M. K. 1992 Food remains, food webs and ecosystems, in A. M. Pollard (ed.) *New developments in archaeological science*. Oxford University Press, Oxford, 209–23.

Jones, R. E. 1986 Identification of materials carried by ceramic vessels, in R. E. Jones, (ed.) *Greek and Cypriot pottery: a review of scientific studies*. British School at Athens Fitch Laboratory Occasional Paper No. 1, Athens, Greece, 839–47.

Jones, S. 1997 *The archaeology of ethnicity: constructing identities in the past and present*. Routledge, London.

Kelly, J. H. and Hanen, M. P. 1988 *Archaeology and the methodology of science*. University of New Mexico Press, Alberquerque, N. M.

Killick, D. 1996 Optical and electron microscopy in material culture studies, in D. Kingery (ed.) *Learning from things: method and theory of material culture studies*. Smithsonian Institution Press, Washington, DC, 204–31.

1996 Materials science and material culture, in D. Kingery (ed.) *Learning from things: method and theory of material culture studies.* Smithsonian Institution Press, Washington, DC, 181–204.

Kinnes, I. and I. Longworth 1985 *Catalogue of the excavated Prehistoric and Romano-British material in the Greenwell collection.* British Museum Press, London.

Knapp, A. B. 1992 Archaeology and annales: time, space and change, in A. B. Knapp (ed.) *Archaeology, annales and ethnohistory.* Cambridge University Press, Cambridge.

2000 Archaeology, science-based archaeology and the Mediterranean Bronze Age metals trade, *European Journal of Archaeology* 3 (1), 31–57.

Knorr-Certina, K. D. 1981 *The manufacture of knowledge.* Pergamon Press, London.

1999 *Epistemic cultures.* Harvard University Press, London and Cambridge, Mass.

Kohl, P. L. 1993 Limits to a post-processual archaeology (or, the dangers of a new scholasticism) in N. Yoffee and A. Sherratt (eds.) *Archaeological theory: who sets the agenda?* New Directions in Archaeology Series. Cambridge University Press, Cambridge, 13–20.

Kovacik, J. P. 2000 A faunal perspective on the spatial structuring of Anasazi everyday life in Chaco Canyon, New Mexico, U.S.A., in P. Rowley-Conwy (ed.) *Animal bones, human societies.* Oxbow, Oxford, 133–45.

Kuhn, T. 1970 *The structure of scientific revolutions.* Chicago University Press, Chicago.

Lakoff, G. 1987 *Women, fire and dangerous things: what categories reveal about the mind.* Chicago University Press, Chicago.

Lakoff, G. and Johnson, M. 1980 *Metaphors we live by.* Chicago University Press, Chicago.

Latour, B. 1987 *Science in action: how to follow scientists and engineers through society.* Open University Press, Milton Keynes.

1991 Technology is society made durable, in J. Law (ed.) *A sociology of monsters: essays on power, technology and domination.* Routledge, London, 103–31.

1993 *We have never been modern.* Harvard University Press, Cambridge, Mass.

1999 *Pandora's hope: essays on the reality of science studies.* Harvard University Press, Cambridge, Mass.

Latour, B. and S. Woolgar 1986 *Laboratory life: the construction of scientific facts.* Princeton University Press, Princeton, N. J.

Lavell, C. 1981 Publication: an obligation, *Archaeological Journal* 138, 91–119.

Leach, E. 1973 Concluding address, in C. Renfrew (ed.) *The explanation of culture change.* Duckworth, London, 761–71.

Leavis, F. R. 1962 *Two cultures? The significance of C. P. Snow.* Chatto and Windus, London.

Lechtman, H. 1984 Andean value systems and the development of metallurgy, *Technology and Culture* 25 (1), 1–36.

Legge, A. J. 1978 Archaeozoology or zooarchaeology, in D. R. Brothwell, K. D. Thomas and J. Clutton-Brock (eds.) *Research problems in zooarchaeology.*

University of London Institute of Archaeology occasional publications No. 3, London, 129–32.

Legge, T., S. Payne and P. Rowley-Conwy 1998 The study of food remains from prehistoric Britain, in J. Bayley (ed.) *Science in archaeology: an agenda for the future.* English Heritage, London, 89–95.

Lemonnier, P. 1992 *Elements for an anthropology of technology.* Anthropological Papers No. 88, Museum of Anthropology, University of Michigan, Ann Arbor, Mich.

1993 Introduction, in P. Lemonnier (ed.) *Technological choices: transformation in material culture since the Neolithic.* Routledge, London.

Lenoir, T. 1998 *Inscribing science: scientific texts and the materiality of communication.* Stanford University Press, Stanford, Calif.

Lévi-Strauss, C. 1966 *The savage mind.* Wiedenfeld and Nicholson, London.

1970 *The raw and the cooked: an introduction to a science of mythology.* Pimlico, London.

Lindauer, O. 1992 Ceramic conjoinability: orphan sherds and reconstructing time, in J. L. Hofman and J. G. Enloe (eds.) *Piecing together the past: applications of refitting studies in archaeology.* British Archaeological Reports: International Series 578, Oxford, 210–16.

Little, B. 1994 Consider the hermaphroditic mind: comment on 'the interplay of evidential constraints and political interests: recent archaeological research on gender', *American Antiquity* 59, 539–44.

Lock, G. and Z. Stancic 1995 *Archaeology and geographical information systems.* Taylor and Francis, London.

Longacre, W. 1981 Kalinga pottery: an ethnoarchaeological study, in I. Hodder, G. Isaac and F. Hammond (eds.) *Patterns of the past: studies in honour of David Clarke.* Cambridge University Press, Cambridge, 49–66.

1985 Pottery use-life amongst the Kalinga, northern Luzon, the Philippines, in B. Nelson (ed.) *Decoding prehistoric ceramics.* Southern Illinois University Press, Carbondale, Ill., 334–46.

Longino, H. E. 1990 *Science as social knowledge.* Princeton University Press, Princeton, N. J.

Lovell, N. 1998 Introduction in N. Lovell (ed.) *Locality and belonging.* Routledge, London.

Lynch, A. 1983 The seed remains in J. W. Hedges *Isbister: a chambered tomb in Orkney.* British Archaeological Reports: British Series 115, Oxford, 171–5.

Mackenzie, M. A. 1991 *Androgynous objects: string bags and gender in central New Guinea.* Harwood, Reading.

Mandal, S. 1997 Striking the balance: the roles of petrography and geochemistry in stone axe studies in Ireland, *Archaeometry* 39 (2), 289–309.

Marciniak, A. 1999 Faunal materials and interpretative archaeology – epistemology reconsidered, *Journal of Archaeological Method and Theory* 6 (4), 293–320.

Marshall, D. 1977 Carved stone balls, *Proceedings of the Society of Antiquaries of Scotland* 108 (1976–7), 40–72.

Martin, E. 1990 The end of the body?, *American Ethnologist* (1990), 121–37.

Mason, R. B. and M. S. Tite 1997 The beginning of tin opacification of pottery glazes, *Archaeometry* 39 (1), 41–59.

Matson, F. R. 1965 Ceramic ecology: an approach to the early cultures of the Near East, in F. R. Matson (ed.), *Ceramics and man*. Aldine, Chicago, 202–17.

Mauss, M. 1925 *The gift: forms and functions of exchange in archaic societies*. Routledge and Kegan Paul, Oxford.

1950 [1936] Les techniques du corps, in *Sociologie at anthropologie*. Presses Universitaires France, Paris.

McNairn, B. 1980 *The method and theory of Gordon Childe*. Edinburgh University Press, Edinburgh.

Meadows, K. 1997 Much ado about nothing: the social context of eating and drinking in early Roman Britain, in C. G. Cumberpatch and P. W. Blinkhorn (eds.) *Not so much a pot, more a way of life*. Oxbow Monograph 83, Oxford, 21–37.

Meillasoux, C. 1972 From reproduction to production, *Economy and Society* 1, 93–105.

Middleton, R. 1994 Flint report from Barnhouse, unpublished manuscript.

Middleton, A. and I. Freestone 1991 *Recent developments in ceramic petrology*. British Museum Occasional Paper No. 81, British Museum Press, London.

Miller, D. 1982 Explanation and social theory in archaeological practice, in C. Renfrew, M. J. Rowlands and B. A. Segraves (eds.), *Theory and explanation in archaeology*. Academic Press, New York, 83–97.

1985 *Artefacts as categories: a study of ceramic variability in central India*. Cambridge University Press, Cambridge.

1987 *Material culture and mass consumption*. Blackwell, Oxford.

1995 Consumption as the vanguard of history: a polemic by way of an introduction, in D. Miller (ed.) *Acknowledging consumption: a review of new studies*. Routledge, London.

Moore, H. 1982 The interpretation of spatial patterning in settlement residue, in I. Hodder (ed.) *Symbolic and structural archaeology*, Cambridge University Press, Cambridge, 74–9.

1986 *Space, text and gender*. Cambridge University Press, Cambridge.

Munn, N. 1986 *The fame of gawa: a symbolic study of value transformation in a Massim (Papua New Guinea) society*. Cambridge University Press, Cambridge.

Mykura, W. 1976 *British regional geology: Orkney and Shetland*. HMSO, Edinburgh.

Neff, H. 1992 *Chemical characterization of ceramic pastes in archaeology*. Prehistory Press Monograph Series No. 7, Madison, Wis.

Nelson, B. A. 1991 Ceramic frequency and use-life, in W. Longacre (ed.) *Ceramic ethnoarchaeology*. University of Arizona Press, Tucson, Ariz., 49–60.

Noddle, B. 1983 Animal bone from Knap of Howar, in A. Ritchie (ed.) Excavation of a Neolithic farmstead at Knap of Howar, Papa Westray, Orkney *Proceedings of the Society of Antiquaries of Scotland* 113, 40–121.

n.d. The animal bones from Skara Brae, manuscript.

Orlove, B. S. 1994 Beyond consumption: meat, sociality, vitality and hierarchy in nineteenth-century Chile, in J. Friedman (ed.) *Consumption and identity*. Harwood Academic Publishers, Switzerland, 119–47.

O'Brien, W. 1994 *The Mount Gabriel project*. Department of Archaeology, Galway, Bronze Age studies Vol. 1. Galway University Press, Galway.

1998 Approaches to the study of metals in the insular Bronze Age, in J. Bayley (ed.) *Science in archaeology: an agenda for the future*. English Heritage, London, 109–23.

1999 *Sacred ground*. Department of Archaeology, Galway, Bronze Age studies Vol. 4. Galway University Press, Galway.

O'Conner, T. 1991 Science, evidential archaeology, and the new scholasticism, *Scottish Archaeological Review* 8, 1–7.

Patrik, L. E. 1985 Is there an archaeological record? *Advances in Archaeological Method and Theory* 8, 27–57.

Peacock, D. P. 1969 Neolithic pottery production in Cornwall, *Antiquity*, 139, 145–9.

Pfaffenberger, B. 1988 Fetishised objects and humanised nature: towards an anthropology of technology, *Man* (NS) 23, 236–52.

1992 Social anthropology of technology, *Annual Review of Anthropology* 1992, 491–516.

1999 Worlds in the making: technological activities and the construction of intersubjective meaning, in M.-A. Dobres and C. Hoffman (eds.) *The social dynamics of technology: practice, politics and world views*. Smithsonian Institution Press, Washington, DC, 147–67.

Pickering, A. 1995 *The mangle of practice: time, agency and science*. Chicago University Press, Chicago.

Piggott, S. 1954 *The Neolithic cultures of the British Isles*. Cambridge University Press, Cambridge.

Plog, S. 1980 *Stylistic variation in prehistoric ceramics*. Cambridge University Press, Cambridge.

Pluciennik, M. 1999 Archaeological narratives and other ways of telling, *Current Anthropology* 40 (5), 653–78.

Pollard, A. M. and C. Heron 1996 *Archaeological chemistry*. Royal Society of Chemistry Paperbacks, Cambridge.

Pollard, J. 1992 The Sanctuary, Overton Hill, Wiltshire: a re-examination, *Proceedings of the Prehistoric Society* 58, 1992, 213–26.

1995 Structured deposition at Woodhenge, *Proceedings of the Prehistoric Society* 61, 137–56.

Prown, J. D. 1996 Material/Culture: can the farmer and the cowman still be friends? in D. Kingery (ed.) *Learning from things: method and theory of material culture studies*. Smithsonian Institution Press, Washington, DC, 19–31.

Putnam, H. 1975 *Mind, language and reality: philosophical papers*, Vol. 2. Cambridge University Press, Cambridge.

Quine, W. V. O. 1966 *The ways of paradox and other essays*. Random House, New York.

Rackham, J. 1987 Practicality and realism in archaeozoological analysis and interpretation, in C. F. Gaffney and V. L. Gaffney (eds.) *Pragmatic archaeology: theory in crisis?* British Archaeological Reports: British Series 167, Oxford, 47–67.

Renfrew, C. 1982 Explanation revisited, in C. Renfrew, M. Rowlands and B. A. Segraves (eds.) *Theory and explanation in archaeology*. Academic Press, New York, 5–22.

1979 *Investigations in Orkney*. Society of Antiquaries Monograph 38, London.
1982 Interfacing problems in archaeological science, in J. S. Olin (ed.) *Future directions in archaeometry*. Smithsonian Institution Press, Washington, DC.
1984 *Approaches to social archaeology*. Edinburgh University Press, Edinburgh.
1992 Meeting summary: the identity and future of archaeological science, in A. M. Pollard (ed.) *New developments in archaeological science*. Oxford University Press, Oxford, 285–95.
Renfrew, C., J. R. Cann and J. E. Dixon 1966 Obsidian and early culture contact in the Near East, *Proceedings of the Prehistoric Society* 32, 30–72.
Renfrew, C. and S. Shennan 1982 *Ranking, resource and exchange*. Cambridge University Press, Cambridge.
Renouf, P. 2000 Symbolism and subsistence: seals and caribou at Port au Choix, northwestern Newfoundland, in P. Rowley-Conwy (ed.) *Animal bones, human societies*. Oxbow, Oxford, 65–74.
Reyna, S. P. 1995 Literary anthropology and the case against science, *Man* (NS) 29, 555–81.
Rice, P. 1987 *Pottery analysis: a sourcebook*. Chicago University Press, Chicago.
1996 Recent ceramic analysis 1. Function, style and origins, *Journal of Archaeological Research* 4 (2), 133–63.
Ricoeur, P. 1976 *Interpretation theory: discourse and the surplus of meaning*. Texas Christian University Press, Fort Worth, Texas.
1981 *Hermeneutics and the human sciences*, Vol. 1. Cambridge University Press, Cambridge.
Richards, C. C. 1990a Postscript: the Late Neolithic settlement complex at Barnhouse Farm, Stenness, in C. Renfrew (ed.) *The prehistory of Orkney*. Edinburgh University Press, Edinburgh, 305–16.
1990b The Late Neolithic house, in R. Samson (ed.) *The social archaeology of houses*. Edinburgh University Press, Edinburgh, 78–91.
1993a Monumental choreography: architecture and spatial representation in Late Neolithic Orkney, in C. Tilley (ed.) *Interpretative archaeology*. Berg, Oxford, 143–78.
1993b An archaeological study of Neolithic Orkney: architecture, order and social classification, Ph.D. thesis, Glasgow University.
1995 Knowing about the past, in I. Hodder, M. Shanks, A. Alexandri, V. Buchli, J. Carman, J. Last and G. Lucas (eds.) *Interpreting archaeology: finding meaning in the past*. Routledge, London, 216–19.
1996 Monuments as landscape: creating the centre of the world in Late Neolithic Orkney, *World Archaeology* 28, 190–208.
1998 Centralising tendencies? A re-examination of social evolution in Late Neolithic Orkney, in M. Edmonds and C. Richards (eds.) *Understanding the Neolithic of North-western Europe*. Cruithne Press, Glasgow.
forthcoming *Dwelling amongst the monuments: excavations at Barnhouse and Maes Howe, Orkney*, McDonald Institute Monographs, Cambridge.
n.d. Report on the Neolithic butchery site at Skaill Bay, Mainland, Orkney, manuscript.
Richards, C. C. and J. S. Thomas 1984 Ritual activity and structured deposition in later Neolithic Wessex, in R. Bradley and J. Gardiner (eds.)

Neolithic studies, British Archaeological Reports: British Series 133, Oxford, 189–218.

Richards, M. P. and R. E. M. Hedges 1999 A Neolithic revolution? New evidence of diet in the British Neolithic, *Antiquity* 73 (282), 891–7.

Richards, P. 1996 Human worlds are culturally constructed 'against the motion', in T. Ingold (ed.) *Key debates in anthropology*. Routledge, London, 112–18.

Ritchie, A. 1983 Excavation of a Neolithic farmstead at Knap of Howar, Papa Westray, Orkney, *Proceedings of the Society of Antiquaries of Scotland* 113 (1983), 40–121.

Ritchie, J. N. G. 1976 The Stones of Stenness, Orkney, *Proceedings of the Society of Antiquaries of Scotland* 107, 1–60.

Rorty, R. 1980 *Philosophy and the mirror of nature*. Blackwell, Oxford.

1989 *Contingency, irony and solidarity*. Cambridge University Press, Cambridge.

1991 *Objectivity, relativism and truth: philosophical papers*, Vol. 1. Cambridge University Press, Cambridge.

Rowley-Conwy, P. 2000 Animal bones and the reconstruction of past human societies, in P. Rowley-Conwy (ed.) *Animal bones, human societies*. Oxbow, Oxford, ix–x.

Rye, O. S. 1981 *Pottery technology: principles and reconstruction*. Smithsonian Institution Press, Washington, DC.

Sahlins, M. 1972 *Stone age economics*. Aldine-Atherton, Chicago.

Sahlins, M. and E. Service 1960 *Evolution and culture*. University of Michigan Press, Ann Arbor, Mich.

Samuel, D. 1999 Bread making and social interactions at the Amarna Workmen's village, Egypt, *World Archaeology* 31 (1), 121–44.

Saunders, N. 1999 Biographies of brilliance: pearls, transformations of matter and being *c*.AD 1492, *World Archaeology* 31 (2), 243–57.

Saussure, F. de 1966 [1916] *Course in general linguistics*. Duckworth, London.

Schiffer, M. 1976 *Behavioural archaeology*. Academic Press, New York.

1988 The effects of surface treatment on permeability and evaporative cooling effectiveness, in R. M. Farquhar, R. G. V. Hancock and L. A. Pavlish (eds.) *Proceedings of the 26th International Archaeometry Symposium*. Academic Press, Toronto, 12–31.

Schiffer, M. and J. Skibo 1987 Theory and experiment in the study of technological change, *Current Anthropology* 28 (5), 592–622.

Schmidt, P. R. 1996 Cultural representations in African iron production, in P. R. Schmidt (ed.) *The culture and technology of African iron working*. University of Florida Press, Gainesville, Fla., 1–28.

1997 *Iron technology in East Africa: symbolism, science, and archaeology*. Indiana University Press, Bloomington, Ind.

Serjeantson, D. 2000 Good to eat and good to think with: classifying animals from complex sites, in P. Rowley-Conwy (ed.) *Animal bones, human societies*. Oxbow, Oxford, 179–89.

Shanks, M. and C. Tilley 1987 *Reconstructing archaeology*. Cambridge University Press, Cambridge.

Sharples, N. 1984 Excavations at Pierowall Quarry, Westray, Orkney, *Proceedings of the Society of Antiquaries of Scotland* 114, 75–125.

Shee-Twohig, E. 1981 *The Megalithic art of Western Europe*. Clarendon Press, Oxford.

Sheridan, A. 1985 The role of exchange studies in 'Social Archaeology', with special reference to the prehistory of Ireland from the fourth to the early second millennium BC, Ph.D. thesis, Cambridge University.

1991 Pottery production in Neolithic and Early Bronze Age Ireland: A petrological and chemical study, in I. C. Freestone and A. Middleton (eds.), *Recent developments in ceramic petrology*. British Museum Occasional Papers No. 81, British Museum Press, London, 306–36.

Sherratt, A. 1990 The genesis of megaliths: ethnicity and social complexity in Neolithic northwest Europe, *World Archaeology* 22, 147–67.

Sillar, B. and Tite, M. 2000 The challenge of 'technological choices' for materials science approaches in archaeology, *Archaeometry* 42 (1), 2–20.

Simpson, D. D. A. 1996 'Crown' antler maceheads and the later Neolithic, *Proceedings of the Prehistoric Society* 62, 293–311.

Skibo, J. M. 1993 *Pottery function: a use-alteration perspective*. Plenum Press, New York.

Snow, C. P. 1959 *The two cultures and the scientific revolution*. Cambridge University Press, Cambridge.

Sofaer-Derevenski, J. 2000 Rings of life: the role of early metalworking in mediating the gendered life course, *World Archaeology* 31 (3), 389–406.

forthcoming Is human osteoarchaeology environmental archaeology?, in U. Albarella (ed.) *Environmental archaeology: meaning and purpose*. British Archaeological Reports, Oxford.

Sokal, A. and J. Bricmont 1998 *Intellectual impostures: postmodern philosophers' abuse of science*. Profile Books, London.

Sperber, D. 1982 Apparently irrational beliefs, in M. Hollis and S. Lukes (eds.) *Rationality and relativism*. Blackwell, Oxford, 149–81.

Star, S. L. and J. R. Greisemer 1989 Institutional ecology, 'translation', and boundary objects: amateurs and professionals in Berkeley's Museum of Vertebrate Zoology, 1909–1939, *Social studies of science* 19, 387–420.

Sterner, J. 1989 Who is signalling whom? Ceramic style, ethnicity and taphonomy among the Sirak Bulahay, *Antiquity* 63, 451–9.

Stocking, G. 1996 *After Tylor*. Athlone, London.

Strathern, M. 1988 *The gender of the gift*. University of California Press, Berkeley.

1991 *Partial connections*. Manchester University Press, Manchester.

1992 *Reproducing the future: essays on anthropology, kinship and the new reproductive technologies*. Manchester University Press, Manchester.

1993 The nice thing about culture is that everybody has it, in M. Strathern (ed.) *Shifting contexts*. Routledge, London.

1998 Social relations and the idea of externality, in C. Renfrew and C. Scarre (eds.) *Cognition and material culture: the archaeology of symbolic storage*. McDonald Institute Monographs, Cambridge, 135–49.

Tacon, P. 1991 The power of stone: symbolic aspects of stone use and tool development in western Arnhem Land, Australia, *Antiquity* 65, 192–207.

Tambiah, S. J. 1990 *Magic, science, religion and the scope of rationality*. Cambridge University Press, Cambridge.

Thomas, J. 1990 Silent running: the ills of environmental archaeology. *Scottish Archaeological Review* 7, 2–7.

1993 Discourse, totalization and 'the Neolithic', in C. Tilley (ed.) *Interpretative archaeology*. Berg, Oxford, 357–94.

1996 *Time, culture and identity*. Routledge, London.

1998 Some problems with the notion of external symbolic storage, and the case of Neolithic material culture in Britain, in C. Renfrew and C. Scarre (eds.) *Cognition and material culture: the archaeology of symbolic storage*. McDonald Institute Monographs, Cambridge, 149–57.

Thomas, N. 1991 *Entangled objects: exchange, material culture and colonialism in the Pacific*. Harvard University Press, London and Cambridge, Mass.

Tilley, C. 1984 Ideology and the legitimation of power in the middle Neolithic of southern Sweden in D. Miller and C. Tilley (eds.) *Ideology, power and prehistory*. Cambridge University Press, Cambridge.

1989a Archaeology as socio-political action in the present in V. Pinsky and A. Wylie (eds.) *Critical traditions in contemporary archaeology*. Cambridge University Press, Cambridge, 104–16.

1989b Excavation as theatre, *Antiquity* 63, 275–80

1991 *Material culture and text: the art of ambiguity*. Routledge, London.

1993 Interpretation and a poetics of the past, in C. Tilley (ed.) *Interpretative archaeology*. Berg, Oxford, 1–31.

1994 *A phenomenology of landscape: places, paths and monuments*. Berg, Oxford.

1996 *An ethnography of the Neolithic*. Cambridge University Press, Cambridge.

1999 *Metaphor and material culture*. Blackwell, Oxford.

Tite, M. 1972 *Methods of physical examination in archaeology*. Seminar Press, London.

1996 Dating, provenance and usage in material culture studies, in D. Kingery (ed.) *Learning from things: method and theory of material culture studies*. Smithsonian Institution Press, Washington, DC, 231–60.

1999 Pottery production, distribution and consumption – the contribution of the physical sciences, *Journal of Archaeological Method and Theory* 6 (3), 181–235.

Todd, L. C. and D. J. Rapson 1988 Long bone fragmentation and interpretation of faunal assemblages: approaches to comparative analysis. *Journal of Archaeological Science* 15, 307–25.

Toren, C. 1999 *Mind, materiality and history*. Routledge, London.

Torrence, R. 1986 *Production and exchange of stone tools: prehistoric obsidian in the Aegean*. Cambridge University Press, Cambridge.

Toulmin, S. 1990 *Cosmopolis*. Chicago University Press, Chicago.

Wachtman, J. B. 1993 *Characterization of materials*. Butterworth-Heinemann, Boston, Mass.

Wainwright, G. J. and I. Longworth 1971 *Durrington walls: excavations 1966–68*. Society of Antiquaries of London Monograph 29, London.

Wardle, J. 1992 *Earlier prehistoric pottery production*. British Archaeological Reports: British Series 225, Oxford.

Watson, P. J., S. A. LeBlanc and C. L. Redman 1971 *Explanation in archaeology*. Columbia University Press, New York.

Weiner, J. F. 1991 *The empty place: poetry, space and being among the Foi of Papua New Guinea*. Indiana University Press, Bloomington, Ind.

Whittle, A. 1996 *Europe in the Neolithic: the creation of new worlds*. Cambridge University Press, Cambridge.

Wiessner, P. 1996 Introduction: food, status, culture and nature, in P. Wiessner and W. Schiefenhovel (eds.) *Food and the status quest*. Berghan, Providence, R. I., 1–19.

Williams, D. F. 1976 Petrological analysis of pottery, in J. N. G. Ritchie (ed.) The stones of Stenness, Orkney, *Proceedings of the Society of Antiquaries of Scotland* 107, 1–60.

1979 Petrological analysis of pottery, in C. Renfrew (ed.), *Investigations in Orkney*. Society of Antiquaries of London Monograph 38, London, 90–6.

1983 Petrological analysis of pottery and stone axe, in A. Ritchie (ed.) Excavation of a Neolithic farmstead at Knap of Howar, Papa Westray, Orkney *Proceedings of the Society of Antiquaries of Scotland* 113, 40–121.

Williams-Thorpe, O. 1995 Obsidian in the Mediterranean and the Near East: a provenancing success story, *Archaeometry* 37, 217–48.

Wilson, B. 1971 *Rationality*. Blackwell, Oxford.

Wittgenstein, L. 1953 *Philosophical investigations*. Blackwell, Oxford.

Wobst, H. M. 1977 Stylistic behaviour and information exchange, in C. E. Cleland (ed.), *For the director: research essays in honour of James B. Griffin*, Anthropological Papers No. 61, Museum of Anthropology, Ann Arbor, Mich. 317–42.

Woodward, A. 1996 Vessel size and social identity in the Bronze Age of southern Britain, in I. Kinnes and G. Varndell (eds.) *'Unbaked urns of rudely shape'*. Oxbow Monograph 55, Oxford, 195–202.

Woodward, A. and P. Blinkhorn 1997 Size is important: Iron Age vessel capacities in central and southern England, in C. G. Cumberpatch and P. W. Blinkhorn (eds.) *Not so much a pot, more a way of life*. Oxbow Monograph 83, Oxford, 153–62.

Wylie, A. 1992 On 'Heavily decomposing red herrings': scientific method in archaeology and the ladening of evidence with theory, in L. Embree (ed.) *Meta-archaeology*. Kluwer Academic Publishers, Dordrecht, 269–88.

1993 A proliferation of new archaeologies: 'Beyond objectivism and relativism' in N. Yoffee and A. Sherratt (eds.) *Archaeological theory: who sets the agenda?* Cambridge University Press, Cambridge, 20–7.

Index

abstraction, 68–9
acculturation, 5
accumulation, 100–1
agency, 20, 71, 170, 171, 172, 176–7, 179–81
animals, 157, 158–60, 161, 179–81
animate objects, 34, 35, 83, 100, 161, 176, 177, 178
anthropology, xiii, 8, 35, 59, 60, 65, 81
archaeological laboratory, 49–50, 54, 60, 63
  site-as-laboratory, 49
archaeological practice, 38, 39, 40, 45, 53, 55, 58–62, 63, 168
  as a science, 49
  linear structure of, 40–4, 46, 56, 62, 77
archaeological record, 10–22, 23–4, 37, 95, 178
  physical model, 11–17, 20, 23, 37, 100
  textual model, 17–20, 23, 37
archaeological science, xi, xiii, 2, 3, 14, 17, 20–2, 38, 39, 45–6, 47, 63–4, 78, 173, 175–6
  practice of, 16, 49, 173–6, 182
  XXXX, xi, 70, 74, 81, 103, 173, 175–6, 178, 179, 181, 182
  processual (or New), 11, 12, 14, 15–16, 26, 37, 70
  social, 3
  theoretical, 1, 2, 3, 20–2, 23, 37–8, 169
art history, 65
arts, 1–3
associations, 35–6

Barnhouse, 111, 113–17, 152, 166, 175
  house, 2 135–8, 141, 148–9, 166
  links to wider landscape, 150–7
  middens, 140–2
  spatial arrangement, 115–17
  structure, 8 138–9, 149–50, 163, 166
  see also Grooved ware, at Barnhouse
Barnhouse Odin, 150, 152

Barton Court Farm, 98
biography, xiii, 82, 83–5
  of artefacts, 83–5, 96, 99 102,
  of humans, 83, 84
  see also Grooved ware, biography
'black boxes', 29, 33, 34, 37–8, 46, 57–8
Blackhammer, 159
botanical analysis, 14, 16, 19, 42, 46, 47, 64, 98
'boundary objects', 75, 178–9
Broken K Pueblo, 93

carved stone balls, 107, 163
categorisation, 5, 7, 8, 35, 54, 76, 97, 168
cattle milk, 30, 33
ceramics, 30, 33, 42, 46, 55, 67–8, 104
  and identity, 105–7
  as cultural indicator, 105
  biography of, 106
  ecology, 86
  neolithic, 105–7
  production of, 68, 87, 91, 92, 93, 94, 97
  scientific analysis of, 76, 88, 91
  see also Grooved ware
chaînes opératoires, 90, 120, 138
clay, 87, 89
  see also ceramics
cognitive psychology, 5
consumption, xiii, 52, 62, 85, 95, 96–9, 157–61, 165–7
  and social identity, 96, 119, 163–4
  see also biography
context, 18–19, 40, 41, 44, 45, 47, 50, 51, 52, 55, 56, 61, 62, 63, 74–5, 76, 78, 84, 101, 175, 181
  and artefacts, 74–5, 78, 84, 97, 102, 106–7
  see also decontextualisation
culture, 1, 11, 26–9, 36–7, 169
culture-history, 11, 51, 70, 117
cultural evolution, 14, 15, 70, 92
Cuween Hill, 159